Dreiser's
Jennie Gerhardt

Dreiser's
Jennie Gerhardt
New Essays on the Restored Text

EDITED BY
James L.W. West III

UNIVERSITY OF PENNSYLVANIA PRESS

Philadelphia

Copyright © 1995 by the University of Pennsylvania Press

Printed in the United States of America
Dreiser's Jennie Gerhardt : new essays on the restored text / edited
by James L. W. West.
   p.   cm.
  Includes bibliographical references and index.
  ISBN 0-8122-3284-4 (cloth : alk. paper). — ISBN 0-8122-1513-3
(pbk. : alk. paper)
   1. Dreiser, Theodore, 1871–1945.   Jennie Gerhardt — Criticism,
Textual.   I. West, James L. W.
PS3507.R55J4   1995
813'.52 — dc20   95-19219
                                                        CIP

PS
3507
R55
J4
1995

Contents

Introduction

Dreiser's *Jennie Gerhardt* has no extensive history of critical interpretation. This situation is in large part a result of its proximity in Dreiser's career to *Sister Carrie* — a landmark in American fiction and a novel around which there has grown up much mythology and apocrypha and a considerable body of scholarship. The wide visibility of *Sister Carrie* has worked to keep *Jennie Gerhardt* in the shadows: *Sister Carrie*, published in 1900 against a background of disapproval and suppression, has functioned readily as the cornerstone of many courses in the twentieth-century American novel. *Jennie Gerhardt*, published in 1911 and (until recently) with no known history of bowdlerization or publisher's interference, has not seemed as teachable or as important historically. There has also been the problem of Jennie herself, as she is presented in the Harper and Brothers first edition. In that text she seems overly pliant and malleable, with no coherent approach to the living of human life. Lester Kane, by contrast, seems focused and whole: with his defiant pessimism and philosophical skepticism, he dominates the first-edition text and makes Dreiser's story appear uncomplicated and didactic. And too *Jennie Gerhardt*, an emotional and deeply moving novel, has been open to the charge of sentimentalism, a mode of writing with which critics of American literature have not been comfortable until very recently.

The present volume of criticism, based on the restored text of *Jennie Gerhardt* published in 1992 by the University of Pennsylvania Press, aims to begin a new examination of the novel. The Pennsylvania edition has been the catalyst for this collection: it has provided a quite different text of the novel, heretofore known only to a handful of readers and until now never subject to interpretation. The 1911 text of *Jennie Gerhardt* was altered profoundly by the editors at Harpers before publication: much of its sexual energy was short-circuited, its criticisms of organized religion were blunted, and its language was smoothed and sentimentalized. Perhaps most important, Jennie's role in the book was reduced by editorial cutting and condensation, making her a less complex and thoughtful character than Dreiser had envisioned. In restoring Dreiser's language and the omitted material, the Pennsylvania edition has provided a text of *Jennie Gerhardt* that is much closer to Dreiser's original conception. The sexual charge of the novel has been restored, its social and religious criticisms have been reinstated, and its language has been made Dreiser's again—blunt, unadorned, and direct. Jennie's character has emerged more fully in the new text, which now reveals itself to be a dialectical novel, with Lester's materialistic determinism counterbalanced by Jennie's equally strong idealism and natural mysticism.

The history of the composition, publication, and reception of *Jennie Gerhardt* is set forth in detail in the full-dress Pennsylvania edition; a condensed version of the story is given in the Penguin paperbound reprint (1994), which is designed as a classroom text. It has therefore not seemed necessary to cover this ground again here, other than to remind readers that the Pennsylvania text differs markedly from the Harpers text, constituting in its restored form a significantly different work of art. The 1911 text has its own validity as an historical artifact, but it bears only a tangential relationship to the restored text.

Brought together in the present collection are readings of the Pennsylvania text by at least three generations of Dreiser scholars and critics: a senior generation that established Dreiser's work securely in the canon and set an agenda for subsequent investigation; a middle generation that has continued to study his writings and has made fresh and illuminating discoveries about his life and career; and a young generation that is beginning to take the Dreiser field in new directions, informed by current interpretive stances and critical vocabularies. This is a healthy situation: it argues for the continued vitality and potency of Dreiser's work.

Some of the readings in this volume are general assessments—examinations of Jennie's and Lester's behavior, treatments of the autobiographical backgrounds on which Dreiser drew, or views of the various literary traditions (realistic, naturalistic, sentimental, ethnic) from which he borrowed. Other essays examine some of the historical contexts that inform *Jennie Gerhardt*—the nineteenth-century culture of death and burial, the sphere of domestic labor, the background of proletarian working conditions, or the demimonde of the luxury hotel and mineral-water spa. No effort has been made to take up every possible approach to *Jennie Gerhardt* or to touch on every historical context. Dreiser's novel is too deep, rich, and suggestive ever to be exhausted in this way. Still, from this collection should emerge a cross-section of approaches and a useful body of contextual information for the scholar, teacher, and student—the collective audience for which this volume is intended. What also should emerge are some worthwhile conversations among the contributions themselves, because many of them are in dialogue with one another.

Some sensitive, acute criticism of the 1911 *Jennie Gerhardt* is in print already. One thinks particularly of essays by Daryl C. Dance, Mordecai Marcus, Carol A. Schwartz, and Warwick Wadlington and of book chapters by Philip Gerber, Richard Lehan, and Donald Pizer.[1] These works of criticism have their own place and usefulness in the Dreiser field, but one must be aware always that they are interpretations of a different work of art from the one addressed in this collection. The edition of *Jennie Gerhardt* published by Harpers in 1911 was a collaborative, negotiated text, socialized and domesticated by the cultural forces of its day so as not to offend convention too strongly and not to risk negative publicity and suppression. Comparison of this 1911 text with the restored version of 1992 is a useful (even an essential) exercise. It reveals much about the climate in which *Jennie Gerhardt* was originally published. No effort has been made in this volume to mount an attack on the 1911 text or to demonstrate, other than in passing, the superiority of the Pennsylvania text. Readers and critics must make their own judgments on these matters, remembering that the Harpers text was a product of its historical moment and that the Pennsylvania text, just as surely, is spoken by the culture of its times.

This volume of essays should begin a productive discussion of *Jennie Gerhardt,* an interchange of ideas, information, and interpretations. This collection should also help to carry *Jennie Gerhardt* into the classroom. Without in any way wishing to set Dreiser's novels against each other, one can say that it would be healthy if *Jennie Gerhardt* began sometimes to be taught instead of, or in addition to, *Sister Carrie.* Our understanding of Dreiser's themes and artistry will gain by this small broadening of his canon, leading perhaps to fresh teaching and criticism of his later works as well— the writings of the middle years of his career and the magnificent *An American Tragedy.*

All elements and materials are now in place for a reexamination of *Jennie Gerhardt*: the Pennsylvania edition, with its explanatory essays, illustrations, and apparatus; the Penguin paperback, with a critical introduction and notes; and this collection, with its new interpretations and fresh historical evidence. It is time now for the conversation to begin.

Note

1. See the checklist of previous scholarship and criticism on *Jennie Gerhardt* at the rear of this volume.

PART I

General Assessments

I

Janus-Faced *Jennie*

ROBERT H. ELIAS

IN PRESENTING DREISER WITH THE American Academy of Arts and Letters Award of Merit in 1944, Professor Chauncey B. Tinker began his citation with the explanation that the Academy was "Janus-faced, looking before and after. . . . Its aim is to seek out and reward ability wherever it appears and in whatever guise" (Tinker 1). Today, with a different emphasis and an extension of meaning, we can call Dreiser's work, and particularly *Jennie Gerhardt*, Janus-faced. For, both autobiographically and thematically, *Jennie* looks before and after and exhibits Dreiser assessing human aspiration and necessity, whatever their guise.

Although his second novel carries a 1911 publication date, Dreiser had a good while earlier imbued his initial draft with the anxieties and reflections that he was contending with in the months following the failure of *Sister Carrie* — a writer with new work in progress but without the readers he had anticipated, facing indefinite days of he knew not what, surely recalling painful deprivations in his past while remembering at the same time hopes for his future aroused by the glamorous individuals whose worldly successes he had observed as a reporter and whose triumphant lives he had explored in interviews for the magazines, there he was, deeply disheartened, on the brink of a breakdown. When his recovery finally enabled him to earn money as an editor and then resume work on his novel confidently, he undertook no radical change in the direction he had plotted nearly ten years earlier but rather, with an awareness enlarged by reconsideration and the comments of friends, brought it to completion with nuances and complexities that the 1911 editors blue-penciled and the Pennsylvania edition now makes fully available.

Like *Sister Carrie* the story contrasts material success and failure, and also like *Sister Carrie* it suggests that there is something elusive beyond material success that the sensitive individual experiences and that no one can definitely verbalize. But where *Sister Carrie* concludes by leaving readers sensing they have followed the account of two ultimately diverging careers, *Jennie Gerhardt* portrays connections.

Fundamentally, *Jennie* is an exploration of how one is to live in a world in which material satisfactions are both necessary for survival and insufficient for fulfillment. It is a world in which circumstance can determine the limits of the will and a world in which feeling qualifies the value of what the will accomplishes in the face of circumstance. In this world, too — and it is the world in which all mortals exist — individuals and society are inescapably defined by symbiosis. Decisions about whether to live as part of society, accepting conventions, or to live apart from society, rebelling against conventions, cannot occur in an ethereal vacuum purged of all other wills. Hence, as Dreiser shows, no individual has the luxury of unfettered rational choice. The mind or will can never escape contingency — indeed, finally cannot attain meaning without it. So it is in the intertwining of their lives, in their interactions and effect on each other, and in their entanglements with the society around them that Jennie Gerhardt and Lester Kane create Dreiser's story.

The title suggests that the story is primarily Jennie's. She does without doubt bear its emotional burden. It is with her that Dreiser's deepest sympathies lie and through her that his own past (or, at least, his family's) engages him. The fear of want, the desperate need to pay for food, the uncertainty of a secure place to live — all part of Dreiser's childhood experience — condition Jennie's motives. Her acceptance of Senator Brander's attentions and later Lester Kane's is inseparable from her familial devotion. Indeed, Dreiser is at pains to establish the purity of her actions. She is instinct with a moral sense. She is self-sacrificing, wide-eyed, unsophisticated, and even after seduction and impregnation, remains as idealized and unsoiled as any heroine in sentimental fiction.

There is, to be sure, a significant difference here. While Dreiser is portraying her as essentially innocent, he is also establishing her sexuality. She is not only a pure woman but also pure woman. And it is precisely in this conjunction that Dreiser establishes Jennie's claim to celebration. The pregnancy of an unwed woman may violate certain community codes, but pregnancy constitutes an affirmation of a life force. Jennie's is to be understood not as an event in itself but as a function of her character. Although the accident of Senator Brander's sudden death creates her critical predicament, Dreiser does not thereby question her morality. Instead, he treats her subsequent maternity as a part of her womanhood, a fact of nature to be accepted, even praised. "The whole earth . . ." Dreiser declares, "is moved by passions hymeneal, and everything terrestrial has come into being by the one common road"; to treat "the method of nature" as "something unclean" is simply the reaction of "a judgement . . . marvelously warped" (92). Had she the knowledge and experience, Dreiser could have had her quote Whitman's chanting about the procreant urge of the earth. For in her conceiving and giving birth she is a vehicle for "one of life's ideal functions" (93).

That role is, moreover, not coldly schematic. Dreiser endows her with a temperament that is integral to all her involvements. Jennie, we learn at the very beginning, is a person for whom life is a "true wonderland, a thing of infinite beauty[:] . . . Trees, flowers, the world of sound and the world of color" (16). This explanation is reminiscent of the interpolated musings Dreiser must have enjoyed reading years earlier in such works of Balzac's as *The Wild Ass's Skin* (Balzac 269). More than once in his first six chapters Dreiser interpolates to associate her rhapsodically with the delights and soothing influences of her natural surroundings. It is this susceptibility of hers that accounts for her relations with others. Her responses are intuitive, without calculation, generated by nature without let or hindrance. She is guiltless of contrivance. Essentially, she comprehends, in both meanings of that word, the processes of nature.

This capacity of Jennie's is part of the novel's challenging duality. Yielding to nature may well be a childhood dream, but in a deeper way it is an act with philosophical implications. In establishing Jennie's responsiveness, Dreiser both looks back to the pastoral geography of his earliest memories and looks ahead, as we can say now, to what he would affirm during his last days in *The Bulwark*. There is in nature something healing that produces an experience essentially religious. It is noteworthy that Dreiser makes a point of showing that the ultimate effect of Vesta's baptismal service on old Gerhardt is the release of "a feeling of natural affection" (117). This association of nature and transcending love is what Solon Barnes feels toward the end of his life.

But if Jennie bears the burden of the story, it is Lester whose career Dreiser subjects to the more radical questioning. His choices are the ones that Dreiser compels us to examine most critically. It is on them that Jennie is totally dependent, whereas Lester can act without considering her. He is a man with no fixed ideas, whether about marriage, polygamy, the best form of government, or the existence of a deity; he can behold "the vastness of the panorama of life" (125) without managing to understand it and is prone to questioning everything — everything, that is, except himself. The "product of a combination of elements — religious, commercial, social — modified by the overruling, circumambient atmosphere of liberty in our national life which is productive of almost uncounted freedoms of thought and action," Lester is "an essentially animal man" (126), seeking to be among the fittest in the struggle for survival. He represents nature in a different guise.

Dreiser does not want us to think ill of him. Portrayed as a rather crude and shallow rake in the novel's first draft, Lester appears in the present, uncut version as a man capable of coupling sensual responses with occasionally Spencerian speculations. He is given, one might argue, to the sporadically examined life, without allowing his examination to interfere with his desires. Where there are no divinely ordained sanctions and everything is permitted, all rules are off. So if Jennie is attractive to him, why should he not possess her on whatever terms he fancies? That does not mean that when he first comes to know her he is unmoved by her plight or insensitive to her family's needs, or that in their later relationship he is indifferent to what he must do for her comforts. It does mean, though, that when the question is about love and commitment he and Jennie are seeming opposites.

But they are also complements. In fact, it is only as complements that they can develop a relationship that embraces their opposition. Jennie finds Lester forceful, decisive, admires his worldly knowledge, and feels secure with his mastery of the practical, whether that relates to setting up a secluded ménage or employing the means of contraception. And she loves him so much that she sacrifices maternal satisfaction to conceal Vesta's existence from him. Why she loves Lester as she does is less clear than why he loves her (if love it be). Lester finds her a comfort, a source of respite from daily striving. She may lack the sophistication, artistic talent, and intellectual endowment of Letty Pace, the sort of woman he ordinarily values, and may have no connection with tradition or experience beyond a parochial one—he could not marry her lest he be the subject of "social comment"—

> But there was a mental and emotional pull to her nevertheless which bigger minds could understand. She thought only of big things in a vague way, formulating any idea or action slowly. But she thought in ways which usually transcended the common, more superficial method, much as the flow of a river might transcend in importance the hurry of an automobile.
>
> But she liked social life of another kind, he saw—that quiet interchange of neighborly ideas and feelings which go to make up the substance and backbone of true social life. When it came to those pleasant things which concern taking an interest in one's neighbor's home, one's neighbor's children, one's

neighbor's health and prosperity or sickness and failure, she was a personality to be reckoned with. (258)

What appeals to Lester here is a feeling for community that derives from her culturally different background and that he misses in the competitive self-seeking society of the rich and ambitious. Yet, whereas for Jennie love is all, for Lester it is not something for which to lose the world. Jennie, despite occasional moments of self-assertion, appears to live only to please Lester. Close to what nowadays we might regard as abject, she wants only to serve him as lord and master; she is willing to be a doll-like presence, his little girl, and ready to give up her own hopes so that he can enjoy the social and financial advantages of status. He, in turn, never wholly content with having parted from Jennie when the opportunity for profit required it, is still unable to declare his love fully until he is on his deathbed and powerless to act on his declaration. Up to that point he satisfies himself with saying to Jennie:

> "I want to tell you something, Jennie. . . . It may seem peculiar to you, after all that has happened, but I still care for you, in my way. I've thought of you right along since I left. I thought it good business to leave you—the way things were. I thought I liked Letty well enough to marry her under the circumstances. From one point of view it still seems best, but I'm not so much happier. I was just as happy with you as I ever will be. It isn't me that's important in this transaction apparently—it's the general situation. The individual doesn't count much in the situation. I don't know whether you see what I'm driving at, but all of us are more or less pawns. We're moved about like chess men by circumstances over which we have no control." (392)

At the end Jennie is bereft, and our sympathies are with her, whatever may be our judgment of Lester and however much we may be impatient with her resolute compliance. "Jennie loved and, loving, gave," Dreiser's coda tells us (575). But we recognize that the crucial choices have been Lester's, not hers, and that, insofar as he is the one needing to come to terms with what he is, the story has been his. It may be difficult to feel an affinity with him—certainly, to his credit, Dreiser, in making him understandably human, does not undertake to make him likable—but when Dreiser has the train-hand who is loading Lester's coffin call to a helper inside the freight car: "Give us a hand here. There's a stiff outside!" (417), we resent it because of Jennie and because Dreiser, after all, has succeeded in making Lester more deserving of respect than that. We can appreciate the way he has struggled in the web of social conventions to reconcile his desire for acquisitive power with his yearning to experience the life that Jennie seems to offer him. Even if he and Jennie act out their gender roles in ways that today can only make us squirm, we feel that Dreiser has conferred arresting gravity on their existence, and in dramatizing their intertwined careers has provided a provocative critique of the nature of individuality and the problem of social definition that he explores more fully in the volumes of the Trilogy of Desire that follow.

It is finally a sense of exploration with which we are left. The story of Jennie and Lester does not conclude with Lester's funeral and Jennie's facing "an endless reiteration of days" (418). That would be merely pessimistic, as *Sister Carrie* would be if *it* concluded with Hurstwood's turning on the gas and muttering, "What's the use?" The 1911 *Jennie* concludes with the coda that Dreiser almost always found essential for his novels, a meditation, never pessimistic, on the events that have preceded, a celebration of the mysterious processes of life that generate suffering, triumph, questioning, delight, and awe. Life remains a riddle: judgments of individuals can be only arbitrary — at best, only understanding is possible, and this requires a respectful recognition of the complex ways in which nature works — an appreciation ultimately aesthetic — so that at the last one can affirm, as Dreiser does in the subtitle of *Hey, Rub-a-Dub-Dub* (and repeatedly elsewhere), "the mystery and terror and wonder of life."

Bibliography

Balzac, Honoré de. *The Wild Ass's Skin.* New York: P. F. Collier, 1900. Quoted in *Theodore Dreiser: Apostle of Nature,* by Robert H. Elias. Emended ed., 76. Ithaca, NY: Cornell University Press, 1970.

Dreiser, Theodore. *Jennie Gerhardt.* Edited by James L. W. West III. Philadelphia: University of Pennsylvania Press, 1992.

Tinker, C[hauncey] B. "Theodore Dreiser. Citation." Typescript (copy). Dreiser Collection, Carl A. Kroch Library, Cornell University, Ithaca, NY.

2

The Biographical Significance of *Jennie Gerhardt*

RICHARD LINGEMAN

IN SEPTEMBER 1910 THEODORE DREISER made a sudden career change. A scandalous affair with a young woman had forced him to resign from his well-paying job as editor-in-chief of a stable of women's magazines published by the Butterick pattern company. Now he was faced with a choice between returning to novel writing, with uncertain financial prospects, or taking a secure magazine or journalistic job.

Although Dreiser told friends he was considering several attractive offers, his heart was not really in them, and he began working on the manuscript of his second novel, called "The Transgressor," which he had abandoned in 1903 after suffering a nervous breakdown. On his recovery he had turned to editing and had had little time for writing, although the novel remained clear and strong in his mind. Freed from the editorial grind, he was able to pick up the threads of the interrupted work and soon was announcing to his friend H. L. Mencken, "I expect to try out this book game for about four or five books after which unless I am enjoying a good income from them I will quit" (Lingeman II:36).

He retitled the new novel *Jennie Gerhardt* after its central character, a young woman from an impoverished family who is seduced by a senator, bears a child out of wedlock, and then becomes the mistress of Lester Kane, the son of a wealthy Cincinnati carriage-making family. After his experiences with *Carrie,* which had been called "immoral" by its publisher, Frank Doubleday, and virtually suppressed, Dreiser feared that his second book with *its* "immoral" heroine would also meet editorial resistance; indeed, his fears had contributed to his psychological block on the book.

But in 1911 he was a different man from the vulnerable first novelist of

A shorter version of this essay was published as "A Few Changes, Mr. Dreiser," *New York Times Book Review,* 7 November 1993:33–34. Reprinted by permission of the *New York Times.*

1900, whose extravagant dreams of literary fame had been dashed by the failure of *Sister Carrie*. His Butterick position had conferred on him money, prestige, and social standing, which enabled him to move more confidently in his imagination in the upper-class milieu of Lester Kane. As for Jennie's background—the world of a poor family headed by a sternly religious German immigrant workman—he copied it directly from his own grim childhood in Indiana.

He could also indirectly draw on the emotional capital of his unrequieted affair with the young woman. "I have just discovered that this is a very sad world," he wrote Mencken in the midst of the turmoil (Lingeman II:29). His grief for his lost love seeped into his novel, darkening the romance of Jennie and Lester, adding a somber ground-bass to his prose. And he brought to bear on the characters of his protagonists a greater maturity and detachment. In the earlier draft, they were unsympathetic, even a little sordid. Jennie's character is an unstable mix of innocent waif and greedy golddigger (as Carrie Meeber was to some degree); Lester comes across as a rake, a coarse sensualist. In the rewriting, Dreiser endowed them with more complexity and more moral and philosophical heft. They increase in symbolic stature by embodying contrasting views of the universe. Jennie is natural, romantic, credulous, a pagan Nature sprite. Lester is skeptical, cynical, stoical, a materialist who accepts the Darwinian scenario of creation but questions why the great machine was started in the first place. Those contrasting attitudes represented two poles within Dreiser's own psyche.

Emotionally unblocked, Dreiser worked furiously on the book and completed a substantially recast version by early 1911. His anxieties about its commercial acceptability were confirmed when it was refused by the first editor who read it and found it too "broad" (i.e., explicit) (Lingeman II:17). But the next house on the list, Harper and Brothers, accepted it and published it that same year. The novel had a good sale and attracted favorable reviews from the younger critics, who saw it as redeeming the promise of a mature realism in American fiction that Dreiser had tendered in *Sister Carrie*. Leading the chorus was Mencken, who applauded *Jennie Gerhardt* as "the best American novel I have ever read, with the lonesome but Himalayan exception of 'Huckleberry Finn'" (Lingeman II:41–42). By then, Dreiser was roaring along on destiny's track, his third novel well under way and the fourth fermenting in his brain.

Jennie Gerhardt is a somewhat neglected title in the Dreiser canon, but the publication of this edition by the University of Pennsylvania Press in its new Dreiser Edition may help remedy that. The original manuscript has been collated with the published book, and the comparison has revealed thousands of changes in what Dreiser had written. More than 16,000 words were cut; sentences and whole paragraphs were rewritten.

Dreiser's correspondence shows that he bridled at the editing but ultimately accepted much of it. Although throughout his career he sought help from a train of "editorial assistants" and, early in his career, Mencken himself, he could be a very stubborn and truculent author. At this stage in his life he was in a precarious position: he was an unemployed editor and the author of one novel, whose troubled publication had marked him along publishers' row as a "daring" and "difficult" writer.

Accordingly, he was more interested in getting the novel published than in testing how liberal publishers and censors had become in the decade since *Carrie*'s debut; indeed, as editor of a genteel women's magazine he had experience in complying with the reigning taboos.[1] Not that he had tried to conform *Jennie* to those same standards; rather, he retained (one guesses) a lingering sensitivity to them and a cynical (or worldly) willingness to play the game by the rules—up to a point. A few years later, of course, when his artistic conscience had been tested and toughened, he would be more uncompromising.

Evidence of his uneasiness is the fact that, before sending the manuscript to a publisher, Dreiser had circulated a draft among eight people, most of them editors, writers, or critics. None of the draft readers seems to have had any moral qualms about the narrative; indeed, Dreiser had quickly drawn the curtains on the few seduction scenes and had made his heroine so sympathetic that for all her moral lapses—the product of irresistible circumstances, he argued—only a Cotton Mather would have cast stones at her.

Fortunately for Dreiser, the editor who read the manuscript at Harper and Brothers was Ripley Hitchcock, who had admired *Carrie* in 1900 and had taken a personal and professional interest in Dreiser's career. But Hitchcock was no literary radical. When he edited Stephen Crane's *Maggie: A Girl of the Streets* and *The Red Badge of Courage,* he pruned them of lewd or "sordid" matter, while preserving enough of Crane's realism to keep the franchise. Hitchcock was a shrewd bookman with sound commercial as well as literary instincts but also an active churchman and a moralist.

Hitchcock could be said to have been the ideal man to tame the barbarian: he was sympathetic with what writers such as Crane and Dreiser were trying to do but enough of a moral businessman to keep them from stirring up Anthony J. Comstock, New York's rampant censor. The Harpers must have hoped that Hitchcock would help Dreiser to produce "'less drastic' but very saleable books" (Lingeman II:41). The publisher, one of America's oldest and most distinguished houses, had tumbled into receivership in 1900 and badly needed best-sellers to clear its debt to the Morgan bank. Hitchcock had made Crane into a best-selling author; why not Dreiser?

The contract that Dreiser signed gave Harper the right to edit the novel as necessary, with the stipulation that Dreiser could withdraw the book without penalty if he did not like the results. Dreiser apparently accepted this provision without much protest, but he did cavil at other clauses in the agreement, and it is a measure of the weakness of his bargaining position that he lost every argument. As he told the British publisher Grant Richards, "They were nervous about [the book] — practically dictating their own terms" (Lingeman II:38).

If Harpers was nervous about the book's suitability (and there is evidence that the firm was), even with Hitchcock on the case, so was Dreiser. Its publication was crucial to the resumption of his literary career, and he wanted it out bearing the imprint of a prestigious publisher, such as Harpers, and with the house's unqualified commercial backing. Memories of Doubleday's grudging issue of *Sister Carrie* still haunted him, but, more practically, he hoped to earn enough royalties to carry him through the writing of his next book. Given those considerations, the fight for fearless, truth-telling American fiction could wait. As he confided to Mencken, "I sometimes think my desire is for expression that is entirely too frank for this time." "I had better be careful," he told Richards. "My turn comes later" (Lingeman II:37).

His strategic caution does not mean that he abdicated his integrity as author. About midway through the editorial process, having heard nothing from Hitchcock and fearing that he would be presented with a fait accompli (which could well have been Hitchcock's plan), Dreiser demanded to see the edited manuscript. When Hitchcock finally produced it, Dreiser grumbled vociferously and succeeded in restoring some 9,000 of the 25,000 words that had been carved out of it. But when it was all over Hitchcock could write Dreiser's agent, with some exaggeration, "He seems to have accepted my final work on the manuscript without any changes of consequence" (Lingeman II:44).

Dreiser still had some qualms, however, for he asked Mencken, who had only seen the original manuscript, to read the published book and tell him if it had been seriously mutilated. Mencken, who had been unaware of the extent of the editorial surgery and did not wish to discourage Dreiser, assured him that no damage had been done. Privately, he was appalled by the cuts, telling a friend, "Such ruthless slashing is alarming" (Lingeman II:41).

The great bulk of the editing had to do with tone and style, rather than with censorship. A few passages were excised on moral grounds — notably one in which Lester tells Jennie in a veiled way about contraceptives (the mention of which would have mobilized Comstock). But the main achievement of the editors was to soften *Jennie,* to transform it from "a blunt, carefully documented piece of social analysis to a love story merely set against a social background" (West 442). Hitchcock and his subeditors tarted up Dreiser's plain style with rewriting that made it closer to that of what was currently popular fiction. The flat, understated language he used in describing scenes of high emotional drama was plumped up; his ironic comments on manners and morals were defanged. (Dreiser was no Edith Wharton when it came to satirizing the empty rituals of high society, but he effectively dramatizes Lester's boredom at some stuffy soirees.) Hitchcock also diligently cleansed the book of impieties and satirical descriptions of religion.

Dreiser's style grew out of his attitude toward his material; it reflected his deterministic vision of fate and society. His protagonists' pathetic schemes for happiness are dashed by implacable social forces and an adamantine universe. He succeeds in presenting two lives down through their days wholly and without melodrama — life as it is lived, without contrived denouements or imposed moral judgments. His art is to seem to tell his story without artifice. The characters are, to be sure, emotional, warm-blooded, unlike the pallid, sexless puppets of the average novel of the period. For all their gropings and thrashings, we sense that they are, as Lester observes, pawns of circumstance — but also, as Jennie exemplifies, possibly redeemed by love, by the life force. And yet, in the end, what does all this shadow play mean? The book closes with Lester dead (after he tells Jennie he has always loved her) and Jennie abandoned, facing "Days and days, an endless reiteration of days, and then — ?" (418).

To show how the editors gussied up Dreiser's style, consider the scene in which Jennie is deciding whether to reply to a letter from Lester, who at this point in the story is aggressively attempting to seduce her. Having already borne an illegitimate child, she is understandably fearful and is possessed by an almost sickening dread of encouraging Lester in any way. As Dreiser quietly shows, she is physically attracted to Lester and senses that encouraging him will lead to another affair, which, given her sexual naïveté, would likely mean another child. At the same time, her father has been badly injured and the family is on the brink of destitution. Lester has promised to help them if she becomes his mistress. In the event, her concern for her family overrides her moral compunctions, and she answers his letter, knowing in her heart that she has turned a fateful corner. Here is how Dreiser describes her decision: "[She] wrote him the briefest note. She would meet him as requested. Please not to come to the house. This she mailed and then waited, with a sort of soul dread, the arrival of the day." The Harper's editors revised the passage to read: "She mailed the letter, and then waited, with mingled feelings of trepidation and thrilling expectancy, the arrival of the fateful day" (153). Dreiser's version has a hectic, tossed-off effect to suggest her emotional turmoil; the phrase "soul dread" cuts to the heart of her fears. The Harper's revision is clichéd and marred by that false note of "thrilling expectancy."

Comparison of the two passages shows that the publisher's objective was to make the book more commercial, more palatable. This was accomplished by softening the language, making it more suitable (as defined by the male editors) for the female readership that still made up the primary audience for novels at that time.

Not that Hitchcock's editing radically altered Dreiser's intentions. The basic story remains; the most moving passages are retained; the pessimism and determinism still reverberate. But Dreiser's indictment of society's hypocrisy has been watered down. His thesis that upper-class morality is an iron fist in a white glove, a form of power used by the strong, the wealthy, to repel undesirables and to quash unruly passions that threaten a family's reputation — that message is diluted. Lester, who finds with Jennie the only genuine love of his aimless life, is forced by family pressure to disown her. Dreiser symbolizes the superiority of financial calculus over love among Lester's class by the device of a will. After his family has discovered his affair with Jennie, the elder Kane stipulates in his final testament that Lester may not receive his inheritance unless he renounces Jennie. He remains loyal to her for a time, but the price of life outside the pale becomes too high. He leaves Jennie, marries a beautiful, wealthy widow, and immerses himself in the pointless pleasures of society. Lester is a decent man, but he believes life itself is pointless, a "silly show" (392). For him, living well is the best revenge.

In the Harpers version, Lester's fate becomes the dominant motif; Jennie becomes a passive handmaiden to his destiny, submitting to his desires, ministering to his needs as a loving mistress, and leaving him when she learns that he has put his fortune in jeopardy rather than abandon her. In Dreiser's version there is much more to Jennie. He intends her as a person of consequence, an untutored but instinctively intelligent woman, affectionate, and, of course, good — society's condemnation notwithstanding. Passages highlighting these traits were cut from the Harpers edition, whereas the descriptions of Lester remained.

With Jennie receding into the shadows, the novel loses the philosophical dialectic that was embodied in Lester's and her contrasting views of life. Her diminution also serves to reinforce Victorian stereotypes of woman's place. Admittedly, as conceived by Dreiser, Jennie is something of a male fantasy figure (she was, Dreiser said, based in part on his own mother) — all-loving, all-giving, all-sacrificing. Even so, Jennie remains a true heroine who is willing to love, even knowing she will become a social outcast. Hers is a fully considered decision, albeit driven by need and distorted by the Victorian double standard.

Dreiser would never again write so fully about his own German immigrant background as he did in *Jennie Gerhardt*. The character of old Gerhardt is a surprisingly sympathetic picture of Dreiser's own immigrant father, whose Old World patriarchal authority, so resented by the son, was undermined by the secular snares of America. And in the character of Jennie Dreiser has evoked not only the sacrificial goodness of the mother he worshiped but the desires and troubles of his sister, Mame, who had a child out of wedlock with a socially superior man. At its deepest level, Dreiser wrote his novel as a fictional apologia for Mame (just as *Carrie* was in part an apologia for his sister Emma) and for his family, who were made pariahs by poverty and conventional morality. He used art partly to cauterize the subconscious wounds inflicted in childhood by the hardships and ostracism his family had suffered. *Jennie* is an indictment of the callous cruelty of a pharisaic morality of "good form" that places an artificial model of feminine virtue above individual happiness.

Jennie's success propelled Dreiser into the most prolific phase of his long career. Between 1912 and 1916 he completed three major novels — two volumes of his trilogy about transit magnate Frank Cowperwood (*The Financier* and *The Titan*) and *The "Genius"*; short stories, poems, and one-act plays; a travel book about Europe; and a ruminative account of a visit to his home state, *A Hoosier Holiday*. After this burst, he was again tripped up by charges of immorality (Harper would refuse to publish *The Titan* — perversely vindicating his wariness with *Jennie*; *The "Genius"* was banned by the Comstock forces), and he did not publish another novel until *An American Tragedy*, in 1925. Conceivably, if *Jennie* had failed, or if Dreiser had rebelled against Hitchcock's editing and withdrawn the book, he would have had to give up the game. The next publisher on his agent's list after Harper and Brothers would have also said no. The head of that house, William Morrow, told Sinclair Lewis, then a fledgling editor, that he regarded Dreiser as a salacious writer (Schorer 186).

For Dreiser *Jennie Gerhardt* was a good career move. Now, with the appearance of the Pennsylvania edition, we can see that it is also a great novel.

Note

1. For example, as editor of *The Delineator* he asked H. G. Wells to tone down a novel submitted for serialization because "it would possibly offend the rank and file." Quoted in Lingeman, II:29.

Bibliography

Dreiser, Theodore. *Jennie Gerhardt*. Edited by James L. W. West III. Philadelphia: University of Pennsylvania Press, 1992.
Lingeman, Richard. *Theodore Dreiser: An American Journey, 1908–1945*. Vol. II. New York: G. P. Putnam's Sons, 1990.
Schorer, Mark. *Sinclair Lewis*. New York: McGraw-Hill, 1961.
West, James L. W. III. "The Composition and Publication of *Jennie Gerhardt*." In *Jennie Gerhardt*, edited by James L. W. West III. Philadelphia: University of Pennsylvania Press, 1992.

3
Jennie Gerhardt: Naturalism Reconsidered

JUDITH KUCHARSKI

IN NOVEMBER 1911 H. L. MENCKEN reviewed the newly published *Jennie Gerhardt* for *Smart Set*, calling it "the best American novel I have ever read, with the lonesome but Himalayan exception of 'Huckleberry Finn'" (Riggio 740). Mencken's boundless enthusiasm and unqualified praise was grounded in what he took to be the novel's "doctrine," expressed through Lester Kane, "that life is meaningless, a tragedy without a moral, a joke without a point" (Riggio 741) — a doctrine, according to Mencken, that Dreiser, alone among American novelists, was able to face unflinchingly. The friendship between the two men during these years was based, at least in part, on Mencken's assumption that they shared a kind of tough-minded, ultrarealistic philosophy, one too bleak and too close to the truth to suit the taste of an American audience that preferred its fictions pretty and sentimental.

Following Mencken, critics have centered their attention on the stark, unemotional, naturalistic aspects of Dreiser's work. And although Dreiser has been recognized as an "inconsistent mechanist" (Vivas 237), as a writer whose fiction often belies his professed belief in a mechanistic, deterministic world, his novels continue to be read as exemplifying "naturalistic" principles.[1] The obvious danger of relegating any writer to a particular genre and generalizing about his or her philosophical or narrative intentions is that works that are anomalous (or tendencies within them that run counter to preconceived notions) tend to be skewed to fit expected patterns. Specifically, Dreiser's sense of the mystical, his sentimentality, his deep sympathy with his characters, are read as curious diversions within an otherwise overarching scheme. I would like to pretend for a moment that we do not "know," as we think we do, that Dreiser is a "naturalist" or a "pessimistic realist" or a "mechanistic determinist." I would then like to suggest the ways in which *Jennie Gerhardt* departs from the constraining tenets of naturalism and represents aspects of Dreiser's thinking that are at

odds with the reductive definitions that do not so much define as essential-
ize both Dreiser and his second novel.

Because of the emphasis on the philosophical import of Dreiser's fiction, individual characters have tended to be explained away as mere func-
tionaries, as pawns in Dreiser's naturalistic game. Jennie has traditionally
been read as Dreiser's version of the sentimental heroine, or as a stock naturalistic character — the weak, helpless individual buffeted about by forces
beyond her control. Readers are frequently troubled by Jennie's almost
unbelievable simplicity and self-sacrificing goodness; even those who find
the novel compelling often do so in spite of, rather than because of, Jennie
herself and feel the need somehow to account for her "superficial and sentimentalized portrayal" (Marcus 61). Discussions of Jennie's character almost invariably include the adjectives "weak," "helpless," and "victimized."
But it is difficult to see how these qualities distinguish her very radically
from the other characters in the novel. There is no question that Jennie is a
victim. Although Dreiser describes her early in the narrative as "only a
helpless victim" of the "unreasoning element of society," she is but one of
many characters who suffer at the hands of "unseeing man, narrowly drawing himself up in judgement" and demanding conformity (94). In Dreiser's
fictional world, everyone is victimized to a greater or lesser degree; victimization is the leveling factor. Even characters such as Carrie Meeber who rise
in the world suffer from the disillusionment that inevitably accompanies a
raised consciousness.

Having said this, one must add that while for Dreiser victimization is
a universal predicament, it is not the defining quality of his characters.
Dreiser established the milieu in which his characters functioned and then
turned to the more interesting question of *how* they maneuvered within the
confines of that world. It matters less that Jennie is a victim than that she is a
"big woman" (292), capable of great joy as well as great sorrow. Put another way, what distinguishes Jennie in the novel is not her vulnerability
but her strength. Attention to her status as a victim of larger forces obscures
the more interesting question — for Dreiser as well as for the reader — of
how Jennie, a poor girl raised in a strict Lutheran home, finds the strength
or faith to commit the multiple "transgressions" that propel the story and to
survive, increasingly isolated, in a world so clearly not of her own making.

Despite his philosophical bias, Mencken sensed this dimension of Jennie. He wrote to Dreiser that he would have preferred Jennie to be "a more
typical kept woman" and less "uncompromisingly exceptional" (Riggio
69). Only a presumption that the novel's point and force would remain

essentially intact with a more conventional Jennie could have prompted Mencken to voice such a preference — that, and a failure to see how personally invested Dreiser was in his "pet heroine" in 1911. In fact, Jennie's voice is as vital as Lester's, and the novel is appropriately read as a dialogue between two equally complex yet conflicting perspectives. *Jennie* is compelling not because it espouses any single naturalistic doctrine, but because of the unresolved tension between the philosophical skepticism of Lester and the spirituality and natural grounding of Jennie — a tension with which Dreiser himself struggled. Any "more typical" character would have eliminated that tension and reduced the story to little more than a sustained lament on life's hopelessness. Such a character would have made it Lester's story in every way. Had Mencken looked at Jennie with an eye toward finding something other than a confirmation of the "profound pessimism" of the naturalist (Riggio 743), he might have seen the ways in which Jennie stands as a challenge to and an implied critique of all that Lester represents. He would also have realized that Dreiser, through Jennie, reveals his impatience with facts and philosophies, his admiration for intuition over intellect, and his longing for the kind of strength Jennie draws from the natural world, a strength that allows her to survive.

Much of Jennie's force as a character derives from her association with nature. Although she seems wholly caught up in circumstance, her bond with nature insulates her from a world that, it is often assumed, controls her. Jennie is, from beginning to end, innately in harmony with and ultimately at peace with the natural world. If this seems a statement of the obvious, it is important to note that there are those for whom Jennie's characterization as a child of nature is, at most, a minor issue, and an inconvenient one at that.[2] But Dreiser could not be more clear on what it is that grounds Jennie and sustains her throughout the novel. Dreiser suggests that Jennie is another type of being entirely, one of those for whom "trees, flowers, the world of sound and the world of color . . . are the valued inheritance of their state." She is an example of those who are "caged in the world of the material" (16) and as such are nearly beyond linguistic description. Jennie is capable by nature, not by design, of experiencing a kind of romantic union with the natural world: "No artist in the formulating of conceptions, her soul still responded . . . and every sound and every sigh were welcome to her because of their beauty" (17).

The association with nature that Dreiser establishes for Jennie in the second chapter does not fade later in the narrative, as Donald Pizer and others suggest. Rather, it is continually reinforced as an explanation for her ability to carry on. Even at her most vulnerable point, after the death of Vesta, Jennie is sustained by the beauty of nature, which persists though "at times certain events were cruel." In a reprise of the rhapsodic tone of chapter II, Dreiser reiterates that, for her, "the flowers, the stars, the trees, the grass" as well as the human spectacle softened "the harsh faces of hunger, cold, indifference, greed." Jennie is not destroyed by events because she perceives the world as ever a wondrous, mysterious, and beautiful place. "She could not understand what it was all about, but still, as in her youth, it was beautiful. One could live, somehow, under any circumstances" (396). As great as Jennie's need is to gather around her those whom she can nurture and care for, it is nature that sustains her.

It is tempting to overlook Jennie's link with the natural world and to see her as a complex heroine who "grows and . . . matures intellectually and socially," thus rescuing both her and the novel from overt sentimentality (Pizer 113). In the end, though, Jennie seems to have changed only in that she, and we, have discovered that her capacity for sorrow is equal to her capacity for joy and that she is able to survive under the nearly crushing weight of circumstance. Jennie's strength lies not in her ability to change and grow with experience but rather to resist the forces — specifically of society and convention — that threaten constantly to destabilize the individual, and to which Lester Kane, "hedged about by the ideas of the conventional world," does eventually succumb (243). The common critical assumptions that Lester's forcefully articulated philosophy is Dreiser's own and that Jennie is a type of tragic heroine, fated to suffer loss upon loss, obscure the fact that it is Lester, not Jennie, who lives an empty, increasingly dissatisfying and disillusioning life. Lester's failure to learn from Jennie, or even to think past his vague notion that "there was something to this woman" (365), dooms him to cynicism and a pathetic, untimely death. The world of *Jennie Gerhardt* is not an entirely fixed and determined one; rather, it is one in which choice, based on experience, is both possible and important. Dreiser presents Lester's choices as real; he could, Dreiser implies, have chosen differently. Much of the novel's pathos therefore arises from his deathbed realization that he has chosen wrongly — according to material, not spiritual, values.

Although Lester possesses a "naturally observing mind," and a "complicated and incisive nature," he is unable to sort out the "vastness of the panorama of life, the glitter of its details, the unsubstantial nature of its forms, the uncertainty of their justification" (125–27). Lester's superior intellect not only fails to provide him with any single settled idea or guiding philosophy, but also, ironically, is actually responsible for his pathetic end. Although his "Rabelaisian" mind is "fairly endowed with the power to see into things," it is not likewise endowed with the power to explain and resolve what it sees, and he is left "overwhelmed" and "confused." Dreiser, with characteristic sympathy, explains Lester's confusion as inevitable in a world of rapidly proliferating "facts and impressions" that succeed in undoing, not enlightening, the "observing mind" (125–27). Jennie is no less confused by the world. She has come, in the end, to "no fixed conclusion as to what life meant" (395). The difference between them is simply that Lester cannot live with his confusion and uncertainty and Jennie can. What Jennie knows, although not consciously, and what Lester is intellectually capable of learning from her, although he fails to do so, is how to survive the gradual disintegration of hope, to emerge from speculations and dreams and live with what life permits. In Dreiser's fictional world, this is as good as it gets.

Lester, the "grizzled example of a philosopher" (403), feels compelled to resort to universal explanations that will fill the gap between what life might be and the reality he confronts. Unable to find meaning or justice in life, he attributes his misfortune to fate and, giving up all faith in free will, "drifts" along satisfying his immediate, material desires, exerting control in the only way he can. It is precisely his intellectual machinations, his inability and unwillingness to "let go," his stubborn refusal to "budge from his beliefs and feelings" (403), and his adherence to the dictates of "policy" (365) that prevent him from making choices. Ultimately, they cause him to conclude that life is show, illusion, farce, and that individual action does not matter. Lester uses his philosophy to distance himself from life: "All the winds of fortune or misfortune could not apparently excite or disturb Lester. He refused to be frightened" (403). But his unwillingness to immerse himself fully in either joy or sorrow is not a sign of strength, and is certainly not endorsed by Dreiser. On the contrary, Lester is much the worse off for his insistence on numbing himself to experience. His need for an overarching, metaphysical philosophy traps him in a destructive cycle: misfortune leads him away from action, which in turn results in still greater misfortune. Lester's intellectual complexity and searching mind do not allow him to be resilient to experience but rather cause him to become paralyzed in the face of it, leaving him spiritually bereft.

Although Lester, like many readers, sees Jennie's vulnerability but only vaguely understands her strength, he does realize that, in contrast to himself, she was "living the thing she was" (314). That is, Jennie does not have a philosophy; she has a life. Whereas Lester, Brander, and even old Gerhardt attempt to explain, justify, and philosophize, seeking an underlying rationale for existence and action, Jennie does not attempt to "put the ocean into a teacup" or "explain or adjust the moral and ethical entanglements of the situation" (393). She does not reduce life to theory or operate according to preconceived notions of fairness or policy. In fact, when Lester universalizes his own struggle by expounding his philosophy of life as the effort merely "to hold our personalities intact," Jennie "did not quite grasp what he was talking about." Significantly, however, she knew what it meant in practical terms: Lester "was not entirely satisfied with himself" (392). If it is difficult for Jennie to "reason about the whys and wherefores of life" and to "think things out" (248), she is deeply aware of the ultimate reality: "They would be dead after a little while, she and Lester and all these people. Did anything matter except goodness — goodness of heart? What else was there that was real?" (308). Jennie neither dreams of what life might be nor philosophizes as to what it should be but rather responds to circumstances as they are presented based on what some feminist ethicists have called a morality of care (Noddings; Gilligan). The priority that guides her actions is care for her family and the well-being of those whose lives she is in a position to affect. When it is within her power to help, by submitting to Brander or to Lester, she does so, and if the least harm will result from misleading her father about her marital status or hiding the existence of Vesta, she does those things as well. Confronted with the death of her only child, Jennie does not resort to an external, metaphysical locus of control — the religion of old Gerhardt or Lester's fatalism — that might serve to explain life or to comfort her in the face of it. Instead she turns back to life itself, adopting two children to whom she will devote her attention, an effort that presumably will sustain her.

Jennie's adoption of children is often overlooked in the haste to read the novel's last line, the "endless reiteration of days" (418), as a demonstration of one of the despairing fundamentals of naturalism: that life is, in the end, without meaning or purpose. But for all his preoccupation with final things and unanswerable questions, Dreiser was consumed not with despair but with curiosity about life. He was less concerned with progress, or with endings, than he was with process — with the individual's ability or inability to adapt to a new environment. If we can judge from the length of his manuscripts, Dreiser was reluctant to end his stories at all. And when he did finally close his first two novels, it was with considerable ambivalence.

Both *Sister Carrie* and *Jennie Gerhardt* ended originally with either impending or actual marriages for their heroines. Fictional concerns, not philosophical ones, led Dreiser to change the ending of *Jennie,* which by no means supplies sufficient closure to allow us to use it in retrospectively interpreting the entire narrative. The process of Jennie's life, her continually renewed effort to adapt to new circumstances, and the positive and life-affirming act of adopting children (one significantly named Rose Perpetua) inform the novel with an element of hope and faith with which it is rarely credited.

Admittedly, Jennie's need to nurture, her willingness to sacrifice her own happiness for others, and her endless capacity to give seem to be signs that she has simply internalized the role that society dictated for women. From a feminist perspective, Jennie seems an obvious restatement of the nineteenth-century essentialized woman who was considered closer to God and nature, whose intuitive and spiritual senses far outstripped her intellectual capacity, and who had no place in men's culture. It is easy to dismiss Jennie as a simplistic and essentialized woman and to assume that her penchant for self-sacrifice, tenderness, sentimentality, and devotion to others was a reflection of Dreiser's ideal of womanhood.[3] And Dreiser's glorification of those qualities that might be called "feminine," as well as his supposed failure to create a self-aware heroine with a well-developed consciousness, seems to be just another reinforcement of the familiar stereotypes.

For Dreiser, though, Jennie's simple goodness, her freedom "from the taint of selfishness" (364), was not associated with feminine weakness but with a strength that at times holds Dreiser in awe. Moreover, the values that Jennie embodies were not, for Dreiser, gender specific. During these early years of his career, he created several male characters who exhibit the same unselfish, sympathetic nature as Jennie. In "A Doer of the Word" in *Twelve Men,* Dreiser valorizes Charlie Potter's commitment to serving those in need even at the expense of his family's material desires. As in Jennie's case, the narrator is curious and mystified by Potter's motivation; Dreiser writes of Potter's explanation for his happiness as though it were an as yet undiscovered secret to success: "I never saw the man or woman yet who couldn't be happy if you could make them feel the need of living for others, of doing something for somebody besides themselves. It's a fact. Selfish people are never happy" (73). And in the *Twelve Men* sketch of his brother Paul, he singles out his "tenderness or sympathy . . . a very human appreciation of the weakness and errors of most of us" as "by far his most engaging quality" (79). Paul was, according to his brother, "generous to the point of self-destruction" and his success was never "purely selfish — exclusive, not inclusive" like the success of "some people" (79).

As with Jennie, both of these characters represent for Dreiser an enviable contentment that inheres in a simple, almost single-minded devotion to others. One of the strongest expressions of the same sentiments comes from Ames in *Sister Carrie* when he advises the now successful and wealthy, if not quite happy, Carrie that her talent will fade quickly if she becomes "self-interested, selfish and luxurious." He elaborates: "If you want to do most, do good. Serve the many. Be kind and humanitarian." Again there is a sense of awe; like Lester, who cannot quite understand Jennie, and the narrator, who is mystified by Potter, Carrie is drawn to Ames, whose advice "appeal[s] to her as absolutely true" but who is a curious figure. "Never had she seen such a man as this" (486). Dreiser's interest in unselfishness and sacrifice has less to do with the effect of charity or philanthropy on those in need than it does with the beneficial effect on the doer. Selflessness brings happiness and contentment to those who give. Clearly Dreiser values Potter, Jennie, and Ames not because they represent ideals of masculinity or femininity, but because in the compendium of fictional characters he created, they come closest to striking that elusive balance that allows for happiness and moral virtue in a world seemingly designed to destroy both.

After the long and difficult years of writing *Jennie,* Dreiser turned quickly and with comparative ease to the Cowperwood novels, which, along with *An American Tragedy,* fixed his reputation as the leading American naturalist. We can only speculate as to whether Dreiser himself would have preferred that we focus more closely on these later novels. In any case, it is important that Dreiser's early fiction be read on its own terms and not simply as prefiguring the ideas more prevalent in his later work. To the extent that Dreiser is stuck with the tough-guy image — aggressive newspaper reporter, ally of H. L. Mencken, active womanizer, author of the lobster and squid metaphor — *Jennie Gerhardt* is a useful corrective. *Jennie* is the fullest expression of an idealism and a sensitivity to life that are often ignored but that were central to Dreiser's thinking. It is possible, in his second novel particularly, to see Dreiser as critiquing the naturalistic philosophy he supposedly endorsed.

Naturalism, like every other "ism," is at once a shorthand that facilitates communication and a reductive term that causes us to overlook the distinguishing features of particular narratives. We are accustomed to thinking of naturalism as an all-encompassing philosophical statement rather than a literary style. This view not only is inadequate to an understanding of *Jennie Gerhardt,* but also is destructive of the range and complexity of Dreiser's thinking. A reading of *Jennie* unclouded by preconceived naturalistic assumptions reveals a sensibility that was not an idiosyncratic deviation but that persisted throughout his life. This sensibility emerged in his final novel, *The Bulwark,* and in his later writings, collected as *Notes on Life,* in which he elaborated on the themes he had written about in *Jennie* twenty years before: nature, feeling, and intuitive knowledge. We do Dreiser a disservice in dismissing as inconsistencies these important aspects of his thought and his fiction and in subsuming his novels beneath a philosophy that was not actually his own.

Notes

1. Vivas does valuable work in separating Dreiser's philosophy from his fiction. But most critics follow Mencken and fail to make this distinction.

2. For example, Donald Pizer, in his essay on *Jennie Gerhardt* (96–130), finds the "early emphasis on Jennie as a child of nature" to be "disconcerting" and damaging to the novel as a whole insofar as it leads to sentimentality and "bathos." Pizer claims that Dreiser redeems the novel by dropping this line of characterization.

3. If this novel is any indication, Dreiser seemed to have been extremely ambivalent on this question. In the original draft of *Jennie Gerhardt,* Jennie was something of a materialist with a practical and frank interest in bettering her lot. Dreiser was troubled by this initial characterization, though, and changed Jennie substantially, eliminating any conflict between the spiritual and the material and creating the self-sacrificing "All-mother" of the published version. We can only speculate on the relation of Jennie's temperament to Dreiser's mother, Sarah, who her son lovingly described as "a magnetic dreamy soul . . . beyond or behind so-called good and evil" (quoted in Matthiessen 8). Since Jennie was written during one of the most trying periods of Dreiser's life, it is tempting to think that Dreiser wanted to create a fictional female character with all the attributes of the mother whose unconditional devotion and instinctive understanding he no longer enjoyed in fact. I would argue, however, that Jennie is not simply a comforting, nostalgic re-creation of his mother. She also represents a side of Dreiser himself that was attracted, early and late, to the idealism Jennie embodies.

Bibliography

Dreiser, Theodore. *Jennie Gerhardt.* Edited by James L. W. West III. Philadelphia: University of Pennsylvania Press, 1992.

———. *Notes on Life*. Edited by Marguerite Tjader and John J. McAleer. University: University of Alabama Press, 1974.

———. *Sister Carrie*. Edited by John C. Berkey, Alice M. Winters, James L. W. West III, and Neda M. Westlake. Philadelphia: University of Pennsylvania Press, 1981.

———. *Twelve Men*. New York: Boni and Liveright, 1919.

Dreiser-Mencken Letters: The Correspondence of Theodore Dreiser and H. L. Mencken, 1907–1945. Edited by Thomas P. Riggio. 2 vols. Philadelphia: University of Pennsylvania Press, 1986.

Elias, Robert H. *Theodore Dreiser: Apostle of Nature*. New York: Alfred A. Knopf, 1949.

Marcus, Mordecai. "Loneliness, Death, and Fulfillment in Jennie Gerhardt." *Studies in American Fiction* 7 (1979): 61–73.

Matthiessen, F. O. *Theodore Dreiser*. New York: Dell Publishing Co., 1951.

Moers, Ellen. *Two Dreisers*. New York: Viking Press, 1969.

Pizer, Donald. *The Novels of Theodore Dreiser: A Critical Study*. Minneapolis: University of Minnesota Press, 1976.

Vivas, Eliseo. "Dreiser, An Inconsistent Mechanist." In *The Stature of Theodore Dreiser*, edited by Alfred Kazin and Charles Shapiro. Bloomington: Indiana University Press, 1965.

4
Chill History and Rueful Sentiments in *Jennie Gerhardt*

VALERIE ROSS

Let the soul be but gentle and receptive, this vast truth will come home; not in set phrases, perhaps, but as a feeling, a comfort, which, after all, is the last essence of knowledge.
—Theodore Dreiser, *Jennie Gerhardt* (88)

STUDENTS, LIKE CRITICS, TEND TO respond forcefully to sentimental literature. Those who do not like it say that they do not precisely because it is sentimental; those who like it insist that it cannot be sentimental. The term itself is at issue: "Sentimentalism," as one of my students put it, "applies to weepy wimpy women and Hallmark cards." Such responses pretty well sum up critical attitudes toward Theodore Dreiser's *Jennie Gerhardt* as a sentimental novel, attitudes to which I turn later. But because I wish in this essay to explore and even celebrate Dreiser as a sentimentalist—as a teacher and theorist of the role of emotions in personal and sociopolitical relations—it is necessary first to address the history of the term "sentimental" itself, given how at once emotionally fraught and vague it has become. Or, more nearly accurate, given how anxious-making any serious consideration of our emotional lives has become—a condition that Dreiser himself predicts in *Jennie Gerhardt*.

What, then, might it mean to call Dreiser's novel sentimental? Is sentimentalism here a genre? A mode? An ideology? A particular set of emotions? A lapse into bad taste? Literary historians have established that the word "sentimental" and a type of literature referred to as the "sentimental novel" became parts of everyday language during the eighteenth century— as terms of approval. Having a finely tuned sensibility, a capacity to experience, represent, and appeal to the emotions, especially strong emotions, signified one's high moral development and distinguished one as having the qualities, if not the capital, of the upper class.[1] However, while sensibility was flowering, relations and definitions of gender were accommodating the twists and turns of emergent industrial capitalism and, more to the point, of print capitalism and the consequently accelerating, democratizing rates of public literacy. The conjuncture of sensibility with print capitalism and the relegation of emotions and emotional labor to women (what Lester, in *Jennie Gerhardt,* calls Jennie's "affectional services") provided women with heightened authority and access to sentimental literature, of which they became enthusiastic readers and expert writers. Indeed, so successfully did they take to this terrain that, by the early nineteenth century, American male critics and writers had come to characterize and denounce the sentimental novel as "feminine."[2] In his preface to *Last of the Mohicans* (1826), for example, James Fenimore Cooper underscores this nascent sense of novels as having gender-specific qualities and appeal when he advises his readers that his book is not intended for "the more imaginative sex" and takes pains throughout to distinguish his protagonist, Natty Bumppo, as anything but sentimental. Thus, when Natty pushes a faithful horse over a cliff to its screaming death or leaves an Indian he has shot to suffer a slow, anguished death, he responds by expressing a mild, workmanlike satisfaction at his frugal use of bullets. Sympathy and weeping are women's work; they are pedagogical and performative obligations dispatched to the women and more effeminate men in the text.

Whether American women writers and readers actually dominated the nineteenth-century literary marketplace remains a matter of debate, but that they were a significant force in shaping the reception and course of the American novel is certain. By the early nineteenth century, sentimental literature and women were tightly linked in the minds of white male writers and readers; to be a *man* of letters virtually obliged one to disavow at every turn any affiliation with the damned scribbling mob. By the third quarter of the nineteenth century, when American departments of literature began to organize and American high-art literary journals such as the *North American Review* were being established as arbiters of literary culture, professors and critics alike defined themselves in great part *against* sentimental literature, which for them was an unchallenged term of opprobrium. Sentimentalism now came to be affiliated not only with the more imaginative sex, but also with what they called mass literature: that literature most likely to be written and read by the uneducated, by which they mainly meant—and typically said—women. As terms, concepts, and literary values, "popular," "mass," and "sentimental," along with variations on "feminine" ("ladies," "French dancing instructors," "schoolmarms," "schoolgirls") and the underclass ("uncouth," "vulgar"), became a virtually interchangeable vocabulary among those who were or wished to identify themselves as members of an elite literary community.[3] To this day sentimentalism, conjoining "women" (as writers and readers) and "money" (mass commercial appeal), connotes a kind of literary prostitution: a sentimentalist is a writer who sells out—who works for Hallmark rather than starves in a garret.

The affiliation of sentimentalism with prostitution seems also to govern what texts academics consider to be sentimental. Until quite recently, the only sentimental books to receive significant critical attention were novels of seduction—stories of fallen women—with Samuel Richardson's *Pamela* and *Clarissa* constituted as founding texts. Consequently, it is this particular strand or subgenre of literature to which Dreiser's critics generally refer when they label *Jennie Gerhardt* a sentimental novel. Such critics observe that *Jennie Gerhardt* clearly employs the fallen woman motif featured by Richardson and other novelists of seduction. They further point out how Dreiser's novel has all the stock elements of what they call sentimentalism: Jennie, the innocent, self-sacrificing virgin, is seduced and abandoned not once but twice—first by Senator Brander and then by Lester Kane, each of whom fits the bill as an upper-class rake and recalls as well the subgenre's longstanding debates about whether rakes can be reformed. *Jennie Gerhardt* has also the cruel, forbidding father, old William Gerhardt, whose understanding arrives too late to be of much use; and it features a host of disapproving family members and friends.[4] But despite their attention to links between *Jennie Gerhardt* and the novel of seduction, Dreiser's critics seem to overlook the most powerful one: *Jennie Gerhardt,* like Susanna Rowson's very popular *Charlotte Temple* and like Richardson's novels, challenges as well as instructs readers about a particular social prohibition—premarital sex for women—and the consequences attendant on its violation. Each of these texts dwells on the as yet unresolved hypocrisies, contradictions, and double standards of a code that, ostensibly moral, seems actually more concerned with enforcing and maintaining unequal relations and consolidations of power, property, sexuality, and reproduction along lines of class and gender.[5] The social, moral, and economic problematics typically articulated by such texts, whether *Charlotte Temple* or *Jennie Gerhardt,* are likelier to touch readers who, late in the twentieth century, must still grapple with the very real and very emotionally fraught issues these books raise—as students' responses to them inevitably remind me. Critics who reduce such novels to what they presume are stock sentimental features are baffled by the persistent, transhistorical appeal of such texts. Predisposed to reject all things sentimental, they are unlikely to notice the extent to which the social, moral, and affective complexity of a novel such as *Jennie Gerhardt* is indebted to its hearty engagement with sentimentalist discourse.

Although agreeing that *Jennie Gerhardt* participates in the tradition of the sentimental novel, critics tend to disagree about whether Dreiser is participating in earnest or engaging in a sophisticated parody or intelligent correction of the presumed naïveté of novels of seduction. In keeping with a long-standing tradition, Oscar Cargill and Leslie Fiedler have ridiculed and dismissed *Jennie Gerhardt* simply by identifying it as sentimental — and therefore bad. Fiedler writes, "The fictional world of Dreiser is the *absolutely* sentimental world, in which morality itself has finally been dissolved in pity; and in such a world, Charlotte Temple is quite appropriately reborn. No theme but seduction can contain the meanings Dreiser is trying to express" (253). Dreiser's novels, according to Fiedler, "are in fact 'uplifting' — which is to say, sentimental rather than tragic" (250). Fiedler notices that Dreiser has "none of the detachment and cynicism of Crane, none of the utter blackness and pessimism of Twain; he is as 'positive' through his tears as any female scribbler." Pointing to Dreiser's work for the Butterick magazines, "purveyors of fashion, fiction, and useful articles ('What to Do When Diphtheria Comes') to lower middle-brow women," Fiedler insists that Dreiser's writing for this female audience was neither an "unfortunate interruption of his career" nor a "prostitution of his talent." Rather, Fiedler charges, "*At the deepest level, he shared their values*" (his emphasis, 249). In short, Dreiser was not even doing it for money, a form of literary deviance that Fiedler could more easily forgive than that of sharing values with women.

In contrast to those who have rejected *Jennie Gerhardt* as mawkishly sentimental, or simply found it the most sentimental of Dreiser's novels, critics such as Cathy and Arnold Davidson, Mordecai Marcus, Carol Schwartz, and Daryl Dance variously consider the novel a critique or revision of sentimentalism.[6] But even here they employ the term "sentimental" pejoratively, as a charge of literary pandering against which Dreiser must be defended. Of the few critics who have given serious scholarly attention to the sentimentalism of *Jennie Gerhardt*, the Davidsons are the most circumspect about its status as sentimental, choosing instead to demonstrate how Dreiser's novel borrowed from and improved on two popular nineteenth-century American subgenres of literature — the "working girl" novel and the "sentimental costume romance." In so doing, they imply that there is indeed more than one kind of sentimentalism and, of course, more than one popular subgenre in which Dreiser was likely participating.

More typical of the general defense against the charge of sentimentalism are the positions taken by Marcus and Schwartz. Like most critics, Marcus presumes that sentimentalism is a unified, easily identifiable, and readily dismissible type of literature. His strategy is thus to point to how Dreiser diverges *from* its conventions, arguing that he "saved his plot from sentimentality" by showing clearly that Lester's final declaration of love for Jennie could not make up for the havoc created by his earlier denial of it (73). Schwartz, although a little more specific about what kind of sentimental novel *Jennie Gerhardt* might be, ultimately shares Marcus's sentiment. She asks her readers not to "relegate *Jennie Gerhardt* to the genre of the sentimental domestic novel," since Dreiser, in changing the ending from happy to bleak, "rejected the formula of the sentimental novel" — with, she feels obliged to add, the unhappy exception of the melodramatic death of Vesta (24).

Rather than trifle with these definitions *of* the sentimental, I think it is useful to dwell for a moment on what critics reveal about themselves and us in their feelings *about* what they consider sentimental — and hence repellent. Sentimental texts, they seem to suggest, are popular; or rather, if a text is popular, it is probably sentimental. A bleak ending is *not* sentimental; a happy ending is. Deathbed scenes, such as Vesta's, are hardly happy, yet they too seem every bit as sentimental as uplifting scenes. Detachment, cynicism, blackness, and pessimism are not sentimental; tears are. Thus, although critics ostensibly object to sentimentalism on the grounds of its adherence to generic conventions (fallen women, rakes, disapproving fathers), what they actually object to is a particular set of emotions and passions — a certain set of affective responses — that are represented, provoked, or solicited by such novels. "Sentimental," as a term, seems to be applied to texts that invoke or evoke powerful feelings from their readers: tears, joy, hope, sorrow. In contrast, affective responses that are subdued, negative, bleak, cynical, grim, detached, and hopeless are the valued features of the emotionally flat, depressive (one might say almost pathologically disaffected) landscape of the nonsentimental writer, the realist or naturalist.

Exposed here is a division of emotional labor within the field of academic criticism that is at once gendered and generic. This division is deeply rooted in the prior century's rationalizations and valuations of gender and genre. Women (and sentimental literature) are responsible for producing and displaying strong emotions such as grief and joy. Men (and realist or naturalist literature) are the tenders of the rational. They are responsible for *not* indulging in their emotions; they must be disaffected. Like Jennie, tearless at the novel's end, their appropriate affective response to horror and splendor alike must be a dull, inscrutable ache. As Dean MacCannell and Juliet Flower MacCannell observe of contemporary culture:

> If we explore the terrain between the sexes, we find a pattern of expressive constraint in "masculine" self-portraiture. . . . Men, in our Anglo-American society, are supposed to be "cool." This requirement operates on every detail of behavior. . . . There are prohibitions and injunctions, not against "showing off," but against *appearing* to be showing off. . . . [A man] should be similarly cautious when it comes to other forms of self-expression-for-women, his behavior, speech, and dress, lest they be seen as *intentionally* produced for the purpose of being attractive to females. (207)

Such gendered prohibitions and injunctions, and the affective charges attached to them, are precisely what enable Fiedler to accuse Dreiser of gravitating naturally to the values and forms of self-expression of lower middle-brow female readers.

Such injunctions, and their unhappy social and political effects, are precisely what Dreiser theorizes and contests throughout *Jennie Gerhardt*. As both the MacCannells's "Anglo-Saxon" and Fiedler's "lower middle-brow" suggest, affective displays (the show of emotions) and affective responsibilities (whose and which feelings matter) are entangled not only with issues of gender but also with class and ethnicity. And Dreiser moves all of this to the foreground in scene after scene of *Jennie Gerhardt*. Critics, falling into the very trap that Dreiser was trying to dismantle, have been too quick to see Jennie as sole bearer and signifier of sentimentalism and Lester as the man of naturalism and realism. A closer look at the novel suggests that Dreiser's distribution of strong emotions and affective displays does not divide so neatly between the sexes, however much they are shaped and tinged by gender. Jennie's father, an underclass laborer and first-generation German patriarch, breaks into reluctant tears on several occasions—for example, when he tries to retrieve his son, Sebastian, from jail. When Sebastian is led out of the cell, "all marked and tousled," Gerhardt "broke down and began to cry. No word could cross his lips, because of his emotion" (64). While Sebastian himself struggles to hold back tears and reassure his father, old Gerhardt is overwhelmed by his utter powerlessness, his inability to post bail, pay fines, negotiate court appearances. Struck by the nearly unbearable realization that poverty feeds on itself, creating ever more desperate situations, he has another "burst of feeling" and is led away shaking "but trying to conceal it" (65). In contrast, Lester's father, Archibald Kane, is an affluent owner of a manufacturing company, a second-generation Irish patriarch, and a man who never displays strong emotions, although on one occasion readers receive an indirect report of his having experienced one, caused by Lester's and Jennie's extended affair. "The old man grieved bitterly," we learn, "and then by degrees he began to harden" (273).

Although one might conclude from this that Dreiser has divided emotional display and labor along lines of class and ethnicity, I think it is more nearly accurate to say simply that strong emotions are generated from situations that deeply affect the lives of those involved. Insulated by prosperity, the Kane family's only real site of affective discomfort is their son's nonconformity—and they have wills and attorneys to deal with it. But there are also affective differences among and between members of both the Gerhardt and Kane families that Dreiser is careful to elaborate. Thus Lester's brother, Robert, is the cooler, more Anglo-Saxon of the two; he has "a certain hard incisiveness" that fits him for "the money relationship" of the Kane business. Lester is more akin to his father, the "big man" who founded the Kane business on the philosophy that "most men [are] honest" and would pay good money for good products. Of a bigger build and thus physically more "masculine" than Robert, Lester is affectively represented as more "feminine": he is not, we are told, "hard and grasping like his brother . . . but rather softer, more human, more good-natured about everything" (137). Thus, within the Kane family, Lester simultaneously signifies and problematizes conventional divisions between masculinity and femininity.

At one point in the novel, when the brothers argue over the treatment of elderly employees, Robert appears to take the more masculine (affectively flat, realist, naturalist?) position and Lester the more feminine (emotionally charged, sentimentalist?). "Robert was for running the business on a hard and cold basis, dropping the aged, who had grown up with his father, and cleaning out the 'dead wood' as he called it." Lester, by contrast, calls for a humane course: "I'm not going to see these old fellows who have grown up with this business thrown out bag and baggage, without anything, if I can help it. It isn't right." He insists that their company "can afford to be decent" and proposes a pension plan. Entertaining their views, Kane senior vacillates, "rather inclined to agree with Robert commercially, though sympathetically and ethically he thought that Lester had the more decent end of the argument" (170). Through this complex of responses to a situation that elicits competing interests and affects, Dreiser contests and complicates conventional masculinity and the privileging of "Anglo-Saxon" conduct. He also quite astutely (and presciently) points up the relationship between sympathy and ethics. He demonstrates how the repression of strong emotions—in this instance, compassion—being doubly valorized by the combined codes of masculinity and capitalism in late nineteenth-century America, was enabling and even encouraging ruthless policies and practices in the marketplace and within the family.

Such scenes participate in an American sentimental tradition that has many sources. However, the two most immediate sources in this country seem to have been an emergent republican discourse of equality and rights and a popular (as opposed to organized) Christianity based on direct readings of the Bible and taking Christ's forgiveness and sympathy as an ethical model. The tradition had other sources as well, from the Scottish Enlightenment philosophers to Jean Jacques Rousseau, Mary Wollstonecraft, and, of course, Richardson.[7] Best exemplified within American literature by abolitionist and feminist writings of the early nineteenth century, such texts assert a sentimental humanism founded on the principle that human beings are affectively equal—that we universally share the capacity to feel deeply and strongly—and that therefore we are equally entitled to happiness. Such an approach seeks to alleviate both the causes and the effects of suffering, and it presumes that persons who contribute to the unhappiness of others are either oblivious to the pain they inflict or have been affectively disturbed by the social conditions in which they find themselves. Jennie speaks the fundamental principle and goal of sentimental humanism when, pondering the course of civilization on her grand tour, she asks, "Did anything matter except goodness—goodness of heart? What else was there that was real?" (308). As in the epigraph to this essay, in which Dreiser refers to feelings as "the last essence of knowledge," the sentimental-activist writer takes goodness of heart as an epistemological and ethical imperative and, by deploying biographical evidence as a site of analysis, instruction, and persuasion, works to move readers to a change of heart. As Harriet Beecher Stowe put it, one must feel right to do right. The affective pedagogy of sentimental humanism thus seeks to change readers' feelings and, as a consequence, their practices, values, ideals, and sometimes laws.

Although in scenes such as the one between Lester and Robert over the treatment of aging employees, Dreiser is not as explicit or sociopolitically ambitious as some of his sentimental-activist predecessors, his work has much in common with theirs. Like the sentimental activists, his first and most pressing task in *Jennie Gerhardt* is to establish the humanity of the targeted group — the underclass — to guide more privileged readers to identify with, feel compassion for, and act to alleviate their suffering. To effect this identification-across-difference, the sentimental activist mainly works to demonstrate the affective equality or even superiority of the disenfranchised group. As becomes far more clear in the Pennsylvania edition, Jennie exemplifies this affective superiority. The task of producing identification *across difference* is quite demanding, for the sentimental activist must manage to prove equality without repressing real differences (in values, habits, preferences, worldviews) between the reading and the represented subject. The danger on the one hand is that of producing unrecognizable or unwittingly offensive caricatures of either group. The danger on the other is of converting the oppressed individuals into mirrors of Anglo-American middle-class values and manners so that privileged readers learn only how to sympathize with people who think, look, and act like themselves. This, of course, is seldom the case with those who have been excluded from and by white middle-class culture.

Writers like Dreiser, who themselves have been members of the groups they set out to represent, are generally more successful in articulating such differences: their topic is more emotionally charged for them, and they have worked both sides of the fence and can draw their stories from real experience rather than from imagining what it might be like to be poor (or a slave, or a woman). Dreiser frequently stages this divergence of subjectivities, as when Lester and Jennie encounter a beggar, "some played-out specimen of humanity whom [Lester] had scarcely noticed" but who attracts Jennie's attention. She is "quick to see ragged clothes, worn shoes, care-lined faces" — signs of poverty she can readily recognize. But it is Lester who blithely assumes the role of the expert: "It isn't always as bad as you think," he explains to her. "Some of these people are professional beggars." The point here is not simply that Lester fails to take her experience into account; only moments before, as a matter of fact, he had been admiring Jennie's view that "people were not as bad as some people thought," a philosophy that "appealed to him as a big, decent way to take life, even if it did eliminate aggressiveness and the ability to gather material things." Now offered an easy opportunity to practice what Jennie preaches ("Let's give him something," she suggests), Lester immediately changes his tune to harmonize with his own privileged position: "If you see anybody who wants anything very badly," he pontificates, "and is capable of enjoying it, he is apt to get it. Not always, but most people get what they are capable of enjoying. Anyhow, sympathizing and worrying won't help anybody. Action is better. A barrel of flour is worth a hundred barrels of tears" (195). Here Lester nicely exemplifies the sentimental principle that social feelings and actions are inextricably linked to personal history, position, and knowledge. Having at his disposal a self-serving, culturally licensed screen of cynicism and ignorance rather than any cultural imperative to understand, sympathize with, and alleviate the sufferings of the poor, Lester is moved not to act but to temporize, while Jennie, silenced, continues to study the crowd. The scene enacts an earlier moment of sentimental instruction by Dreiser: "As yet, we are dwelling in a most brutal order of society, against the pompous and loud-mouthed blusterings of which the temperate and tender voice of sympathy seems both futile and vain," he observes. "Although able to look about him" and thus to sympathize with others, "in the teeth of all the winds of circumstance, and between the giant legs of chance, struts little man — the indifference, the non-understanding, the selfishness of whom make his playground too often a field of despair" (93).

Those out to criticize or excuse Dreiser's sentimentality have inevitably seized on the fact that Dreiser, having been raised in poverty, openly expressed his deep sympathy for the poor. This "admission" is often enough attached to his own criticisms of the "sentiment and mush" that he confessed to having once enjoyed; and these are used as proof that his portrayal of the Gerhardts is more sentimental and thus not as well-crafted as his more realist construction of the Kanes.[8] Exemplifying Dreiser's observations about the futility of sympathy in a culture trained to be indifferent, such critics neither evaluate nor challenge the *realism* of the impoverished Gerhardts; rather, they discount the representation of the Gerhardts' lives *because* it solicits and, one would hope, provokes strong emotional responses. Critics seem to prefer — and defend in the name of "realism" — a literary tour guide who, like Lester, provides a reassuring distance, cynicism, and detachment from suffering with which they might otherwise be prompted to feel rueful and complicit. Acutely aware of this high-culture predilection for indifferent texts, Dreiser faced a challenge that his sentimental predecessors had not. Somehow he had to acknowledge and account for what his readers had been trained to feel was an appropriately artistic *and* affective response to the sufferings of others. If critics' responses are any measure, he was only half successful in providing the kind of mirror reflection of their own values, problems, and assumptions that they demanded of texts and, in *Jennie Gerhardt,* found only (if at all) in the Kanes.

That Dreiser felt entangled within the competing demands of sentimental activism, popular-commercial appeal, and high-culture realism is
intricately figured by the story-within-the-story newspaper account of Jennie and Lester's relationship. Dreiser opens this account by observing,
in sentimental (activist) fashion, that the "American public" liked gossip
about the rich, and "was inordinately interested in all that concerned the
getting of money and the spending of it, for that was almost the sole and
vital interest of the nation." Here he attempts to guide his readers away
from identification with such a public, even as his own text assumes a reader
interested in stories about the getting and spending of money and the lives
of the rich. We then learn that, it being "the business of the newspapers to
chronicle" such lives, various minor society leaflets and magazines were
making passing references to Lester's "rather distinguished romance." Dreiser continues:

> The fact that [Lester] might not be married seemed to be courteously ignored
> by these items, the romance of a real marriage between a man of wealth and a
> poor working-girl seeming to have a greater appeal for the paragraphers. It
> seemed rather astonishing to the poor and, in many cases, underpaid workers
> of the smaller press that any such thing should be. (284)

This passage is intriguing, given that Dreiser began his writing career as one
of those underpaid workers of a small press, whereas his sisters — poor
working girls — variously dated or actually married into wealth. Thus the
newspaper's "astonishing" story — like *Jennie Gerhardt* — reflects real events
in the lives of Dreiser and his sisters. Indeed, his original manuscript was a
more faithful biography of his sister Mame, the predominant model for
Jennie, insofar as it culminated (as in the newspaper story) with her marriage to the son of a well-to-do Irish family. Ironically, Dreiser revised the
ending partly at the urging of Lillian Rosenthal, a wealthy young woman
who felt that readers — like herself — would find the marriage unrealistic
and unsatisfying. If he knew it, this fact should have been cautionary to
Fiedler, suggesting as it does that male critics who prefer bleak endings
might be sharing the values of upper-class women. Had he, taking Dreiser's
lead, struggled against his fear of feminization, Fiedler might even have
noticed the extent to which he was partaking in tastes cultivated by and for
those with rather poor reasons for cherishing hopelessness and despair.

When the story of Jennie and Lester becomes a full-page Sunday feature in a Chicago newspaper, Jennie's response (in the Pennsylvania edition) demonstrates yet again her powers of sympathetic identification.

Titled "This Millionaire Fell in Love With This Lady's Maid," and replete with photos and sketches of herself and Lester, Jennie studies it and then "turn[s] the matter over ruefully in her mind." She "did not know how she ought to feel, really." She anticipates and analyzes Lester's reaction: " She did not mind so much what it meant to her — as a matter of fact it was rather flattering, that she could see — but Lester, Lester, how must he feel? And his family!" She acknowledges that "she had come, in her private conscience, to think rather badly of his family of late," but nonetheless "she felt sorry for Lester. He would mind. He loved his family" (289). She tries to keep calm, "to exert emotional control, but again the tears would rise, only this time they were tears of opposition to defeat." She wonders, "Why couldn't the world help her, instead of seeking to push her down?" (289–90).

Lester, as the reader knows, has already read the article; it made him feel "stunned and chagrined, irritated beyond words to express." He exclaims, "To think the damned newspaper would do that to a private citizen who was quietly minding his own business!" Not alerting Jennie to the story, he tears it out of the paper and leaves the house "to conceal his deep inward mortification." He rides about Chicago in a trolley car, wondering "what his friends were thinking." "Wrath," he concludes, "was useless." So he calls on his attorney, who advises him, "Let's not cry over spilled milk" and points to a possible silver lining, that the story "will make a sort of popular hero out of you with the working classes — the so-called proletariat." Lester, darkly frowning, replies, "To the devil with them." He again protests "this damned country of ours!" where a "man with a little money hasn't any more privacy than a public monument" (286–88). On "mature deliberation," he decides to tell Jennie about the story and assure her that it "did not make so much difference, though to him it made all the difference in the world. The effect of this chill history could never be undone." When he does tell her of the story — "I didn't know I was such an ardent Romeo" — Jennie observes that "Lester did not express his real feeling — his big ills (ills so big that they could not readily be corrected by human effort) in words." She sees herself as responsible for his troubles, as a "great detriment." She considers leaving him but reminds herself that he wanted her and would not let her go — which in any case she was very reluctant to do. Lester, however, is still lost in thoughts of his "newspaper notoriety" and how he would be shut out of his old world (290–91). Finally his thoughts turn to Jennie:

> What a rough thing it all was. Jennie was growing in mental acumen. She was beginning to see things quite as clearly as he did. She was not a cheap, am-

bitious, climbing creature. She wanted to be fair by him; she had his real interests at heart. She was a big woman in her way. (292)

Undoubtedly, the Harpers edition, which, like Lester, all but erases Jennie's subjectivity, has contributed to critical dismissals of *Jennie Gerhardt* as a sentimental novel. In it Jennie is viewed as a passive, self-sacrificing, sentimental heroine rather than a generous, loving, resourceful, powerfully analytical underclass woman with a child born out of wedlock — a "big woman" who has grown to love a relatively weak, passive, self-centered "little man" who, brutalized by the callous act he commits in abandoning Jennie, eventually dies from the effects of his self-indulgence.

In the Pennsylvania edition, Jennie comes far more clearly into focus as a figure drawn from Dreiser's own experiences and, to the extent he could grasp them, his sisters'. About his sisters he wrote in *Dawn,* "I might attempt to disentangle what was unquestionably a knot or network of emotions and interests, all relating to the particular love life of each," and then adds, "but I would fail for lack of any real knowledge of the underlying subtleties and beauties" (172). Rejecting the moral and practical sense of proscribing women's sexuality, he concludes that his sisters were strong, desiring women who "were their own masters, or might be if they would" (173).

One can only wonder at the portrait of Jennie Gerhardt that might have emerged had Dreiser not been compelled, by the forces of chance and circumstance, to tailor his novel to a readership that preferred its playgrounds to simulate fields of despair. Those in search of hopelessness are likely to miss the underlying subtleties and beauties, the knot of interests and emotions that he so brilliantly and painstakingly analyzes in *Jennie Gerhardt.* They are unlikely, as well, to notice that Dreiser actually ends the novel in good dark cheer as our gaze converges with that of Jennie Gerhardt, alive and well, watching Lester fade into the world of indifference he helped to create.

Notes

1. See, for example, Todd, Bell, Brissenden, and Kaplan.

2. For discussions of the rise and reception of the American sentimental novel in relation to gender and print capitalism, see Davidson, Baym, and Kelley. For histories of print capitalism and the profession of literature in the United States, see Charvat, West, Warner, and Ziff.

3. I discuss more extensively the function of gender and class in the organization and identity of the American profession of literature in "Too Close to Home: Repressing Biography, Instituting Authority."

4. Daryl Dance, for example, provides a brief history of American sentimentalism, which she says is "patterned for the most part after Samuel Richardson's *Pamela*," and follows with a succinct list of its "almost standardized plot and stock characters" (129). By means of this, she argues that in *Jennie Gerhardt* "Dreiser comes closer to creating a purely sentimental heroine that he does in *Sister Carrie*" (136).

5. For discussions of how this discourse of female sexuality both challenges and works to consolidate power along lines of gender, race, and class, see Carby (especially 20–39) and Armstrong.

6. Another strategy for saving Dreiser from sentimentalism is that of Warwick Waddlington, who, in response to "the memorable instance by Lionel Trilling to excoriate the 'doctrinaire indulgence' of Dreiser's 'brooding pity' as a form of sentimentalizing the proletariat," argues that *Jennie Gerhardt* is a novel of "pathos" and should thus be situated in the (firmly masculine, high-culture) company of Euripides, Shakespeare, Milton, Flaubert, Ibsen, Camus, and Nietzsche.

7. Along with Davidson, Kelley, and Warner, see Douglas and Tompkins (especially 122–46). For a history of antebellum sentimental-activism, see Yellin; for debates about the relationships between feminism, abolitionism, and sentimentalism, see Sanchez-Eppler and Romero.

8. Critics are fond of quoting a few passages from Dreiser's *A Book about Myself* as evidence of his incurable sentimentalism. The most common of these is: "The saccharine strength of the sentiment and mush which we could gulp down at that time, and still can do to this day, is to me beyond belief. And I was one of those who did the gulping; indeed I was one of the worst" (151). Although he is here speaking specifically about drama and his experiences as a drama critic for the *St. Louis Globe-Democrat* this passage (or portions of it) are taken out of context to imply that he was an unabashed (and unrecovered) reader of "mush," that is, sentimental texts. A second passage relied on is Dreiser's contemplation of the effects of his impoverished childhood, about which he observes, "I was filled with an intense sympathy for the woes of others, life in all its helpless degradation and poverty, the unsatisfied dreams of people, their sweaty labors, the things they were compelled to endure" (151). Daryl Dance, for example, uses both passages to establish that "Dreiser's reaction to poverty and suffering was essentially sentimental" (127).

Bibliography

Armstrong, Nancy. *Desire and Domestic Fiction: A Political History of the Novel.* New York: Oxford University Press, 1987.

Baym, Nina. *Novels, Readers, and Reviewers: Responses to Fiction in Antebellum America.* Ithaca, NY: Cornell University Press, 1984.

Bell, Michael. *The Sentiment of Reality: Truth of Feeling in the European Novel.* London: George Allen & Unwin, 1983.

Brissenden, R. F. *Virtue in Distress: Studies in the Novel of Sentiment from Richardson to Sade.* New York: Macmillan, 1974.

Carby, Hazel. *Reconstructing Womanhood: The Emergence of the Afro-American Woman Novelist.* New York: Oxford University Press, 1987.

Cargill, Oscar. *Intellectual America.* New York: Macmillan, 1941.

Charvat, William. *The Profession of Authorship in America, 1800–1870.* Columbus: Ohio State University Press, 1968.

Dance, Daryl. "Sentimentalism in Dreiser's Heroines, Carrie and Jennie." *College Language Association Journal* 14(December 1970):127–42.

Davidson, Cathy N. *Revolution and the Word: The Rise of the Novel in America.* New York: Oxford University Press, 1986.

Davidson, Cathy N. and Arnold E. Davidson. "Carrie's Sisters: The Popular Prototypes for Dreiser's Heroine." *Modern Fiction Studies* 23, 3(Autumn 1977): 395–408.

Douglas, Ann. *The Feminization of American Culture.* New York: Doubleday, 1977.

Dreiser, Theodore. *A Book About Myself.* New York: Boni and Liveright, 1927.

———. *Dawn.* New York: Horace Liveright, 1951.

———. *Jennie Gerhardt.* Edited by James L. W. West III. Philadelphia: University of Pennsylvania Press, 1992.

Fiedler, Leslie A. *Love and Death in the American Novel.* New York: Stein and Day, 1982.

Kaplan, Fred. *Sacred Tears: Sentimentality in Victorian Literature.* Princeton, N.J.: Princeton University Press, 1987.

Kelley, Mary. *Private Woman, Public Stage: Literary Domesticity in Nineteenth-Century America.* New York: Oxford University Press, 1984.

Lingeman, Richard. *Theodore Dreiser: An American Journey, 1908–1945.* Vol. II. New York: G. P. Putnam's Sons, 1990.

———. *Theodore Dreiser: At the Gates of the City, 1871–1907.* Vol. I. New York: G. P. Putnam's Sons, 1986.

MacCannell, Dean and Juliet Flower MacCannell. "The Beauty System." In *The Ideology of Conduct: Essays in Literature and the History of Sexuality,* edited by Nancy Armstrong and Leonard Tennenhouse, 206–38. New York: Methuen, 1987.

Marcus, Mordecai. "Loneliness, Death, and Fulfillment in *Jennie Gerhardt.*" *Studies in American Fiction* 7, 1(Spring 1979):61–73.

Romero, Laura. "Bio-political Resistance in Domestic Ideology and *Uncle Tom's Cabin.*" *American Literary History* 1, 4(Winter 1989):715–34.

Ross, Valerie. "Too Close to Home: Repressing Biography, Instituting Authority." In *Contesting the Subject: Essays in the Postmodern Theory and Practice of Biography and Biographical Criticism,* edited by William H. Epstein. West Lafayette, IN: Purdue University Press, 1991.

Sanchez-Eppler, Karen. "Bodily Bonds: The Intersecting Rhetorics of Feminism and Abolitionism." *Representations* 24(Fall 1988):28–59.

Schwartz, Carol A. "Jennie Gerhardt: Fairy Tale as Social Criticism." *American Literary Realism 1870–1910* 9, 2(Winter 1987):16–29.

Todd, Janet. *Sensibility: An Introduction.* New York: Methuen, 1986.

Tompkins, Jane. *Sensational Designs: The Cultural Work of American Fiction, 1790–1860*. New York: Oxford University Press, 1990.

Waddlington, Warwick. "Pathos and Dreiser." In *Critical Essays on Theodore Dreiser*, edited by Donald Pizer. Boston: G. K. Hall, 1991.

Warner, Michael. *The Letters of the Republic: Publication and the Public Sphere in Eighteenth-Century America*. Cambridge: Harvard University Press, 1990.

West, James L. W. III. *American Authors and the Literary Marketplace since 1900*. Philadelphia: University of Pennsylvania Press, 1988.

Yellin, Jean Fagan. *We Are Your Sisters: The Antislavery Feminists in American Culture*. New Haven, CT: Yale University Press, 1989.

Ziff, Larzer. *Writing in the New Nation: Prose, Print, and Politics in the Early United States*. New Haven, CT: Yale University Press, 1991.

5
Jennie One-Note:
Dreiser's Error in Character Development

LAWRENCE E. HUSSMAN

IN THE HISTORICAL COMMENTARY appended to the Pennsylvania edition of *Jennie Gerhardt,* James L. W. West III rightly contends that the intellectual tension of the novel has its source in the clash between Lester Kane's and Jennie's points of view. West justly characterizes Kane as a "pragmatic cynic" and Jennie as "unreasoning," an "instinctive romantic." West further argues, again correctly, that Lester and Jennie transcribe two warring sides of the novelist's own nature. Dreiser is most successful artistically, West finds, when he creates characters by dramatizing the conflict between the "pessimistic determinist" and the "religious mystic" within himself (446–47). What West fails to note, however, is the radically different way in which Dreiser fashioned Jennie compared with that of his usual practice. This departure from the norm remains the overriding reason, despite the restoration of details about Jennie in the Pennsylvania text, for the novel's failure as first-rate literature.

Each of Dreiser's other major characters throughout his fiction emerged from the novelist's creative crucible as a psychological alloy. The strong Aristotelian probability of each, in fact, resides in the varying degrees of balance or contention between opposite impulses that his or her actions, emotions, or both demonstrate. Witness Carrie, conflicted between her personal longing for things and pleasure and her somewhat feeble but discernible feeling for the poor. Or Clyde at the last, hopelessly confused about whether strong desire can or should be checked by duty. Or even Cowperwood, simultaneously a ruthless robber baron and a philanthropist. Lester Kane is such an "alloy" character. Because of the way Dreiser softened him from the materialistic lecher of the ur-manuscript, Lester exhibits a satisfying complexity. He takes what he wants, including Jennie, but there is a side of him that is giving, that is capable of comforting as well as calculating, that allows him to fault his brother Robert for being insufficiently "warm-hearted or generous." No such cross-currents inform Jennie's character. Although a few restored passages in the Pennsylvania text add ever so slightly to her still scant worldly sophistication, there is little evidence to justify Thomas Riggio's claim in his preface to the restored novel that "her power as a woman is clearer, and we are less likely to see her as a weak sentimental heroine" (x). In fact, she remains a plaster saint, her every action (and far too many of her thoughts) devoted to serving others. Most readers know too much of human nature through introspection and observation, one would hope, to buy into Jennie's characterization.

Part of the reason that empathy for Jennie becomes so difficult involves Dreiser's utter failure to explain her motivations. No such problem renders Lester less than comprehensible. His self-serving pragmatism flows logically out of his skeptical worldview, as Dreiser explains at several points. Much of his civility and occasional magnanimity, however, represents the kind of concession that materialists must make if they are to receive anything in return, or if they value civilization, which depends on restraint. Any additional acts of charity by Lester can be seen as gratuitous, the inexplicable but sometimes operative behavior of professed materialists.

When it comes to Jennie, however, Dreiser scarcely tries to explain what causes her programmatic self-immolation. The reader must be content with the narrator's assertion that our heroine, moved by "innate feeling in her [that] made for self-sacrifice," represents an "anomaly" (88, 16). Such an evasion need not have compounded the problem of Jennie's believability. Dreiser could have tried to explain her actions on the basis of her religious training, though Jennie's one-dimensional portrait would doubtless have defeated even such a sensible effort. She has, after all, been educated in the Lutheran schools, which might have been expected to inculcate the kind of values Jennie improbably intuits. Indeed, in a restored passage on the second page of the novel, Dreiser tells us that Jennie and her siblings "learned little" in school "outside of the prayers and precepts of the Evangelical faith." Although Dreiser has his heroine ultimately reject any "fixed conclusion as to what life meant," he allows her to wonder if a "guiding intelligence" might not be responsible for life's beauty (395–96). But he never makes the possible connection between the Christian precepts she had learned, or her willingness to entertain the possible existence of a guiding intelligence, to the unfailing charity with which Jennie approaches all her interactions with others.

We should not be surprised. Dreiser was too thoroughly blocked by bitterness toward his own Catholic upbringing to credit such connections.

Significantly, he never seems to have entertained the possibility that what he perceived as the beautifully giving nature of his beloved mother, on whom Jennie's character is partially based, might have owed a debt to her Christian background. Instead, he invariably pays tribute to his mother's "pagan" spirit. In the same way, he never seemed to think it possible that there might be a link between the deep compassion for which his novels and much of his later public life were to become justly noted and the impression made on him by the Sermon on the Mount. He had read it and other biblical passages with relish in the otherwise detested parochial schools. His negative experiences with "religionists" in his youth served not to suggest such a link but to inspire the creation of characters like Jennie's father and the Gerhardt family's minister, Pastor Wundt, both of whom are often blinded by bigotry because of rather than in spite of their Christian faith.

Interestingly, Jennie becomes even more selfless as she grows away from her religious roots. She exhibits isolated instances of personal longing early in the novel, occasionally imagining herself in affluent circumstances, for example. These bits of self-consideration are probably remnants of Dreiser's characterization of Jennie in the ur-manuscript, where she was conceived as a much more worldly, even semi-sluttish woman. In the Harpers first edition and the Pennsylvania version, both of which reflect Dreiser's subsequent rethinking of Jennie's character, her self-considerations disappear completely by chapter V. Early in her relationship with Lester we are told that she chooses public education for her daughter, Vesta, because "religious forms did not exactly explain life" to Jennie now (192). But her own actions, far from drawing on the self-devoted example of her atheistic lover, become ever more self-effacing.

Jennie's selflessness probably causes most readers to reject or at least to puzzle over her. And Dreiser must bear the blame. As Jennie's creator, he had access to her deepest thoughts. And as author of this "realistic" novel, he was under some obligation to make her character square with our experience. But surely none of us has ever known so pure, all-giving a person as Jennie, her two "illicit" liaisons notwithstanding. How often would one be likely to meet a real-life woman who could crown her hyper-obsessive devotion to family and others by pointing out to her lover rival beauties he might find more desirable and then, when he locates one on his own, offer to step aside for fear he might "suffer" (311–13). Surely, in real life, Dreiser's much-admired St. Francis of Assisi must have been capable of occasionally thinking that his love for all those birds was enhancing his personal standing with God. Or to use a contemporary example, Mother Teresa must sometimes bask in the belief that her good works are scoring her personal points with the pope. Such lapses from perfection help define sainthood, which does not, after all, involve the complete transcendence of human nature. Even readers hooked on lives of the saints demand some inner turmoil from their spiritual exemplars. Conversely, although the list of literary villains runs to some length, they are usually ancillary characters in realistic fiction. When they do take center stage, it behooves their inventors to remember that historians tell us even Hitler and Stalin loved their mothers.

One rule of thumb in twentieth-century fiction, conditioned as it is by modern discoveries in psychology, dictates that the complexity of a character should be proportionate to the significance of that character in the story. In *Sister Carrie,* for example, the reader is not troubled by not knowing much about the "Captain" who begs money to provide beds for the homeless, the Sisters of Charity who run soup kitchens for the unemployed, or Fleischmann, the baker who donates bread to derelicts. These minor characters are merely faces in the fictional crowd, symbols of giving that Dreiser uses to contrast with the grasping majority. But when a character's role calls for more than a cameo appearance, modern readers expect some rounding. In *Jennie Gerhardt,* only Jennie fails the test. Not only did Dreiser's reworking of Lester Kane's ur-character give her second lover an agreeable mixture of motives, but the novelist's revision of her first lover's makeup also showed a profit. Although Senator Brander plays a relatively limited role in the novel, seducing Jennie and dying before he can make her an honest woman, he becomes a person of more parts than she. At one restored point in the Pennsylvania text, for example, Brander sends Jennie's mother a shawl as a gift. The narrative voice explains the senator's motivation as "mingled charity and self-gratification" (39). But Dreiser misses a parallel opportunity to locate the psychology behind Jennie's programmatic giving in some hidden agenda of at least partial self-gratification à la Senator Brander.

Riggio's preface to the Pennsylvania edition of *Jennie Gerhardt* asks pointedly why the editorial staff at Harpers insisted on weakening Jennie's character and not Lester's when they edited Dreiser's manuscript for the 1911 edition (x–xi). Riggio wants to cast these revisions in the context of turn-of-the-century sexism, to make them the chauvinist responses of staffers offended by an uppity heroine bent on having more of her way. But there are simply too few instances of such tampering to make the case. Even those that West adduces in his historical essay do not make Riggio's position wholly convincing. In one, West highlights a restored section in which Jennie points out to Lester a beggar on a New York street and urges that they give him a handout. Lester cautions that beggars can be professional con artists. He talks Jennie out of contributing by arguing that "anybody who wants anything very badly" will likely get it, because "fortune is a thing that adjusts itself automatically to a person's capabilities and desires" (447–48).

West correctly asserts that Jennie's family history has taught her otherwise and that the denouement of the novel will reinforce her understanding and change Lester's mind. West therefore laments the excision of what he sees as this highly ironic scene from the Harpers edition, because its absence diminishes Jennie's role in the novel's philosophical debate. It could also be argued that dropping the scene represented an unwillingness by the editors at Harpers to weaken Lester's character, since he is so obviously in error. But just how this restored scene bespeaks what Riggio calls Jennie's "power as a woman" is less clear. After all, she exhibits here the same characteristic sympathy for life's victims that she does throughout the novel. And although West may be right in inferring that she knows better than Lester about human suffering, she does nothing to set her lover straight. Instead she is "overawed by his mighty sentences," bows to his will, and remains silent (448). Rather than illustrating a sexist plot at Harpers, the excision of this scene probably resulted from the editors' feeling that it added nothing new about Jennie.

When West juxtaposes another of Dreiser's manuscript passages to the altered version from the Harpers edition, with a view to showing that the former carries more stylistic force than the latter, an instance of the original publisher's "preferable" characterization of Jennie is inadvertently revealed. The passage closes out chapter XIX. At this point in the novel a series of family misfortunes, capped by old Gerhardt's injury, has convinced Jennie she must consider becoming Lester's mistress. In Dreiser's version, Jennie, after sending Lester a note agreeing to meet him, awaits their assignation with "soul dread." Such an emotion typifies Jennie as Dreiser portrays her after chapter V. It underscores her willingness to sacrifice herself to help her family. When the Harpers editors revised the passage in question, they did soften Dreiser's tone by conventionalizing language to make it less forceful, as West notes. But they also made Jennie more a real person by changing her "soul dread" to "mingled feelings of trepidation and thrilling expectancy" (448–49). In so doing they provided her, perhaps unconsciously, with a measure of the inner mix missing from Dreiser's portrayal after the first few chapters. Rather than weakening her character, or certainly her believability, at least in this instance the Harpers editors strengthened it.

Contemporary feminists are unlikely to be convinced that the Pennsylvania edition marks a significant advance in Jennie's character over the Harpers text. And although some critics may be tempted to approve of Jennie in both versions because she seems to know her own mind (or feelings) and remains unchanged despite the buffeting of circumstance, such approval would be illogical. Her actions make more sense (if they make any sense at all) as the necessary concomitant of her powerlessness. She is a woman battered by poverty and male dominance into a willing doormat. And it is Dreiser, after all, who, within a restored section of the novel, apparently approvingly notes that his guileless heroine shares an equal allotment of assertiveness with the average mouse (199).

Moreover, Dreiser endorsed in Jennie an emotional response pattern that he did not approve of in men. In an early portrait of Jennie's father, for example, Dreiser complains that the old man "felt, rather than reasoned" because he was "incapable of a broad mental perspective" (50). This complaint stemmed from Dreiser's disapproval of his own "religionist" father, but in the context of *Jennie Gerhardt* it also demonstrates the novelist's susceptibility to the gender stereotypes of his day. For Dreiser, men were supposed to be the thinkers, and women ideally would do the feeling. In fact, Dreiser later wrote to Mencken that *Jennie Gerhardt* would have strong appeal for "emotionalists — especially women" (214).

In contrast, Dreiser's imputation of superior feeling to women constituted the core of his respect for them. His own strong suit was the depth of his emotional reserves, and he gravitated to women in search of soul sustenance. He sometimes led with his heart in his fiction as well, and this accounts for his intention to have Jennie and Lester marry and live happily ever after in early revisions of the novel. The same romantic wishes led to a similar matrimonial consummation for the originally projected ending of *The "Genius."* In the case of *Jennie,* nothing could be more telling than the advice given Dreiser by his friend Lillian Rosenthal, quoted by West in the Historical Commentary, about his plan to marry Jennie to Lester. Rosenthal, who had read and liked the rest of the novel, cautioned Dreiser that because "poignancy" was crucial to the story, he must see to it that his heroine be denied Lester as part of her regimen of "persistent want" (431). Rosenthal failed to grasp the fact that Jennie seeks little or nothing for herself at any point in the novel. Still, the idea of having to advise the author of *Sister Carrie* to create a heroine consistently disappointed in desire could hardly be more ironic. It is consistent, however, with Dreiser's giving in to other temptations to side with Jennie elsewhere in the novel. For example, during Lester and Jennie's visit to Egypt, Dreiser included a long passage valorizing his heroine's "goodness of heart" (307–8). And he originally appended to the novel a terse coda preferring Jennie's way of life over Lester's.

Because Dreiser remembered the tribulations he experienced in the effort to bring *Sister Carrie* before the public, he decided after producing the ur-manuscript of his second novel that Jennie's character as he had fashioned it was in "error" (424). Perhaps making Jennie a virtuous woman could lessen Dreiser's potential difficulties with publishers. It may be that the calculation was correct. If he had submitted another "seamy" tale about a kept woman with a weak conscience, the novelistic career he was trying to renew might have been aborted. But the cost of his capitulation to prevailing tastes proved ruinous. In refashioning Jennie's character, he made a far greater error. He allowed his humanistic side free rein, unchecked by his deterministic, thinking side. Jennie became, as a result, a wish-fulfillment stick figure of self-sacrifice. Even Dreiser seems to have recognized this later. Approximately ten years after the novel was published he told Indiana newspaperman Claude Bowers: "No, I don't like *Jennie* so much. I formed a dislike for it almost as soon as I had finished it. I wrote it in an emotional mood and liked it immensely in the process of composition, but almost immediately afterward I concluded that I had overdrawn Jennie. I think so still." When the journalist suggested that he had "known some women after whom she might have been patterned," Dreiser countered: "I can't say I have" (156). As proof of his sincerity, he never created another major character anything like her.

The Pennsylvania text represents a clear advance over the Harpers original in at least one important way. Much of the restored material concerning Lester Kane's interaction with his family enhances the novel. The machinations of the Kane family in pressuring Lester to give up Jennie are far more richly detailed here than in the Harpers edition. The fuller treatment intricately reproduces the labyrinthine web of upper-class conventions, duties, rituals, and prejudices that make for an inhibiting social determinism—so intricately, in fact, as to cast into doubt Norman Mailer's received contention that Dreiser's understanding of the workings of society ended at the drawing-room door. But the fatal flaw in the novel remains Jennie herself. Despite the added details from the manuscript that Dreiser submitted to Harpers, the Pennsylvania Jennie never exhibits the "power as a woman" claimed for her. Half a century ago Oscar Cargill complained, in comparing Jennie with George Moore's Esther Waters, that Dreiser's heroine was "so much dough" (118). After all these years, the dough still refuses to rise.

Bibliography

Bowers, Claude. "Memories of Theodore Dreiser." In *My Life: The Memoirs of Claude Bowers.* New York: Simon and Schuster, 1962.

Cargill, Oscar. *Intellectual America.* New York: Macmillan, 1941.

Dreiser, Theodore. *Jennie Gerhardt.* Edited by James L. W. West III. Philadelphia: University of Pennsylvania Press, 1992.

———. *Letters of Theodore Dreiser.* Edited by Robert H. Elias. 3 vols. Philadelphia: University of Pennsylvania Press, 1959.

6

Dreiser's Ideal of Balance

LEONARD CASSUTO

GIVEN DREISER'S EXTENDED AND unsystematic philosophizing in both fiction and other media, it is hardly surprising that the philosophical aspect of *Jennie Gerhardt* has provoked the bulk of the critical attention accorded the novel. Indeed, Dreiser's original version of the novel may be persuasively read as a dialectic between Jennie's mystical, romantic view of life and Lester's harsh, traditionally naturalistic perspective. But reading the novel as an extended philosophical argument between Jennie and Lester minimizes the action in the first part of the story and thus slights the position of the other man in Jennie's life: her austere, God-fearing Lutheran father. Jennie's philosophical opposition with Lester follows (and partly overlaps with) another completely different ideological conflict, this one between Jennie's active desire for happiness in life and her father's repressive conventional morality. If we concentrate on Jennie's perspective through the novel, the book becomes the story of a woman who is the only character capable of finding the midpoint between male extremes of behavior and who, in the process of doing so, pulls these extremes toward her own equilibrium.

This equilibrium is philosophical and social, but above all it is psychological. Dreiser has only recently begun to get his due as a psychological novelist, the long delay part of a general reluctance to recognize naturalism as a literature of characters as well as ideas. Dreiser's early critics were quick to equate the size of his books with a certain looseness, perhaps believing that one who evinced so much trouble with the minutiae of language could hardly grasp the minutiae of personality. In fact, Dreiser is among the most psychologically acute of the naturalists, and the meticulous accretion of detail he brings to his fictional portraiture is the way that he conveys the psychological weight and measure he has taken of his subjects.[1]

Although the restored *Jennie Gerhardt* bears that hallmark detail, it stands as one of Dreiser's least characteristic performances. Jennie is a Dreiserian anomaly because she understands something that Dreiser's other protagonists almost never do: how to live contentedly in the world.[2] More-over, she is capable of communicating that knowledge to others. With Jennie's reemergence in the restored text, she becomes the linchpin of two related psychoanalytic readings. First, *Jennie Gerhardt* may be seen as a kind of allegory of Freud's triadic metaphor, in which Jennie's healthy ego gradually balances the social demands of the superego (William Gerhardt) and the unrestrained appetites of the id (Lester Kane). Second, Jennie plays the role of psychoanalyst to her father and lover, her healthy ego guiding the two unbalanced personalities to a level of mature mental health that neither had previously experienced. Jennie's balancing act is unusual for Dreiser, whose fictional vision more often falls on the less dexterous, spotlighting those who fall from this psychological tightrope.

Dreiser's fiction invites psychoanalytic approaches because his project was broadly similar to Freud's: both writers tried to explain human behavior in terms of the complexities and contradictions of desire. Although *Jennie Gerhardt* was published before Dreiser's documented encounter with Freud's psychoanalytic writings—which he read with great interest soon after they became available in the United States—the novel harmonizes with Freud's ideas, as it shows Dreiser's own struggle to understand character in terms of division and conflict in the mind.[3] Moreover, the interrelationships among Jennie and her father and Lester strikingly anticipate the ego-id-superego model that dominated Freud's later thought.[4]

Dreiser anticipates this metaphor in *Jennie Gerhardt,* personifying the opposing forces as his three main characters and showing not only how they oppose one another, but also how they depend on one another to form the fragile equilibrium that Freud held necessary for a person to function effectively in the world. As ego, Jennie is both a guiding and a binding force. Always learning from experience, she proves consistently equal to the demands of her unifying task.

As lay psychoanalyst, Jennie is delicate but straightforward. Freud says that the analyst should ally himself with the patient's ego, with the goal of revealing the workings of the unconscious—thus making it conscious, the first step to managing its inchoate urges. The analyst, says Freud, relies not on lectures to the patient but on reaction and mirror-like reflection in the analytic dialogue, so that the analysand (the patient) can come to understand what the unconscious is doing. This effort is always accompanied by unconscious "resistance" from the patient, which requires that the analyst proceed in a careful, circumspect way.[5] Therefore, says Freud, "We avoid telling [the patient] at once things we have often discovered at an early stage, and we avoid telling him the whole of what we think we have discovered" (*Outline* 35). This unhurried, reactive stance describes Jennie's behavior exactly. She slowly and gradually guides her father and Lester to a point at which they can see their own excesses. It is of more than passing significance, I think, that the climactic scene of recognition for each man takes place with Jennie sitting before his bed, a near approximation of the classic arrangement of the psychoanalyst and patient, in which the doctor sits and listens to the patient, who lies on a couch.

Jennie reins in her father's overdeveloped fear of social reproach, leading him to value her despite her unconventional relationships and illegitimate offspring. She and her daughter give the old man the only real pleasure in his life. At the same time, Jennie works on Lester's desire to live almost entirely for himself, which leads not only to his risky flouting of social conventions but also to his slighting of Jennie's wants. Her influence on him endures even after he leaves her, leading him finally to declare that he should have married her. Old Gerhardt and Lester both testify on their deathbeds to their love for Jennie, but Dreiser makes it clear that the changes in their attitudes take place over a long period, motivated always by her patient, honest, and forgiving nature. From opposite sides, they are slowly pulled toward her position in the center.

For most of the novel, Jennie's father is a man strangling in the grip of his superego. He fears having others think badly of him. This fear of reproach drives old Gerhardt (as Dreiser calls him) to an unceasing dedication to his work and a fervent devotion to his Lutheran religion. His faith draws its strength not from meditative spirituality but from a deep-set conviction that "everything spoken from the pulpit of his church was literally true" and that if he obeyed its dictates "the Lord would have no excuse for ruling him out" (52–53). This description corresponds almost exactly to Freud's view of religion as an external representation of the superego. He cites early religious teaching as one cause of "the domination of the superego over the ego later on" (*Ego* 24–25).[6] This domination is felt, says Freud, in the form of neurotic guilt. Old Gerhardt fits the type precisely, having been brought up in a home in which "the influence of the Lutheran minister had been all-powerful" (51). A brief period of youthful wildness, once repented, leaves him in perpetual "dread" of the wrath of God the Father.[7]

Freud describes the superego as both "super-moral" and "cruelly prohibiting" (*Ego* 44). This is an accurate description of old Gerhardt's parenting. He establishes a repressive regime marked always by the order to conform to external standards of morality.[8] Dreiser's narrator says early on that the "one criterion [of society] is the opinion of others" (87). Old Gerhardt is a perfect mirror of such sensibilities. When Senator Brander takes Jennie out walking, her father worries that "it looks bad, even if he don't mean any harm" (56). Harm does indeed result when Jennie becomes pregnant, but old Gerhardt seems chiefly concerned over how this misfortune will be seen by others. He turns his daughter out of the house, his fury fueled by the knowledge that "my daughter walks the streets and gets herself talked about" (83). This rage leads him to bury for years any warm feelings for her.

Jennie is at first too innocent to oppose her father's strictures. But she learns from her adversity, and when her father challenges her union with Lester she parries his moralistic attacks with a kindness that gradually melts his opposition. Rightly suspicious of the legitimacy of Jennie's union with Lester, old Gerhardt resists her on the grounds that she was "not leading a righteous life" (241). But she perseveres, and, in a major victory, she persuades him to come to live with her (253). Although in despair over his feeling of uselessness, old Gerhardt is resuscitated by Jennie (265). Vesta, his illegitimate granddaughter, finally loosens the rigid control old Gerhardt had maintained over himself since he had been a young adult. Her playfulness wins him over, after which "there was no more fight in [him]"; he relaxes and accepts the "attention and affection" he "craved" (272).

From Jennie, old Gerhardt finally learns to take pleasure. In Freudian analytic terms, his strengthened ego loosens the nearly exclusive hold that his powerful superego had over him. Importantly, he does not lose his sense of propriety; instead he learns to balance it by liberating his long-suppressed desire for pleasure. Jennie draws him to this change, bringing him into touch with his own desire for intimacy. His deathbed conversation with her leaves no doubt of the completeness of his reversal. "I understand a lot of things I didn't," he says (345). Aware of his own impending death, he tells Jennie that he sees her as "goodness itself," thanking her for her kindness and asking for forgiveness (344). His grateful last words to her: "You've been good to me. You're a good woman" (346).

As Jennie urges her father to give in and satisfy his wants, she does the opposite with her male lovers. George Brander and Lester Kane are both very sensitive to their appetites — generally to the exclusion of Jennie's own desires. Her task as lay analyst in their cases is to make her lovers sensitive to the value of living for others as well as themselves. In contrast to her loosening of her father's strictness, Jennie has to help her lovers harness their superegos to domesticate their ids. In effect, she socializes the two men, bringing them into the orbit of others.

Jennie's influence is essentially the same on both of her lovers, since Brander in many ways represents an early version of Lester. Dreiser points to this similarity by having the two characters share a highly telling courtship line; each says to Jennie, "You belong to me."[9] In addition, Dreiser describes each man's successful seduction of her in terms of the eager possession of flowers. He says that Lester wants to "seize" Jennie as he would pick a "rare flower" (124). When Brander succumbs to temptation and seduces her, the narrator compares his fall to that of one who is offered a bouquet of beautiful harebells after long desiring them (74).

Brander is taken with Jennie's wholesome beauty and openness; his desire for her overwhelms his sense of propriety. Although faced with pangs of conscience over his treatment of Jennie, his id wins the battle, its victory signified by the rhetorical question he asks himself: "Why die unsatisfied?" (40).[10] When Jennie wins Brander over by the purity of her selflessness, Dreiser describes her attraction as a "bigness of emotion" that exerted a magnetic pull (72–73). This image directly reflects Dreiser's interests in the behavioral sciences of his day, but it also shows how Jennie draws her antagonists toward the psychological stability that she represents even at a young age. It is perhaps no coincidence that Dreiser also describes her pull in Freudian language, as "an unconscious power" (22). When Brander falls under the influence of that power, it draws him close enough for him to see that she represents "what he most desired — love, a woman whom he could love" (73). His readiness to enter into adult love points to a change from his earlier self-absorption, for as Freud says, love involves a shift of libidinal energy from self-love outward, to another (*Outline* 8).

Younger and coarser than Brander, Lester is also more clearly self-absorbed. Dreiser uses predatory imagery to describe his seduction of Jennie.[11] The diction leaves no doubt that Lester is a man ruled by his undisciplined, "non-moral" id.[12] He is "Rabelaisian," an "animal man" with strong appetites for wine and women, and he pursues Jennie out of "pleasure-seeking" (125–28). When his pursuit proves successful, he claims Jennie as "his prize" (160) and proceeds to devote considerable effort to making her look "truly worthy of him" (167). He sets Jennie up in an apartment as his mistress and settles into a routine with her that "was not only a comfort but an appetite with him" (213). In frank language cut from the first edition of the novel, he desires her "in a feral, Hyperborean way" (243).

Lester quickly sees that Jennie is more than a sex object, but he cannot bring himself to choose between his unconventional relationship with her and the conventional life in which he retains a part-time membership. Lester's life in high society gives him pleasure — and so do his hours and days with Jennie.[13] As a creature of appetite, Lester wants both lives. He is willing to endure certain social hardships for the sake of continuing to live with Jennie, but these cannot be considered sacrifices. Acting according to the pleasure principle, he decides that keeping Jennie brings him more pleasure (in spite of social reproach) than giving her up would.[14] Although he foresees problems for both of them, he admits that "he was not sure . . . that he really wanted to" resolve them (178). He tells himself that his love for Jennie is "selfish," but he cannot bring himself to renounce this "comfortable . . . bed of down" (187, 220).

Following his appetites, Lester analyzes the situation primarily in terms of his own desires for a long time. When he accidentally discovers the existence of Vesta (whom Jennie had been keeping from him), he feels personally affronted: "How could she be guilty of any such conduct toward him — he who had picked her up out of nothing, so to speak, and befriended her?" (207). His accusatory tone develops into a full-blown legal scenario in his mind, as he sees himself as judge and jury deciding Jennie's fate (212). Similarly, after a showdown with his brother Robert at which the pressure increases on Lester to give up Jennie, he continues to view Jennie foremost in terms of his own life, arguing to himself that "usefulness and adoration for him seemed to justify her" (236). Even after Jennie moves to leave him, Lester will neither let her go nor marry her, maintaining both of them (and Vesta) in an increasingly uncomfortable state of limbo (247).

Jennie builds up Lester's ego by degrees and enables him to exert more control over his id, a progression that allows him to hear his previously muffled superego at last. Like Brander, Lester feels from Jennie "a big, emotional pull of some kind" (264).[15] Held in this way, he learns (as Brander did) to live for others. A notable sign of his increasing willingness to do so is his attitude toward Vesta, which gradually evolves into a parental relation; in an interesting echo of his initial possessiveness of Jennie, Lester "felt as though the little girl belonged to him" (222). The difference between these two kinds of "belonging" illustrates Lester's progress toward the psychological center.

As a parent, common-law husband, and reasonably tolerant son-in-law figure, Lester integrates himself into a social system to which he actively contributes, a striking contrast to his original rebellion. In effect, his life with her becomes "unconventionally conventional." Freud says that the task of a healthy ego is to "appropriate fresh portions of the id" (*New Introductory* 80).[16] Jennie's domestication of Lester accomplishes exactly that: her example helps Lester shape his desires within the constraints of the real world. This "reality-testing" of the id is an important task of the ego that Jennie eventually helps Lester to fulfill for himself (*Ego* 45). Her devoted patience eventually causes him to temper his desire to have her *and* his social position; he sees the necessity of this choice on his own, of course, but Jennie helps him feel comfortable with it, albeit long after he has chosen incorrectly. Lester cannot remake his past, but his now-mature superego enables him to make peace with it, and with Jennie. He unburdens himself on his deathbed by declaring his love for her and his regret of the choices he made. She needs this testimony: "Now she could live happily. Now die so" (411).

Just as psychoanalysis cannot cure every mental disorder or help every patient, Jennie's moderating influence is limited to those with the depth and willingness to take advantage of it. Certain characters in the book, such as her brother Bass, lie beyond her reach because they have no desire to change. Jennie is able to bring her father and lover to equilibrium because they have within them both the potential and the desire for balance. Lester is not all appetite, nor is old Gerhardt all restraint — and that is precisely Dreiser's point. Their divisions — and their discontents with these divisions — already lie within them. If old Gerhardt lived for appearances alone, for example, he would easily have been able to shut his daughter out of his life without a second thought. But to his credit, he has deep feelings for her that his slavishness to convention does not let him express. In exerting her gentle, guiding pressure, Jennie follows Freud's dictate that the analyst collaborate with the analysand's ego, leading but not forcing, showing but not telling. In practicing her own intuitive version of what Freud called the "intellectual work" with the patient's unconscious, Jennie encourages her father and Lester to draw on their own unconscious minds, enabling them to become better balanced, better integrated personalities.

Dreiser supplies considerable evidence of the (frail) presence of a superego in Lester early on. Lester is not ruthless in business or in life generally, at least partly because — as Dreiser often emphasizes — he perceives the puzzling complexities of existence (305, 368–69). Such depth makes Lester into a "man of doubts" (234), in contrast to his decisive but shallow brother Robert. This conflict is noticeable within Lester from the beginning, when he deliberates over whether to go to a dreary party at which he is expected. Although his annoyance at such obligations is clear, he is only "*half*-defiant" (140, emphasis added). And he does go. Years later, when his unconventional union with Jennie is exposed in a newspaper story, he wonders "what his friends were thinking" (286). His worry over the opinions of these "friends" affects his judgment about Jennie; when he discovers that she has a child, he decides that "it would be useless to ever think of marrying her. It couldn't be done, not by a man in his station" (213).

Lester's ambivalence about his place in society puts him astride a moral fissure of his own making. As he remarks to Robert, "There's really nothing to be said. I have the woman, and the family has its objections. The chief difficulty about the thing seems to be the bad luck in being found out" (232). This framing of the problem permits no middle ground between Lester's competing desires. Eventually, when faced with an all-or-nothing choice between all-out defiance and cooperation with society's dictates, he rejects Jennie. Letty Pace Gerald, the voice of convention, is described as a "temptress" (337), an epithet that shows Lester's attraction to her world and the degree to which it has shaped the very appetites that have brought this trouble to him.

These appetites notwithstanding, Lester comes to feel a moral obligation to Jennie, but in finally "making a sacrifice of the virtues" to "policy" (365), he essentially succumbs to appetite. His increasingly harsh naturalistic worldview — that life is "a silly show" (403) — is often noted by critics and mistakenly held up as Dreiser's creed, but it is nothing of the sort. Instead, it is a highly individual complaint by Lester himself, and it arises directly from the action of his superego, grown much stronger over the years with Jennie. His cynical comments displace onto the world his hostility toward himself for choosing selfishly. They arise from guilt, born of his awareness that something is missing from his life. This unarticulated "something" is Jennie (377, 390, 393). When Lester tries to mask his shortcomings beneath naturalistic truisms (e.g., "The individual doesn't count much in the situation"), only Jennie sees through them: "She knew it meant that he was not entirely satisfied with himself and was sorry for her" (392). Lester looks for revenge on the world for forcing his hand and even gets some, but he receives no satisfaction or contentment until he confesses his mistake to Jennie on his deathbed.

Jennie is a telling contrast to the two men in her life; she is "a perfect balance between conflicting emotions" (147). She acts consistently as a psychological counterweight, a moderating influence in different directions. She goes one way to counter her father, another for her mother, another for her brother Bass, and another for Brander and Lester. Contrary to the implication of the severely edited 1911 version of the text, Jennie is not invariably a generous mother superior, nor is she a typically self-abnegating heroine of a sentimental novel. Instead, she is a desiring, pleasuring, flesh-and-blood human being with material and physical urges to go with her oft-noticed altruism and organic spiritual bent.

Dreiser makes sure that we see Jennie's desires from the start. When she looks about the hotel that she and her mother enter in search of work in the first scene in the novel, she takes in all the finery (including a glimpse of Brander's gold cane) and sighs, "I wish we were rich" (9). When Brander later asks her if she would like a watch, her desire for one is almost palpable. When she receives it, "her eyes fairly danced" with "ecstasy" (40–41). Dreiser makes Jennie's sexual desires similarly evident. He describes her attraction to Lester as "something terrific, inviting, urging, [that] was speaking to her" (123). After the two take up together, Jennie's wants are similarly distinct: she hopes that "he might really someday want to marry her" (257). When he leaves her, she is (not surprisingly) "depressed to the point of despair. . . . she wanted him so" (366, 378).

Jennie's distinctiveness lies not in total, saintly self-denial — her desire to be happy is clearly very much in evidence — but rather in her ability to integrate her own wants into her striving for the more important goal of psychic equilibrium. She keeps her balance from the very start because she proves able to place her appetites under the yoke of her ego. Her psychological stability enables her to survive in a social world that constantly buffets her about. Despite such treatment, she is the only character in the novel who can say "I ought" and mean it as an honest gesture for another's sake. Between her father on one side and Lester on the other, Jennie lives a life within the boundaries set by convention, and she maintains a realistic awareness of its power.

Such emotional synthesis is rare in Dreiser's fiction. Jennie's psychological balance is for Dreiser directly linked to her philosophical depth and may even be said to be its source. She sees the "strange, muddled" depth of life, with all of its beauty and inscrutability (307). Although she learns much from Lester, she applies it in a deeper way than he does, seeing a need for "goodness of heart" that he misses (308). Like Lester's acerbic naturalism, Jennie's gentler, mystical view of the world has its roots not so much in eternal truths as in the joys and sorrows that she has known personally.[17]

Central among Jennie's formative experiences is motherhood. In an early narrative aside, Dreiser describes Jennie as living in harmony with a blurry life force that he calls the "All-mother" (92), an especially notable phrase because the author clearly sees motherhood as the state that links the opposite poles of individual desire and responsibility to others. As representative mother, Jennie is a virtual avatar in Dreiser's eyes. Her thoughts, he says, "transcended [those of others], much as the flow of a river might transcend in importance the hurry of an automobile" (258). This image has a certain ironic resonance, given that the speed (and pecuniary value) of cars generally lead the shortsighted to value them over rivers. Jennie is similarly unappreciated in the novel, her value overlooked for long periods of time. Indeed, "her queendom was really not of this particular social world" (257), and Dreiser seems hardly surprised that she does not fare very well there.

Dreiser's descriptions of Jennie are suffused with what can only be described as awe. He admires his fictional creation because she is a perfectly integrated personality who can do what almost none of his other characters can: consistently execute the balancing act between personal desire and social stricture. The essence of Freud's later thought is that people must learn to manage an existence that they cannot master and that they ultimately must part with. Jennie understands from the beginning that she "was never a master of her fate" (413), but she learns to live productively in the face of this knowledge. She has wants, but she does not allow herself to be dominated by them. Appetite (from her id) and selflessness (from her superego) intertwine gracefully in her life. Her therapeutic gift — the ability to share her healthy ego — brings the two men in her life into harmony with her, themselves, each other, and the world.

Notes

1. The novelist came upon Freud's ideas in 1914–15 and, not surprisingly, was much taken with them. Dreiser's time spent reading Freud probably peaked in the years 1918–19, but psychoanalysis continued to give insight and voice to many aspects of Dreiser's own preoccupation with desire during the years afterward as well. Freud prominently informs much of Dreiser's later fiction, most explicitly in the play *The Hand of the Potter* and of course in *An American Tragedy,* in which the murder blow is described as having been "all but unconsciously" administered (493). It is possible that *Jennie Gerhardt* may be informed by Dreiser's secondhand reading about Freud, but this seems unlikely to account for much of an effect.

2. Freud first crystallized his triadic metaphor in *The Ego and the Id* (1923). He developed it in the linked contexts of the individual and the group (i.e., society) for the remaining fifteen years of his life.

3. It is not necessary to take Freud's oedipal allegory literally to appreciate its salient points: that the superego forms out of the need for obedience to an external authority and that its internalized representation in the form of a generalized sense of morality and guilt is the psychic residue of the collision between a child's expansive desires and the reality of the world.

4. There has been considerable theoretical and practical debate in psychoanalytic circles about where the real power lies within the ego-id-superego dynamic. At one extreme is "ego psychology," a branch of psychoanalytic praxis whose members teach that the healthy ego efficiently manages all of its competing demands. At the other pole is Jacques Lacan's reading and application of Freud, in which he describes an ego that is permanently disconnected from a preoedipal unity that it will always seek but will never again experience. Freud himself fell somewhere in between, one of his favorite analogies being a comparison of the ego to a rider on a high-spirited horse (*The Ego and the Id* :15; *New Introductory Lectures* :77).

5. Resistance—which originates in the unconscious portion of the ego—arises from the ego's desire to keep repressed material firmly in the unconscious, where it was originally placed to avoid its unpleasantness. Hence, it resists the effort to make it conscious. See, for example, *New Introductory Lectures on Psychoanalysis* (68–69).

6. Freud says that "the longing for the father is the root of all religion" (*The Future of an Illusion* 22). He locates the origins of religion in "an infantile model," drawing a parallel between "the father-complex" and "man's helplessness and need for protection" and the child's version of the same crisis—a crisis that results in the development of the superego for alliance with and protection from the father (23). Dreiser more explicitly equates religion to superego-like forces in numerous essays written after *Jennie Gerhardt*. See, for example, his collection *Hey, Rub-a-Dub-Dub*.

7. Old Gerhardt's angry fascination with the amusements of the young (52–53) suggests the extent to which he fights his own long-held desire for such pleasures. Freud warns that "the id cannot be controlled beyond certain limits. If more is demanded of a man, a revolt will be produced in him, or a neurosis, or he will be made unhappy" (*Civilization and Its Discontents* 90). Freud would likely classify old Gerhardt as a neurotic in this mold.

8. In chapter five of *The Ego and the Id*, Freud describes how the superego can transform love into aggressiveness. Old Gerhardt seems to be a classic case study of this shift.

9. Brander says this once (75); Lester says it five times during his courtship of Jennie (123, 132, 133, and twice on 134).

10. This quotation of course echoes the oft-repeated motto ("I satisfy myself") of Frank Cowperwood, the hero of Dreiser's Trilogy of Desire.

11. Jennie is described as "like a bird in the grasp of a cat" (123), a motif that Dreiser also uses to describe Jennie's memories much later of their coupling: "He had seized her, much as the cave man had seized his mate—by force" (409).

12. Freud, *The Ego and the Id* (44). He describes the id as the seat of the "passions" (15).

13. Although Freud equates "society," by virtue of its strictures, with what he called "the cultural superego," Lester's self-dictated social life follows most strongly from the pull of his id; there is little sense of "ought" to his high-society contacts, and every sense of "want." He simply likes being with his friends.

14. The pleasure principle, or a striving for as much pleasure as possible, "reigns unrestrictedly in the id," says Freud (*The Ego and the Id* 15).

15. Following further the idea of Jennie as analyst, this "emotional pull" can be seen as a loose analogy to the phenomenon of transference, in which the patient identifies with the analyst as a parental figure. Freud warns against the analyst's misuse of this power, counseling a strict policy of restraint — a quality always apparent in Jennie's behavior.

16. Similarly, he says that "psycho-analysis is an instrument to enable the ego to achieve a progressive conquest of the id" (*The Ego and the Id* 46). One should not construe from this comment that the ego ever totally masters the id in anyone, but Freud describes mental health as a state in which the conscious ego exerts increasing influence over the id's unconscious drives.

17. Dreiser pointedly juxtaposes the late beliefs of Lester and Jennie in this passage. Jennie is the one who benefits from the comparison. Lester becomes "critical" and "phlegmatic," whereas Jennie gradually moves toward a personal creed that encompasses both ambiguity and beauty (395–96). Jennie's religious philosophy, built up from ideas earlier "badly jumbled in her mind," contrasts sharply with her father's rigid religious beliefs (52).

Bibliography

Dreiser, Theodore. *An American Tragedy.* 1925. Reprint. New York: New American Library, 1964.

——. *Jennie Gerhardt.* Edited by James L. W. West III. Philadelphia: University of Pennsylvania Press, 1992.

Freud, Sigmund. *Civilization and Its Discontents.* Translated by James Strachey. New York and London: W. W. Norton & Co., 1961.

——. *The Ego and the Id.* Translated by Joan Riviere; revised and edited by James Strachey. New York and London: W. W. Norton & Co., 1960.

——. *The Future of an Illusion.* Translated by James Strachey. New York and London: W. W. Norton & Co., 1961.

——. *New Introductory Lectures on Psychoanalysis.* Translated by James Strachey. New York and London: W. W. Norton & Co., 1965.

——. *An Outline of Psycho-Analysis.* Translated by James Strachey. New York and London: W. W. Norton & Co., 1949.

7
Triangulating Desire in *Jennie Gerhardt*

SUSAN ALBERTINE

THE OPENING OF *JENNIE GERHARDT* presents the reader with two women — not, as it turns out, incidentally. The two, Mrs. Gerhardt and her daughter Jennie, are applying for work at the best hotel in Columbus, Ohio. From the lobby, the sympathetic male clerk directs their attention upward: the main staircase needs sweeping. Their subsequent move from the lobby up the stairs and to the room of Senator Brander is an ascent/assent to material well-being at the price of Jennie's body — a price the women silently agree must be paid. The opening of *Jennie Gerhardt* projects the unity of the two women in their climb and in their sacrifice. As the story unfolds, the pattern repeats itself several times. I argue that the psychic space between women is a locus of power; yet in Dreiser's variation on the theme of exchange or "traffic" in women, female relations are meaningless without a man to whom this power is bartered.[1] In *Jennie Gerhardt* power relations are triangular and triangulated. As the term "triangulation" implies, the third point, the man, cannot be determined or located without reference to the two other points, the women.

Such relations of power are evident in the 1911 Harpers first edition, but they emerge in mere outline. A significant contribution of the Pennsylvania edition is fuller characterization not only of Jennie but also of other major figures, including Mrs. Gerhardt and Letty Pace. The novel draws in important respects on sentimental traditions, but at the same time Dreiser's restored characterization resists much of the melodramatic flatness of the Harpers version.[2] The Pennsylvania edition allows Jennie to appear much more powerful and thoughtful, her relations with others deeper, more complex, and more disturbing.

Selected examples illustrate how Jennie's force of character appears in the text established for the Pennsylvania edition. In Jennie's first private interview with Senator Brander, when she calls for his laundry, Brander responds unconsciously: "Not recognizing the innate potentiality of any creature, however commonplace, who could make him feel this, he went glibly on, lured, and in a way, controlled by an unconscious power in her. She was a lodestone of a kind, and he was its metal; but neither she nor he knew it" (22). The passage does not appear in the Harpers edition. Without it, the attraction between Brander and Jennie is of a different quality. It is also the case that the bond between Jennie and her mother in their allegiance to Brander is weakened without this passage. For in the Pennsylvania edition Dreiser links Jennie's unconscious sexuality to Mrs. Gerhardt's powers of sympathy. Mrs. Gerhardt knows that she should not tell her husband about the extra money Brander is giving them; she thinks instead "how good he must be, or how large was his heart." For her part, Jennie "reflected this attitude toward the senator, and feeling so generously, talked more freely" (24). The women's sharing of the senator's laundry becomes a metonym for this intimacy.

As the relationship with Brander grows, we see much more complexity and far more emotional substance in the Pennsylvania Jennie. In chapter IV when, just before kissing her, Brander gazes at Jennie, the Harpers edition has the following:

> He looked at her, and the playful, companionable directness of her answering gaze thrilled him through and through. He studied her face in silence while she turned and twisted, feeling, but scarcely understanding, the deep import of his scrutiny. (35)

The restored edition enriches the moment, making it an exchange of feeling that accords Jennie a womanly power:

> He looked at her, and the playful, companionable way in which she seemed to take him, thrilled him. It was the essence of human comfort in another that he was feeling. How long had it been since the touch of a human hand had the thrill and warmth in it for him that hers did. How cold was the general material of life beside this warm, human factor, a woman dealing sympathetically with him. He studied her face in silence, while she turned and twisted, feeling, but scarcely understanding, the deep import of his scrutiny. (34)

Again, the keynote is Jennie's sympathy, the quality she most abundantly shares with her mother. In the Pennsylvania text, when Brander gives Mrs. Gerhardt gifts, they are sent "to the mother, through the daughter" (39), a line that does not appear in the 1911 edition. When mother and daughter decide to pawn the gold watch that Brander has given Jennie, "Secretly Mrs. Gerhardt wept" (48), another line that is cut from the 1911 edition. But Mrs. Gerhardt's weeping matters because when Jennie admits what she and her mother have done with the watch, she too sobs (48). It is significant that moments of mutuality between mother and daughter often appear in the Pennsylvania text just at the point of sexual expression. Jennie's sobbing over the watch occurs just before Brander "had got to the place where that wondrous something about her made it constantly more difficult for him to keep his hands off of her" (49), a line suppressed in the 1911 edition.

Just as Jennie and her mother speak as one to Brander, so they join another triangle when they manage Gerhardt *père,* as, for example, when he criticizes his wife for allowing Jennie to go out with the senator. The Harpers edition (58–59) gives the reader less insight into Mrs. Gerhardt's self-justification than does the Pennsylvania edition (55–56), so that once again the women's complicity and inchoate awareness of their moral dilemma are slighted. The same is true of the passage in which Jennie decides to approach Brander for help when her brother Bass has been jailed for stealing coal, a much-condensed scene in the Harpers edition. Deleted, for example, is a passage in which the narrator tells the reader, "The problem which this daughter of the poor had undertaken to solve was a difficult one, though she did not see it wholly in that light. She was compounded at this moment of a sense of pity and a sense of hope" (70). Here, in the restored text, Dreiser emphasizes the fact that Mrs. Gerhardt knows what Jennie's errand has been: "She was so glad to see [Bass] back that she stroked his hair, all the time, however, thinking of her mother. So she knew. She must tell her — what?" (76). The pronominal blending in this passage, deleted in the Harpers text, indicates the women's near identity.

As the triangular relationship among Brander, Jennie, and Mrs. Gerhardt suggests, Dreiser uses relations between women to confer power on a man. Power here is explicitly sexual but not crudely so in Dreiser's imagining: "All her attitude toward sex was bound up with love, tenderness, service" (Pennsylvania 136; Harpers 144). In relations with Brander, power resides in Jennie's sympathetic womanliness and rejuvenating sexuality, which Mrs. Gerhardt tacitly fosters. In the triangle, the women collude for the sake of the man, an agreement that entails Jennie's moral and social sacrifice for the material gain of herself and her family. In simplest terms, the women agree that one should become a medium of exchange, her body the currency of the transaction. Once this pattern has been established in the women's relations with Brander, the grounds for commerce with Lester Kane are prepared.

The Harpers bowdlerization of the novel is especially evident from the beginning of Jennie's pregnancy to her seduction by Lester. Chapters are rearranged and subdivided, and long passages are deleted. Once again, key phrases indicating Jennie's womanly power and her closeness to her mother are dropped from the narrative. In the restored text of chapter VIII, when Brander's death is announced in newspaper format, two contiguous paragraphs discuss the reactions of daughter and mother. Concerning Jennie: "The vigor of the blow which Fate thus dealt to Jennie was too much for her to ever get a full *conception* of it. . . . and in this condition her mind was not capable of feeling either sorrow or pain to any great extent." Concerning Mrs. Gerhardt: "No *conception* of the real state of affairs ever having crossed her mind, she was largely interested in the loss Jennie would feel in this sudden annihilation of her hopes. She could never be a foreign minister's wife now, and the influence of the man who had been so kind to them all was completely obliterated" (79, emphasis added).[3] *Conception* is indeed the issue; but Dreiser is equally attempting to reveal degrees of consciousness and moral sensibility, mirroring the mother's and daughter's states of mind.

An equation of economic and sexual desire, having been implicit in Jennie's and her mother's earlier relations with Brander, guides their joint response to Lester as well. The Harpers version shows this in outline; the Pennsylvania edition makes it articulate. The opening of chapter XIX shows Jennie thinking "deeply . . . not only concerning Lester, but also concerning her home, her child and herself . . . in rapid order for immediate consideration and answer" (147) as she considers Lester's desire for her. The Harpers edition describes Jennie only as "deeply moved" and shifts attention to her daughter, Vesta (152). In the passage in which Jennie tells her mother that she is going to New York with Lester, partly condensed in the Harpers version, a telling line is deleted: "[Mrs. Gerhardt] drifted in her mood, contrasting their present state of poverty with that other of possible comfort" (162; cf. Harpers 169). And so Mrs. Gerhardt lets Jennie go, colluding with her to conceal the truth from Mr. Gerhardt. Yet despite their material gains, once the women make this sacrifice, they lose their shared power and effectively their bond. In terms of the narrative, Mrs. Gerhardt can do nothing more once Jennie has been given to Lester; thus, the mother dies. The power that the two women share is of narrative interest only until it is irrevocably given to a man.

Having been twice repeated, the pattern is set for Jennie's relations with Letty Pace. Although the two women seldom encounter each other, they enact mutual sympathy and respect out of proportion to any claims they might have. Again, in mercantile language, the two women conduct a transaction in which Jennie gives up the man so that Letty can take him. Like the relations between Jennie and her mother, the agreement between Letty and Jennie is an inversion of the "traffic in women" described by Gayle Rubin. In the sex-gender system of capitalism, as in other forms of political economy, Rubin argues, women have long been the medium of exchange, connecting man to man in the bargain. Dreiser's innovation in creating this third triangle is to bond two unrelated women in the exchange of the man. Although this relationship happens on the periphery, it is central to the narrative. Here, the currency of sex and money is held first by female hands, and the object of desire is male. Yet power and authority (vested in sex and money) are finally transferred to Lester Kane. In the three-way relationship, the women triangulate or empower the man.

The Harpers version of the novel, however, makes the force of the women's relations less noticeable and compelling because the characteriza-tion is flatter. Both women are presented as less acute intellectually than they are in the Pennsylvania edition. When the women meet in London, for example, phrases describing the thoughtfulness of each are cut (Pennsylva-nia chap. XLIV; Harpers chap. XLV). A passage on Jennie's "intuitive knowledge" (311) does not appear in the Harpers edition; a phrase men-tioning Letty's having "grown more beautiful—physically, intellectually, and in every other way" is gone (312). A passage in the Harpers version imposes the idea that Jennie is becoming jealous (312) and cuts two key sentences, restored in the 1992 text, in which Jennie considers the social price that Lester has paid for his relations with her (Pennsylvania 313). A sentence in the 1911 text describing Letty's "charming" behavior specifically to Jennie is altered to "Mrs. Gerald continued to be most agreeable in her attitude toward the Kanes" (312). The overall impression of the Harpers version is that the women are less thoughtful and less connected than Drei-ser originally had it.[4]

As relations among the three progress in Cairo, the women's mutu-ality, even their sympathy, emerges in the Pennsylvania edition. Having met in the garden of the hotel, Jennie encourages Letty to "take" Lester, a verb both editions use, but in the restored text, Jennie "smiled at her temporary guest" (316). Following immediately is an exposition of Jennie's thoughts, much cut and softened in the Harpers edition (cf. Pennsylvania 317–18 and Harpers 317–19). The Harpers narrative goes so far as to make Jennie cry as she imagines Letty dancing with Lester (319). In the Pennsylvania edition,

Jennie thinks rationally and unregretfully about death, but no tears fall (318). For her part, Letty returns Jennie's sympathy, as, for example, in the following sentences, cut from Harpers: "But if he could and would—Jennie might look out for herself, and yet she felt sorry for her at that. She was lovely, but Lester needed another kind—herself—the Letty Pace that was" (319). On the voyage home, during which the three share passage, Jennie thinks further about Letty:

> She could not help liking her at that, for of all the society people she had met this one was the nicest to her. Letty went out of her way to do Jennie little services, to bring her delicacies, to make pleasant suggestions of things to do and so on. She made no attempt to monopolize Lester, but Jennie gave her ample opportunity to talk, for she wanted them to have a good time if they wished to. If Lester liked her, why shouldn't he talk to her? Basically she realized that she would have a hard time forcing him to neglect her or to turn entirely away from her. He was so considerate and fair that only a thing like death—her death—would straighten matters out for him. And she felt also that basically he liked her best—some of the emotional things about her anyhow. He had said so, and it was probably true. (320)

Again, in the restored text, pronominal blending joins the women. In the Harpers version, the passage is reduced to a few bland sentences that conclude, "Perhaps time would solve the problem; in the mean time the little party of three continued to remain excellent friends" (321).

Schwartz has argued that the relations between Jennie and Letty are those between dark queen and fair victim, in the mode of archetype and fairy-tale (25). Indeed, Letty tempts and seduces Lester. Yet Snow White and the evil queen are less apt prototypes for the women of the Pennsylvania edition than for the women of the Harpers edition because Dreiser evidently intended that Letty's and Jennie's self-awareness and mutuality should not create antagonism. Moreover, Dreiser shows each member of the triangle to be more aware of the social and economic realities that subsist for the other two than the Harpers version reveals. A good example occurs at the beginning of Pennsylvania chapter XLIX (Harpers chap. L), in which several important passages are cut, namely, those in which Letty and Lester think about love and money in connection with Jennie. A passage telling us that Jennie has read in the papers of Mrs. Gerald's move to Chicago is also cut (cf. Pennsylvania 336 and Harpers 335–36). Finally, the Harpers edition reads the connection between the two women as oppositional, when in fact Dreiser set the two side by side. A telling alteration of diction appears in Harpers chapter LVI: "For think as [Lester] would,

these two women were now persistently opposed in his consciousness"
(381). The Pennsylvania edition has *juxtaposed,* not *opposed* (375). It is an
emendation that betrays a failure to comprehend Dreiser's point.

As in the case of Jennie's relations with her mother, the bond between
Jennie and Letty is severed as soon as Lester leaves Jennie in Sandwood.
The final encounter between the two women, at Lester's funeral, allows for
no verbal contact, although the women are united in grief. Both versions
depict them "curiously" as "sobbing convulsively" at the same moment
(Pennsylvania 415; Harpers 428). Dreiser underscores the fact that what
brought the two together is irrevocably gone, however, and he does so by
giving them one last chance to speak with each other — which they do not
take. In the depot, where Jennie has come to see Lester's casket put aboard
the train, she is described as being "apprehensive lest she should be de-
tected." Yet, Dreiser adds, "The Kane family were scarcely aware of her
existence any more. Mrs. Kane and Watson were too grieved and employed
to bother at this point" (415). The Harpers version, which does not show
the affinity between the women, deletes this passage entirely. In the 1911
version Jennie is invisible in the depot.

The women of the novel are more fully depicted and more powerful in
the Pennsylvania edition than in the melodrama of the Harpers edition.
They are also more disturbing in the restored text. This is perhaps an effect
of their greater realism, for the more complex they appear, the less apparent
the stereotypes from which they have been drawn. As I have noted, the
women's connections matter only with reference to male empowerment.
Even Vesta's bond to her mother cannot survive Lester's departure; the girl
soon sickens and dies. While they may have convincingly realistic domestic
and social skills, in both editions the women display nothing more than an
intuitive awareness of economic realities. In other words, they are domestic
and social in keeping with their class status, but they are not participants in
the public world of the market. What would have been called their womanly "influence" in the Victorian period emerges in Dreiser's imaginings
as the power of sibyl, muse, earth mother — types of the early twentieth-
century conception of woman as sexualized, dynamic force.

This conception of womanly power aligns itself with ideas expressed
by Dreiser in his apprenticeship period at *Ev'ry Month* in the 1890s, as Amy
Kaplan has noted.[5] Signing himself "The Prophet," Dreiser wrote two columns intended to encourage American women of wealth to marry American men of genius rather than seeking titled spouses abroad. The idea that
wealth in female hands must be transferred to the control of American male

genius through the bond of marriage is also foremost in Letty Gerald's mind as she pursues Lester: "She was terribly weary of the superficial veneer of the titled fortune-hunter whom she met abroad. A good judge of character, a student of men and manners, a natural reasoner along sociologic and psychologic lines, she saw through them and through the civilization which they represented" (Pennsylvania 309; Harpers 308). Letty knows the man she wants; whether he is rich or poor makes no difference so long as he is the ideal American male. It is precisely because Jennie understands the kind of power Letty can give to Lester that she lets him go. Relations between the two women must not be antagonistic if this kind of exchange is to occur. It is as if *Jennie Gerhardt* is meant to be prophetic as well, a fictionalized form of wish-fulfillment that had been merely didactic in the *Ev'ry Month* columns written for a female readership.

Jennie Gerhardt was quite plainly not intended to portray the actuality of women's participation in the marketplace. In her discussion of the working girl as literary type in Dreiser's fiction and in popular literature, Laura Hapke notes that Dreiser's "true subject is her emotional, not her work life" (3–4). Locating *Jennie Gerhardt* in the tradition of the "cross-class labor romance of the 1900's" (4), Hapke concludes that Dreiser was unwilling "to explore the identity of the wage-earning woman" because he could see such a woman "as one who has only herself to sell" (16). Such a reading holds for both versions of the novel. What has not been noted is that Dreiser's attention to female emotional life rather than to female work life is apparent in his construction of Letty Gerald as well.

Dreiser might, of course, have depicted Letty differently — as the businesswoman she evidently was. Possible models abounded in the Chicago Dreiser knew, in fiction and in the actual city.[6] As a journalist for women's magazines and a writer aspiring to popularity, he would have known fictional types of businesswomen.[7] The community of professional women in Chicago included an impressive array of members, many of whom gathered in preparation for the World Columbian Exposition of 1893.[8] Surgeon Frances Dickinson, attorney Catherine Waite, businesswoman and temperance activist Matilda Carse, newspaper owners Helen Starrett and Antoinette von Wakeman, restauranteur and patron of the arts Harriet Moody — all represent Chicago careerwomen who belonged to a larger community that included the Hull House and *Poetry* magazine circles.[9]

Among women in the forefront of Chicago business at the turn of the century, Nettie Fowler McCormick serves instructively in the role of real-life counterpart to Letty Gerald. In 1858 Nettie Fowler married Cyrus Hall

McCormick, industrial magnate and inventor of the mechanical reaper, a man twice her age. By 1871, thirteen years before her husband's death, Nettie McCormick had become de facto director of the McCormick Reaper company. Although she never took a formal title, her managerial role in the company is well documented.[10] Among her achievements was a consolidation of farm equipment manufactories into the International Harvester Company. After her husband's death she became a leading philanthropist. In her time Nettie McCormick would have been called a "silent partner." Such partnerships were numerous in the late nineteenth century, for in this period of industrial-capitalist expansion women of wealth were quietly encouraged to know the management of the family estate.[11] They were more active in business through their families than the dominant ideology could acknowledge. Hence the euphemistic *silent* partnership, a term of identity that was the functional equivalent of a veil. My point is that silent partnerships were often more active than silent. Occasionally, as in Nettie McCormick's case, an interest in the estate came to mean direct management.

As Dreiser presents her, Letty Gerald has the strength of mind and character to direct her own affairs, much as Nettie McCormick did. Letty is far too shrewd to be as ignorant of her own business as she professes to be. Furthermore, Dreiser was likely to have known women like her. In fiction and the actual world, then, businesswomen offered a range of models that Dreiser chose not to imitate. His conception of the sphere of woman remained firmly rooted in nineteenth-century ideology. His innovation, more in keeping with his time, was to sexualize the women and to explore their intellect—to give them powers to serve and enable men far more profoundly than the Victorian angel could do. Engaging new stereotypes of strong femininity, he resisted the easier characterization of Jennie as romanticized innocent and Letty as grasping witch.

It is also true that if the actuality of women's work in the marketplace is not Dreiser's concern in *Jennie Gerhardt*, the world of men's work is likewise unimportant. In fact, Dreiser pays little attention to Lester's business. We get the big picture of his work in carriage manufacturing, at least insofar as the family is engaged in management; the most detailed information about Lester's career appears in the chapters devoted to his failed real estate venture (Pennsylvania chaps. XLVII–XLVIII; Harper chaps. XLVIII–XLIX). The novel is more concerned to reveal intimacy and self-awareness in the interactions among characters than to examine their work. Herein lies the critical difference between the two versions of the novel. In the Pennsylvania *Jennie Gerhardt* the writer gives us an intricate rendition of consciousness in moments of sympathy and exchange. Interestingly, these passages were most susceptible to Harpers cutting. Perhaps this is because they are often sexually charged. But sexuality is not the only issue. It is striking that so many correlative moments of female consciousness were targeted as well. Given Dreiser's intentions to embody female self-awareness, one can only note, ironically, that the cuts reveal women's minds as they discover what they can give to men.

Notes

1. On the "traffic in women" see Rubin; see also Hartsock's rejoinder.
2. For discussions of sentimentalism in Dreiser's work, see Kaplan (140–60) and Dance.
3. The Harpers edition deletes the first paragraph and much of the second, which is placed at the opening of chapter IX (84).
4. The Harpers version also cuts references to Lester's intellect, as if to imply that he is caught up in the emotion of sexual attraction. It may have been Dresier's frankness about the intellectual character of sexual attraction — the exercise of free will in the pursuit of sex — to which the editors objected.
5. See "Review of the Month," *Ev'ry Month* 1 (December 1895):2–3; and "Reflections," *Ev'ry Month* 2 (May 1896):5–6. Both are signed "The Prophet" and are reprinted in Pizer (36–37, 53–55). For analysis, see Kaplan (121–22).
6. Among dramatic changes in the work force through the turn-of-the-century period, one notable development is the movement of women into professional and managerial positions. The actual numbers were small in proportion to the numbers of female domestic, industrial, and clerical workers. The published census also makes it difficult to identify women's nontraditional careers. Yet it is also true that such women were socially visible and powerful. Information on women's employment in the professions in the late nineteenth century can be found in U.S. Cong., *Report on Condition of Woman and Child Wage-Earners*. Manuscript census documents are also a good source of such information. See also Kessler-Harris, Amott and Matthaei, and Conk.
7. Economic fiction about women of the period includes such titles as Hamlin Garland's *Rose of Dutcher's Coolly* (1895), a Chicago novel in which the main character, Rose Dutcher, journeys to Chicago to become a writer; Robert Herrick's *The Gospel of Freedom* (1898), a Chicago novel in which the central character, Adela Anthon, begins a search for a meaningful career by investing in art and in business; F. Hopkinson Smith's best-seller *Tom Grogan* (1896), an antiunion romance concerning a stevedore who assumes her dead husband's name and trade; and Margaret Deland's *Iron Woman* (1911), in which a steel magnate comes into her business through inheritance and widowhood. Deland, a highly popular writer, had published fiction about women and the marketplace as early as "The House of Rimmon," in *The Wisdom of Fools* (1897), as well as numerous articles and advice columns for women's magazines, including pieces on women's careers.

8. For women's participation at the World Columbian Exposition, Chicago, 1893, including names and professions or affiliations, see Weimann.

9. See Massa; and Albertine, "Cakes and Poetry." James et al., eds., *Notable American Women* includes profiles of most of the women named here. The forthcoming *Historical Encyclopedia of Chicago Women,* edited by Adele Hast, will provide additional biographical essays. See also Bremer on Chicago women's fiction, Smith on women in Chicago fiction, and Taylor on economic fiction in general.

10. Nettie McCormick's papers are in the McCormick Manuscript Collection, State Historical Society of Wisconsin, Madison. An important source is Burgess. For discussion of Nettie's life in the context of her husband's career, see Hutchinson.

11. The term "silent partner" itself was current enough by 1871 to serve as title to a popular novel by Elizabeth Stuart Phelps (the daughter). See Albertine, "Breaking the Silent Partnership." See Cromwell for a representative advice book for widows.

Bibliography

Albertine, Susan. "Breaking the Silent Partnership: Businesswomen in Popular Fiction." *American Literature* 62(1990):238–61.

———. "Cakes and Poetry: The Career of Harriet Moody." In *A Living of Words: American Women in Print Culture,* edited by Susan Albertine, 94–114. Knoxville: University of Tennessee Press, 1995.

Amott, Teresa L. and Julie A. Matthaei. *Race, Gender, and Work: A Multicultural Economic History of Women in the United States.* Boston: South End Press, 1991.

Bremer, Sidney H. "Lost Continuities: Alternative Urban Visions in Chicago Novels, 1890–1915." *Soundings: An Interdisciplinary Journal* 64(Spring 1981):29–51.

Burgess, Charles O. *Nettie Fowler McCormick: Profile of an American Philanthropist.* Madison: State Historical Society of Wisconsin, 1962.

Conk, Margo Anderson. *The U.S. Census and Labor Force Change: A History of Occupation Statistics.* Ann Arbor: University of Michigan Press, 1980.

Cromwell, John Howard. *The American Business Woman: A Guide for the Investment, Preservation, and Accumulation of Property.* New York and London: G. P. Putnam's Sons, 1900.

Dance, Daryl C. "Sentimentalism in Dreiser's Heroines Carrie and Jennie." *CLA Journal* 14(1970):127–42.

Hapke, Laura. "Dreiser and the Tradition of the American Working Girl Novel." *Dreiser Studies* 22(Fall 1991):2–19.

Hartsock, Nancy C. M. "Gayle Rubin: The Abstract Determinism of the Kinship System." In *Money, Sex, and Power: Toward a Feminist Historical Materialism,* 293–303. Boston: Northeastern University Press, 1985.

Hast, Adele, et al., eds. *Historical Encyclopedia of Chicago Women.* Bloomington: Indiana University Press (forthcoming).

Hutchinson, William T. *Cyrus Hall McCormick: Harvest, 1856–1884.* New York: Century, 1935.

———. *Cyrus Hall McCormick: Seed-Time, 1809–1856*. New York: Century, 1930.

James, Edward T., Janet Wilson James, and Paul S. Boyer, eds. *Notable American Women, 1607–1950*. Cambridge, MA: Harvard University Press, 1971.

Kaplan, Amy. *The Social Construction of American Realism*. Chicago: University of Chicago Press, 1988.

Kessler-Harris, Alice. *Out to Work: A History of Wage-Earning Women in the United States*. New York: Oxford University Press, 1982.

Massa, Ann. "Form Follows Function: The Construction of Harriet Monroe and *Poetry, A Magazine of Verse*." In *A Living of Words: American Women in Print Culture,* edited by Susan Albertine, 115–31. Knoxville: University of Tennessee Press, 1995.

Pizer, Donald, ed. *Theodore Dreiser: A Selection of Uncollected Prose*. Detroit: Wayne State University Press, 1977.

Rubin, Gayle. "The Traffic in Women: Notes on the 'Political Economy' of Sex." In *Toward an Anthropology of Women,* edited by Rayna R. Reiter, 157–210. New York: Monthly Review Press, 1975.

Schwartz, Carol A. "*Jennie Gerhardt:* Fairy Tale as Social Criticism." *American Literary Realism* 19(1987):16–29.

Smith, Carl S. *Chicago and the American Literary Imagination, 1880–1920*. Chicago: University of Chicago Press, 1984.

Taylor, Walter Fuller. *The Economic Novel in America*. Chapel Hill: University of North Carolina Press, 1942. Reprint. New York: Octagon Books, 1964.

U.S. Cong., Senate. *Report on Condition of Woman and Child Wage-Earners in the United States: History of Women in Industry in the United States,* by Helen Sumner. 61st Cong., 2nd sess., S. Doc. 645. Washington, DC: U.S. Government Printing Office, 1910.

Weimann, Jeanne Madeline. *The Fair Women*. Chicago: Academy Chicago, 1981.

PART II

Critical and Historical Contexts

8
Jennie Gerhardt: A Spencerian Tragedy

PHILIP GERBER

AS THE SUMMER OF 1915 LENGTHENED and as his novel *The "Genius"* was readied for publication, Theodore Dreiser joined his illustrator friend Franklin Booth on a 2,000-mile automobile trip that would take them from New York to Indiana and back again. They drove a new and shiny sixty-horsepower Pathfinder. Late on an August evening, as they traveled roads westward that paralleled the Great Lakes, they approached Erie, Pennsylvania. The city had recently been the scene of a devastating rainstorm-induced flood. Awakening the next morning and probing about the town, Dreiser was struck by two impressions. The first concerned the havoc wrought by the storm. The other was a conviction that this lakeside city of 75,000 looked precisely like Columbus, Ohio, the home town of Jennie Gerhardt, whom he affectionately referred to as his "pet heroine."

Dreiser had never visited Erie, but neither had he ever set foot in Columbus. That fact had not deterred him from assigning Columbus as the locale for Jennie's story. He readily admitted that he had actually modeled Jennie's birthplace on yet another city (probably his own birthplace, Terre Haute, Indiana), but the ultimate implication remained the same: any typical, midsized American city would have served to provide the representative slice of American life that he needed for the initial chapters of *Jennie Gerhardt*. Erie, he wrote, was equally perfect as a locale, from the small houses lining its tree-shaded residential streets to its impressive churches and great factories. Indubitably, he declared, Erie could be "the world in which Jennie originally moved, breathed, and had her being." The pretentious central Erie hotel where he spent the night could easily have been the grand Columbus establishment where Senator Brander had lived, whose brasses Mrs. Gerhardt had polished and whose stairs she had scrubbed. The lobby, with its plate-glass windows and comfortable lounge chairs, seemed just the thing to attract "all the fascinating forces of so vigorous and young a town," right down to the inevitable corps of traveling salesmen and the "idling bigwigs" of local politics. "Jennie's world to the life," wrote Dreiser; "Poor little girl" (191).

Like Columbus, the city of Erie seemed wholly representative. In it dwelled both the complexity and the inherent hypocrisy that Dreiser had come to associate with late Victorian society in America. Not one of the "simple" American towns that he and Booth had passed through in driving toward Erie, he conjectured, could be said to lack its quota of saloons and other "dives" that served to balance the grandiosity of its churches and its "honorable homes." Erie, like Columbus, Dreiser perceived, could be considered either "honest or reprehensible," depending on whether one preferred to focus on those in the population who gathered for a virtuous family supper after an honest day's work and were seen Sunday mornings holding down the family pew or those who patronized the prostitutes and the bars. Erie, in short (like Columbus), might serve ideally as a microcosm for the full spectrum of American society. It would include at one extreme the most notorious vices and at the other the heralded virtues of that "weak man's shield," religion. For Dreiser, the one extreme seemed no more censurable or commendatory than the other, because he envisioned the city's population, "the vast majority," as being driven by necessity down difficult roads they had never planned on traveling.

Consider the great storm that had flooded Erie, for instance; he thought you might choose to view it from either of two polar opposites. It represented the unfathomable and gratuitous visitation of disaster on undeserving virtue — or else it demonstrated anew that the wages of sin truly were death. Dreiser himself, naturally, subscribed to neither of these extremes. For him the storm held little pertinence beyond its service in illustrating the forceful intervention of accident in human affairs. It seemed purely a chance circumstance, came close to being a roll of the universal dice. As a phenomenon, the disaster could be traced to its causes, of course. As Dreiser saw it, this is what had happened: Throughout the region a cloudburst had swelled a small brook, whose course ultimately took it through Erie; along this waterway, somewhere in the near countryside, a barn had washed away, its debris blocking a culvert that ordinarily would have been copious enough to carry nearly any flow of water. As a consequence of this unexpected blockage, the large gully leading to the culvert rapidly swelled to overflowing. Eventually the debris blocking the culvert gave way to the mounting pressure of the backed-up water. The deluge that was released then rushed down upon Erie. Chimneys fell, foundations cracked, houses washed away, debris piled up in mountains. Dreiser, his active sense of irony alerted, made rapid notations for the book he was already planning to write about his trip: "In one house eight [were] instantly killed — a judgment of God, no doubt, on their particular kind of wickedness. In another house three, in another house four; death being apportioned, no doubt, according to the quality of their crimes" (194). Thus it happens, the judgmentally minded might say, that transgressors of the law reap the whirlwind. This should remind us that Dreiser, only four years previously, had employed a rather similar irony in the working title for his novel: "The Transgressor" — the work that ultimately was renamed *Jennie Gerhardt.*

By making his appeal to the immutable natural laws of physics as a means of explaining the catastrophe in Erie, Dreiser revealed his continuing reliance on the notions expressed in Herbert Spencer's *The First Principles,* a book whose bomb-like impact on him during the early 1890s, he says, exploded his previously held concepts of life and then established a radically new pattern for his thinking. Spencer had more than once used gravity and the inevitability of water seeking its own level to illustrate his philosophy. And Dreiser borrowed from *First Principles* also the generalized notion concerning transgression of immutable laws, paraphrasing it in the manner of Spencer for *Jennie Gerhardt*:

> In this world of ours the activities of animal life seem to be limited to a plane or circle, as if that were an inherent necessity to the creatures of a planet which is perforce compelled to swing about the sun. A fish, for instance, may not pass out of the circle of the seas without courting annihilation; a bird may not enter the domain of the fishes without paying for it dearly. . . . and we are content to note the ludicrous and invariably fatal results which attend any effort on their part to depart from their environments. . . . When men or women err — that is, pass out from the sphere in which they are accustomed to move — . . . . People may do no more than elevate their eye-brows . . . and yet so conditional is the well-defined sphere of social activity that he who departs from it is doomed. (235–36).

By the time Dreiser completed *Jennie Gerhardt,* his reading of Spencer was fifteen years in the past. He gives Spencer great credit for shaping him, for providing him with a modern philosophy with which to face coherently the newly industrialized world in which he moved. But in all reality, it seems quite probable that, rather than receiving a bundle of epiphanic revelations, what was most valuable to Dreiser was finding in Spencer solid confirmation of his own most privately held convictions — thoughts about life perhaps not yet voiced even to himself but steadily building nevertheless, shaping themselves from recent practical experiences in the "school of hard knocks." What was needed to confirm his own dark inklings, to support them and bundle them together into a solid philosophical point of view concerning human existence, was precisely the catalyst that he found in Spencer: a voice of authority.

The post-Pittsburgh Dreiser, the Spencer-recycled Dreiser, was always afterward the Dreiser whom Americans came to know, and he never seemed more the Spencerian Dreiser than when motoring westward that summer of 1915 enroute to his Hoosier roots. He had begun his fictional application of Spencer's principles as the century turned, at sporadic intervals halting the action in *Sister Carrie* (1900) to take the pulpit concerning one law or another that he discerned as governing the progress of society in America. In so doing, he caused *Sister Carrie* to ape Spencer's practice of generalizing first, then moving to illustratory examples:

> A man, to hold his position [in society] must have a dignified manner, a clean record, a respectable home anchorage. (85)
> For all the liberal analysis of Spencer and our modern naturalistic philosophers we have but an infantile perception of morals. There is more in it than mere conformity to a law of evolution. (87–88).
> People in general attach too much importance to words. (118)

It was in *Carrie* that Dreiser first gave direct fictional expression to the great "forces" (employing that term, borrowed out of Spencer) that govern life, forces of cosmic power against which the meaningless efforts generated by human desires seemed no more than wisps in the wind. A dozen years after *Carrie*, Dreiser published *The Financier* (1912) and two years later *The Titan* (1914), novels in which his application of *First Principles* might be said to have achieved their maturity, with precise and extended expression, to serve as infrastructure for the Cowperwood story.

Even while laboring toward composition of *The Financier*, however, Dreiser was completing his manuscript of *Jennie Gerhardt* (1911), and it was no accident that *Jennie* should prove to be weighty with Spencerian influence. Held under the British philosopher's thrall, Dreiser must have thrilled with fulfillment as he sat in one of those comfortable reader alcoves in the imposing new Carnegie Library across the river from Pittsburgh and dug his laborious way through dense paragraphs of Spencer's most reader-resistant prose. After enduring pages of tedious and abstract argument concerning planetary motion, the effects of chlorophyll, and "those complex movements of aerial, liquid, and solid matter on the Earth's crust"

(418), it must have come as revelation to read Spencer's assurance that the laws he was codifying never would have more pertinence than when applied to human society, to "all the subtle products of social life" (384). To hear the printed voice of Spencer declare that "certain agencies which we call desires move [people] in the direction of least resistance" (402) was one thing; it was quite another to be offered clear, explicit, and convincing instances taken from life as Dreiser recognized it. The experience surely would have had the effect of causing Dreiser to leap forward mentally, to push beyond the British examples supplied by the text toward examples of his own that were considerably closer to home, instances drawn from his own twenty-three years of accumulative wondering at the ever-changing, often-disturbing spectacle of human life in America and from his restless postadolescent prowlings through a group of emergent urban-industrial societies—Chicago, St. Louis, Pittsburgh, and others—societies in which by virtue of his work as a journalist he had been immersed.

In *First Principles* Dreiser would come upon passages of truly epiphanic power such as this:

> If there be any locality which, either by its physical peculiarities or by pecu-liarities wrought on it during social evolution, is rendered a place where a certain kind of industrial action meets with less resistance than elsewhere, it follows from the law of direction of motion that those social units [persons] who have been moulded to this kind of industrial action will move toward this place, or become integrated there. (403)

Spencer's statement of principle may be convoluted, but the illustratory ex-ample given was plain and simple. Focusing on Glasgow, Spencer pointed out that the city's serendipitous proximity to coal and iron mines and to a navigable river had provided it with a natural advantage over less favored places when it came to the building of iron ships (a burgeoning new indus-try at that time). It followed, then, in the social context, that the total labor required to produce a steamship in Glasgow would be less than it could be in most other localities. If, then, the trade-off (labor's equivalent in food, clothing, and lodging) also were least in Glasgow, a concentration of iron-ship builders would be produced there (as it demonstrably had been). In other areas of endeavor, such as mercantile occupations, the principle would be the same and would produce a similar effect.

When Dreiser read *First Principles* he was newly resident in an Ameri-can corollary to Glasgow and had simply to glance at the busy metropolis spread before him to comprehend the working out of the least-resistance principle in terms of the immense concentration of iron and steel manufacture that were building Pittsburgh into the center of American industrialism. In *Sister Carrie* he had spoken of such a phenomenon in terms of the Chicago of the 1880s, pointing to all the great industries, not the least of which was the huge railroad corporations, which had recognized the potential of the place and had set their course for the future on the certainty that Chicago would continue to grow, prosper, and dominate.

Consider for a moment this law of least resistance; is it not precisely that which Dreiser is describing in his account of the Erie flood? The natural, gravity-propelled, downhill flow of water moves toward the culvert; is balked by the resistant force of massed debris; subsequently backs up, swelling to create a powerful new, antagonistic force; bursts its way at last through the debris as the force of pent-up waters overwhelms the blockage; and inundates the city. That law of least resistance had been central to *Sister Carrie*, whose heroine, in her private, social, and professional lives, forever and consistently follows the path of least resistance, acting ever as a result of applied forces (which often are economic in nature). What had served as a relatively subtle subtext in *Carrie* was then written large in the Cowperwood novels, books (along with *The "Genius"* and *Carrie*) in which Herbert Spencer is named. The aim of the Trilogy of Desire (a title that itself leans heavily on Spencerian terminology) was to tell a story encompassing as fully as possible the entire range of Spencer's social thought: taken together the three volumes describe the evolution of a force (Frank Cowperwood) that might dominate society and then, reaching the pinnacle of its mature stage and stimulating its own opposition of antagonistic forces that would work to hasten its "devolution," slide toward obliteration, leaving society basically unchanged and in the (desirable, inevitable) state of equilibrium that it constantly sought and toward which it eternally moved. In Spencer, Dreiser saw this principle—nature's love of balance—illustrated in a variety of ways, none more clear and simple than the observation that raising one's arm brings into play a rhythm of opposing mechanical forces that soon cause the arm to be lowered again to its original position. Dreiser's Trilogy is huge, encompassing major lines of thought that affect an entire social order. It is massive, continental in scope, city and nation shaking in theme. *Jennie,* by way of contrast, drives toward an opposite and lesser pole, is perhaps the most intensely personal of all Dreiser's novels, fills the smallest canvas possible, and exists deliberately and necessarily on the outer fringes of society. The Trilogy is flamboyantly public, whereas *Jennie* is intensely private. The book never flaunts, never shakes foundations in the way the Trilogy does. In *Jennie,* the hero's desires and their consequences, just as deliberately, as necessarily, cause the story to shrink back, hide away, and retreat from the white-hot bustling center of life.

Nonetheless, *Jennie Gerhardt,* although sometimes less explicit in its reliance on Spencer and certainly less burdened with terminology that is outright Spencerian, shares with *Carrie* and the Trilogy a pronounced tendency to cite and then to illustrate laws derived from *First Principles.* Here we see, for instance, Dreiser's pronounced tendency to present the human being (like everything else in the natural world) as a mechanism created, directed, and determined by exterior influences. We might examine his presentation of Lester Kane as a representative example of this inclination. He describes Lester as being "a product of a combination of elements [read *forces*] — religious, commercial, social — modified by [another force,] the overruling, circumambient atmosphere of liberty in our national life which is productive of almost uncounted freedoms of thought and action" (126). He more specifically portrays Lester, in his relationship with Jennie, as being "instinctively, magnetically, and chemically" attracted to her.

> She was his natural affinity, though he did not know it, — the one woman who answered somehow the biggest need of his nature — a quiet, sympathetic, *non-resisting* [my emphasis] attitude of mind. . . . [She] seemed to combine the traits of an ideal woman — sympathy, kindliness of judgement, youth and beauty. . . . Somehow this ideal was located fixedly in the back of his brain, and when he thought he was in the presence of the right one he instinctively drew near. (124)

Of considerable interest to Dreiser now is Spencer's disquisition on forces of attraction and forces of repulsion, between whose rhythmical pull and push the individual finds a way. Inherent in this presentation, perhaps even central to it, is that same central law of least resistance that I have mentioned and that expresses the principle on which Spencer insists human beings always act when faced by a mélange of attracting and repelling forces. When added to all this is the dictum that says that any force as it evolves is certain (in the interest of final equilibrium) to generate its own oppositional force or forces, then *Jennie Gerhardt* can be seen rather clearly as being a fictional equivalent of Spencerian argument, an "objective correlative" of sorts.

The Jennie-Lester story does represent the working out of the least-resistance principle; but precisely how, given the social gulf that separates them, can Jennie and Lester be brought together? Spencer said that the direction of least resistance was always determined by the distribution of forces to be overcome — those standing in formation on one side of the equation relative to those marshaled on the other. So the lovers must be joined (if joined they be) through the superiority of attracting forces (physical beauty, sexual desire, financial need) over those that repel (disparities in age, religion, social position, financial status). This impressive array of repelling forces is summed up, amalgamated, in the rigid opposition of the Kane family. The fact that this force is removed physically and geographically, so that Lester and Jennie exist in something of a social vacuum when their paths cross in the Bracebridge home in Cleveland — worlds away from his home in Cincinnati and hers in Columbus — does much to explain why Dreiser should feel the need to resort to a form of mesmerism as he strives to portray the power of Lester's desire (and Jennie's also) as being irresistible:

> He looked into her big, soft eyes with his dark, vigorous brown ones. There was a flash that was hypnotic, significant, insistent.
>
> "You belong to me," he said. "I've been looking for you. . . . I like you. Do you like me? Say?"
>
> She looked at him, her eyes wide, filled with wonder, with fear, with a growing terror.
>
> "I don't know," she gasped, her lips dry.
>
> "Do you?" He fixed her grimly, firmly with his eyes.
>
> "I don't know."
>
> "Look at me," he said.
>
> "Yes," she replied.
>
> He pulled her to him quickly. "I'll talk to you later," he said, and put his lips forcefully to hers.
>
> She was horrified, stunned, like a bird in the grasp of a cat, but somehow through it all something terrific, inviting, urging, was speaking to her. (123)

That Dreiser should manage to get away with this scene, to make it palatable, at least, and perhaps even plausible, is a tribute to the long foreground that precedes it, in which are presented with great skill the differing personalities (and of course the circumstances) of the would-be lovers, and in which is foreshadowed the manner of their coming together.

In *Jennie Gerhardt* action most often springs from character, and both Jennie and Lester are presented by Dreiser as essentially passive individuals whose primary traits include confrontational weakness. Neither is inclined to "face up" to society (on the simplest level, their families); much less is either of the principals prepared to "slug it out" with an opponent in asserting any right to individuality. So they both rather easily accept the roles assigned to them as guilty transgressors of social law, and they act accordingly. Jennie takes the line of least resistance in hiding from Lester the fact that she is a mother, the result of her unsanctioned liaison with Senator Brander. But Lester himself takes the same path because, as Dreiser notes, he *could* have had Jennie's entire story had he insisted: "He had asked her once tentatively about her past. She had begged him not to" (208). Taking the immediately easier way, he had not pressed the issue, seeming to recognize it as a potential Pandora's box. Lester assumes the same, "easier" position when he conceals from his family the fact that he has taken Jennie as his mistress. And so he and Jennie begin their life together secretively and in self-imposed exile, moving to what they hope and believe to be a safe neutral ground, Chicago, where they expect to escape detection, the notoriety that might attach to it, and those hard decisions that disclosure would impose on them. Their flight is fruitless, of course; that is the point of the novel.

Spencer wrote that "social units" (i.e., people) move "toward the object of their desires in the directions which represent to them the fewest obstacles" (205). Could a more useful example than that of Jennie and Lester be produced? "You are my niece," Lester declares to Jennie as they begin their affair, much like the declaration of Charles Drouet to Carrie Meeber ("Now, you're my sister") in a similar, unworkable ploy; as if that subterfuge will fool anyone for very long. And as for Jennie, Lester proposes that she employ duplicity rather than deal frankly with her family. "There couldn't be any objection to that, could there?" he asks in a rhetorical question, which Jennie takes seriously, providing the automatic reply, "Not if they didn't find out" (163, 157).

Not being found out then becomes a prime objective of both lovers. On Jennie's part, the object is to keep Lester oblivious of the fact of her daughter's existence. On Lester's, it is to hide from his family the truth about his private life — in short, to prevent a retributive social group from discovering his transgression. To this end, secrecy becomes indispensable. But, given the actualities of their lives — particularly of Lester's, he being necessarily involved in the quite unprivate world of big business — this is not a very real possibility. "Lester's private career with Jennie," writes Dreiser, "was not a matter which could be easily concealed" (223). Some of his many social and commercial associates are bound to (and do) observe the couple driving together in Lester's private carriage. More than once the lovers are spied in each other's company at the theater, and when this happens, Lester introduces Jennie simply as "Miss Gerhardt" and lets it go at that. But his friends, having a natural human curiosity and being "keen observers," a fact that Lester unwisely discounts, are alerted to something more than has met the eye.

Rather early on, even before the lovers run away together, Dreiser set the stage for an eventual exposé, writing of this epoch of American life as being a time in which "the impact of materialized forces is well-nigh irresistible," quite powerful enough to overwhelm the spirit. Cataloguing these forces in an extended paragraph, Dreiser arrives finally at the communicative media, "the express and post-office, the telegraph, telephone, the newspaper and, in short, the whole art of printing and distributing [which] have so combined as to produce what may be termed a kaleidoscopic glitter, a dazzling and confusing showpiece [composed of] the vast army of facts and impressions which present themselves daily." He predicts the death of personal privacy trapped in the "white light of publicity" (125).

A "social movement," Dreiser had learned from Spencer, once it is established in a given direction, tends to continue moving in this direction, "maintains its course for a long time after its original source has ceased; and requires antagonistic forces to arrest it" (208). Here is described the parabolic curve taken by the "social movement" that is Jennie and Lester's life together. In arriving at those pages in which that glaring light of publicity is to be thrown in all its cruelty on the "love nest" in South Hyde Park, Dreiser enlists the aid of his new force, the newspaper. Its introduction here is necessary because, for one thing, the disclosure to the Kanes that the scion of their family is living with a declassé woman in a Schiller Street apartment has not ended the love affair but only caused Lester to retreat farther from the central city, with its possibility of public exposure, to the seeming safety of the Chicago suburbs.

As an exnewspaperman himself, and one who from his early manhood was transfixed by the immense potential of the press for effecting positive social change (a potentiality more often honored in the breach than the observance, he was soon to discover as a young reporter), it was wholly natural for Dreiser to arrange for leakage of Jennie and Lester's irregular ménage to a local gossip sheet, the *South Side Budget*. Dreiser was arguably the very first of our socially conscious novelists to recognize the increasingly significant role that the print media would play in the national life. He had written for the elaborate and magazine-like Sunday supplements himself, and by the time he composed the final sections of *Jennie Gerhardt* his editorial experience with the Butterick combine had considerably augmented his knowledge of the powerful new mass-circulation monthly periodicals. But *Jennie* being a small-scale story, it is more appropriate that the exposure of the lovers begin with a small, local sheet. Dreiser had begun paying attention to media power in *Sister Carrie,* in which the newspapers exert a demonstrable impact on the lives of the characters. Their reports of Hurstwood's theft, spread by wire in every direction from Chicago, like an electronic spiderweb calculated to snare its fly, soon catch up with Hurstwood in Montreal, where he reads his name in the local paper and knows that the jig is up. He never learns anything of good use to him in the papers, whose want ad pages stimulate his brief, disastrous career as a scab during the Brooklyn streetcar strike.

By way of contrast, the newspapers have a consistently positive effect on Carrie, serving to spread news of her theatrical successes in a manner that amounts to free advertising. She and the papers are meant for each other. Symbiotically, she fills empty space for them with entertaining accounts of show business; they in turn promote her fame and fortune. She is courted by reporters, who happily return to their offices with usable interviews. Her sad-mouthed likeness, in rich sepia, graces the pages of the recently introduced Sunday rotogravure sections, and this exposure helps make her a "celebrity" to readers who number in the tens of thousands and more. Her rise, like Hurstwood's fall, is tied directly to her connection with the daily papers.

Once that new and powerful social force, the newspaper, is introduced into the story, the novel's resemblance to the dynamics of the Erie flood becomes even more pronounced. The tiny driblets of water that may have found their way past or around the blockage at the culvert are nothing compared with the pent-up force of the overfull pond that, urgently pressing against the debris, eventually sweeps it away. In *Jennie* the niggling little discoveries and exposures of Jennie and Lester, bothersome as they may be, do little to overcome their suppression of the truth, but the entrance of the newspapers into the affair sweeps away the blockage created by their deception and allows disclosure to rush down on them, devastating their territory. It is altogether consistent with Spencerian thinking that the new and antagonistic force should not be malevolently motivated but, rather, should bear as much resemblance as possible to the essentially neutral forces of nature; the irony of the disclosure is intensified by Dreiser's calling to our attention the fact that the writers and editors who work on the exposure stories have no personal axe to grind. "It was not the idea," writes Dreiser, "to be cruel or critical, but rather complimentary" (285). All of the "bitter things," such as the illegitimacy of Jennie's daughter and the immorality of the affair's masquerading as a marriage, were to be ignored. The journalistic emphasis was to be placed instead on the most affirmative, Romeo and Juliet aspects of the story: "Lester should appear as an ardent, self-sacrificing lover, and Jennie as a poor and lovely working-girl being lifted to great financial and social heights by the devotion of her millionaire lover" (286).

Innocence of motive aside, the preparation of the exposure story for the Sunday supplement involves not only the routine *sub rosa* purchase of a photograph of Lester from his photographer in Cincinnati "for a consideration" but also the penetrating invasion of the couple's privacy by the 1890s version of paparazzi, a candid-cameraman who, unbeknownst to Jennie, takes a snapshot of her one morning as she leaves her South Hyde Park home to go shopping.

The very last wish of Jennie and Lester is to become local, or even neighborhood, celebrities; yet, given the ubiquitous circulation of the big newspapers, this is what inevitably occurs as soon as the story appears, with its bold headline: "This Millionaire Fell in Love With This Lady's Maid" (289). Little difference is made by the fact that the photographs of Lester and Jennie are flattering portraits or that the newspaper has kept free of caricature the bevy of accompanying sketches worked up by one of the professional staff artists employed for that purpose and purporting to give the public a peep at Jennie at work in the Bracebridge home, at Jennie and Lester on one of their carriage rides, and at Jennie standing in the window of a mansion gazing out on the modest cottage of a working man. The result is the same. The pair at once become public property, notorious. Characteristically, Lester's strong initial urge is somehow to suppress knowledge of the newspaper story, to "kill" it, as it were, by ripping out the page on which it appears before Jennie has a chance to come upon it. But her neighbor, "meaning no harm" (288), of course, takes care of that gap in communication by calling Jennie's attention to the Sunday paper's coverage of her "love romance." Jennie is stunned and at once realizes that the newspaper has provided Lester's family with "another club with which to strike him and her" (289). Lester, on reflection, also faces the immense implications of this new force in the story, understanding that his position in society, already weakened by his sister's earlier discovery of his living "in sin" with Jennie on Schiller Street, has been greatly weakened by the notoriety associated with the exposure story. He and Jennie, a "choice morsel" for the scandalmongers, have been devoured.

Dreiser's use of the media in *Jennie Gerhardt* marks a significant advance in fictional technique compared with his use of the newspapers in *Sister Carrie* a decade previously. Whereas in *Carrie* the papers always play a subordinate, if important, role and exist on a secondary plane of the narrative, in *Jennie* the papers are brought to the forefront and serve as a plot device of considerable importance. They become the decisive Spencerian "antagonistic force" that is essential in nudging toward dissolution the "social movement" (the illicit "marriage"), which, as Spencer had said, once set in a given direction tends to continue and maintain its course, even though its original impetus may have dissipated — a social paraphrase of the entropy principle. Lacking the opposing power of this antagonistic force, the liaison of Jennie and Lester would stand a good chance of continuing to drift along its wonted way, disregardful of the temporary embarrassments to be expected from a few accidental sightings by the curious over the years. But the intervention of the papers changes all this. The importance with which Dreiser credits the exposure story may be measured by its position in the plot and the space apportioned to it. It occurs roughly five-eighths of the way through the narrative (interestingly enough, in somewhat the same position that one might expect to come upon the structural turning in the plot of a Shakespearean tragedy; it is at this approximate spot in *Hamlet* that Claudius screams, "Give me some light!"). In a total of sixty chapters of narrative, the exposure story stands as number forty. The whole of this chapter, as well as a good bit of the next one, is given to delineating the preparation of the news story, its publication, and its immediate personal impact on Jennie and Lester.

The protective dam of silence once broken, the waters of social retribution rush down on the lovers, swiftly, catastrophically. Society's agent, appropriately, is the Kane family, and now no time is lost as Dreiser continues on to the death of old Archibald Kane and the reading of his angry will, which spitefully disinherits Lester unless he abandons Jennie. Predictably, faced with this alternative and following his usual path along the line of least resistance, Lester chooses his inheritance, not without a considerable surface display of suffering and regretful anguish. And Jennie, true to her own least-resistance pattern, passively encourages his desertion.

At novel's end Jennie Gerhardt watches from the shadows, without intervening, as persons who loved Lester less than she load his coffin onto a train that will take it to its burial place, far away from her, of course, in Cincinnati, in the family vault of Letty Pace, the society woman he married after abandoning his faithful longtime companion. Dreiser's "pet heroine" is left in a stoic position, facing the wreckage of her life. With the possible exception of old Solon Barnes in *The Bulwark* (1946), and notwithstanding the title of Dreiser's final novel, *The Stoic,* Jennie seems the most thoroughgoing stoic in all of his fiction and the most overt. Faced by the immensity of forces ranged against her and seeing that nothing effectual is to be done in her defense against them, she surrenders herself to the acceptance necessary for the psychic survival of one caught in a hopeless situation, exhibiting that "grace under pressure" that another, later, and younger American writer would speak of when presenting his own characters, faced with inevitable loss against overwhelming odds, in works such as "The Killers" and *A Farewell to Arms.*

Bibliography

Dreiser, Theodore. *A Hoosier Holiday.* New York: John Lane Company, 1916.

———. *Jennie Gerhardt.* Edited by James L. W. West III. Philadelphia: University of Pennsylvania Press, 1992.

———. *Sister Carrie.* Edited by John C. Berkey, Alice M. Winters, James L. W. West III, and Neda M. Westlake. Philadelphia: University of Pennsylvania Press, 1981.

Spencer, Herbert. *The First Principles.* New York: H. M. Caldwell Co., 1880.

9
Jennie Through the Eyes of Thorstein Veblen

CLARE VIRGINIA EBY

THE CAPACITY OF AMERICANS FOR self-deception and sophistic reasoning, particularly in the matter of sexual mores, is one of Dreiser's great themes. The title of his 1920 critique, "Neurotic America and the Sex Impulse," remains startlingly accurate today. In *Jennie Gerhardt,* Dreiser exposes a sexual double standard that is bolstered by a second American peculiarity, the status system. Characters from the highest social classes to the lowest — from Lester Kane's father and Lester's wife, Letty, to the poor and disabled old Gerhardt — assume that Jennie should be cast aside like a soiled garment because she is a poor, unmarried, and sexually experienced woman. Dreiser's contempt for the society that casts her out becomes clear not only when Jennie's common-law husband is rehabilitated socially and financially at the end of the novel, leaving her a pariah, but also when Lester censures her after discovering Vesta: "Senator Brander's child, he thought to himself. So that great representative of the interests of the common people was the undoer of her — a self-confessed washer-woman's daughter. A fine tragedy of low life all this was" (210). Dreiser's exposure of such self-satisfied hypocrisy throughout *Jennie Gerhardt* constitutes one of his most focused pieces of cultural criticism.

The ostracism of Jennie appears particularly odious because she is such an attractive character. Her personality is as unusual in the Dreiser canon as the themes of sexual hypocrisy and the status system are familiar. Unlike Carrie — the character with whom she has most often been compared — Jennie's most passionate desires are not for pretty clothes or fancy restaurants. In contrast with Roberta, Clyde, Carrie, and Hurstwood, Jennie enjoys working, particularly at menial tasks that will be of service to others. Unlike Cowperwood or Witla, Jennie is not ambitious. As Lester describes her, " 'Jennie is of a peculiar disposition. She doesn't want much' " (373). One of the narrator's generalizations helps to clarify what makes Jennie peculiar: "We live in an age in which the impact of materialized forces is well-nigh irresistible; the spiritual nature is overwhelmed by the shock" (125). Jennie resists; she is not overwhelmed.

Critics have disagreed sharply over this anomalous Dreiserian character. H. L. Mencken, who greatly admired his friend's second novel, was the first to suggest that Jennie's character was its one weakness; that opinion has been echoed by Lawrence Hussman and Mordecai Marcus (*Dreiser-Mencken* 69, Hussman 64, Marcus 61). Other critics, such as Warwick Wadlington and Donald Pizer, however, have warmed to Jennie's "remarkable wholeness" and tragic stature (Wadlington 226, Pizer 125). The divergence of opinion is not simply a matter of readers seeing different things in the same text; it is sharpened by *the way* Dreiser depicts Jennie's uniqueness. Her integrity, as I would call it, is inseparable from Dreiser's view of her femininity. She is "a big woman, basically . . . worthy of any man's desire" (72–73). An "ideal mother," as the narrator calls her several times, Jennie is so fertile that she becomes pregnant after her first sexual encounter, and she gives birth almost effortlessly. Jennie's actions and reactions are presented in stereotypically feminine terms.

Dreiser's enthusiasm for the essentialist woman he has created may embarrass the modern reader, as for instance when it leads to apostrophes to "the All-mother" (92). His view of Jennie's femininity will seem to many readers old-fashioned, if not reactionary.[1] But by suspending retrospective judgment on Dreiser's conception of femininity in *Jennie Gerhardt,* we can examine to what ends he *uses* it in the novel. In the early years of the twentieth century, the question of whether women had an essential nature was hotly argued. American sociology provides a useful context for looking at how *Jennie* participates in this debate, especially because Dreiser often aspires to an air of quasi-scientific seriousness in his own writings. Sociological analyses of gender based on essentialist premises were not the exclusive province of conservatives who wanted to restrict women to a limiting sphere. Champions of women's rights such as Lester Ward, Charlotte Perkins Gilman, and Thorstein Veblen invoked essentialist logic to call for recognition and expansion of women's role in American life.

Lester Ward's 1903 treatise, *Pure Sociology,* challenges popular wisdom. As Ward sees it, "while female superiority is a perfectly natural condition, male development requires explanation" (323). Advancing his "*gynaeco-centric* theory," Ward argues that, "in a word, life begins as female" (296, 313). Males, evolving later, are "a mere afterthought of nature" (314), and contemporary male superiority is merely "make-believe" (331). Ward looks forward to the "*gynandrocratic*" stage "in which both man and woman shall be free to rule themselves" (373). In *Women and Economics* (1898), Charlotte Perkins Gilman uses a similar argument to advance her claim of original female superiority. She is dismayed that the modern conflation of the sexual and the economic realms—the "sexuoeconomic relation" as she calls it—has left women on the sidelines of social evolution (74). Modern women, Gilman argues, should be freed from their economic bondage so they can earn money, because productive labor can give meaning to their lives and because unleashing "female" qualities such as coordination and conservation will benefit the entire species (157, 130).

The influence on Dreiser of the conservative evolutionary sociologist Herbert Spencer is a matter of established importance and has been much discussed. Progressive social theoretical ideas, however, open up new aspects of *Jennie Gerhardt* for interpretation. For instance, Ward's theory that male superiority originates in the discovery of paternity (345) may shed light on Lester's response to Vesta, and Gilman's sensitivity to the devaluation of women's work is certainly relevant to Dreiser's novel.[2] It may give pause that Ward and Gilman would combine evolutionary theory (the essence of which is change) with an argument about essence. But for liberal social theorists at the turn of the century, woman's "essence" could provide the grounds for increasing her freedom in society.

It is particularly the sociology of Veblen, also progressive, evolutionary, and essentialist, that illuminates *Jennie*. In a 1935 letter, Dreiser described Veblen's *The Theory of the Leisure Class* as "marvellous," but there is no evidence of his systematic study of the sociologist (*Letters* 750). In his penetrating poetic sketch, Robert Penn Warren describes Dreiser's brooding temperament: "Nothing could help nothing, not reading Veblen or even Freud" (6). In fact, greater familiarity with Veblen's social theory would certainly have comforted Dreiser, for they wrote in response to many of the same cultural circumstances, frequently arriving at nearly identical conclusions. The logic of *Jennie Gerhardt*, like many of Veblen's works, depends on an essentialist conception of women's work, which is aligned with motherhood, to criticize the values of capitalist America.[3]

Veblen is best known for his scathing analysis of business and the leisure class, but he also theorized about a stage of human evolution that preceded capitalism. The era of peaceable savagery, characterized by small groups of people working in cooperation to satisfy their simple wants, resembles the social organization under which the elder Gerhardts try, with scant success, to raise their family. Disputing the many followers of Auguste

Comte who held to the creed of human progress, Veblen looks backward
for signs of heaven on earth. Veblen commends the savage mode of existence,

> characterized by a considerable group solidarity . . . living very near the soil,
> and unremittingly dependent for their daily life on the workmanlike efficiency
> of all the members of the group. The prime requisite for survival . . . would be
> a propensity unselfishly and impersonally to make the most of the material
> means at hand. (*Instinct* 36)

During this early, peaceful stage, the two human "instincts which make
directly for the material welfare of the community" were allowed free rein
(*Instinct* 25).

The first, the instinct of workmanship, is the human tendency to make
useful things; its "functional content is serviceability" (*Instinct* 31). The
word "serviceable" recurs throughout Veblen's writings, always with a favorable cast. The second positive instinct, which he considers inseparable
from workmanship, is the parental bent (*Instinct* 25). Veblen carefully
distinguishes the parental bent — which includes sympathy for all living
things — from the merely "tropismatic" reproductive instinct (*Instinct* 26).
The instinct of workmanship and the parental bent are manifested in the
behaviors that Veblen considers as rare in modern America as they are
praiseworthy: productive work, generosity, virtue, concern for others, and
service. Dreiser's Jennie Gerhardt, who is nothing if not willing to be of
service, is a perfect Veblenian heroine. She apprehends, as do Veblen's
peaceable savages, the connections between human beings, other living
things, and the planet. "Quick to see ragged clothes, worn shoes, care-lined
faces" in others, Jennie instinctively helps and gives to them (195).

Jennie is also distinguished by her attitude toward work. In *Tales of the
Working Girl*, Laura Hapke credits Dreiser for raising "the working girl
story into art" but faults him for "censoring" Jennie's "involvement" in
menial jobs (71, 82). She notes that Dreiser does not give Jennie's work
even the few pages of description that he gives Carrie's — a wise observation, yet one that leads Hapke to grant Dreiser less than his due. As Thomas
Riggio has remarked, no male writer of this period, with the lone exception
of Henry James, shows as much interest in women's lives as Dreiser does
(*American Diaries* 26). Dreiser's sympathy for working women emerges on
the first page of *Jennie Gerhardt,* which depicts Jennie and her mother
seeking employment. Rather than censoring their labors, Dreiser saturates
the novel with women's instinct of workmanship. Left pregnant by Senator
Brander, Jennie finds "the pleasure of work lifting her out of herself" (95).

"'I must work. I want to work,'" she tells Lester when he asks her to become his mistress (133). Jennie holds a job outside the home for a time when she does not need the money (173). Even after she becomes Lester's common-law wife, Jennie's "natural industry" prompts her to do much of her own housework (197, 252, 268). Dreiser calls, likewise, for acknowledgment of Mrs. Gerhardt's labors; she "worked like a servant and received absolutely no compensation either in clothes, amusements or anything else" (108). Looking at work in Veblen's terms — as a serviceable instinct aligned with a propensity toward virtue, rather than as a particular set of tasks to accomplish for remuneration — brings women's work to the center of Dreiser's novel.

Like Ward and Gilman, Veblen distinguishes between women's contemporary status and their essential nature. His analysis of women's "work" best known today — featuring wives as conspicuous consumers of goods to advertise their husbands' wealth — comes into play at a late stage of human evolution, after the emergence of private property. Veblen says numerous times that women are instinctively better endowed than men with workmanship and the parental bent (*Leisure* 353, 358; *Instinct,* passim). Furthermore, women, according to Veblen, occupied "the chief place in the technological scheme" during the era of savagery (*Instinct* 94). Consequently, the savage social order was "peaceable, non-coercive . . . with maternal descent and mother-goddesses, and without much property rights, accumulated wealth or pecuniary distinction of classes" (*Instinct* 153). Veblen's language here is more restrained than Dreiser's tribute to the "All-mother," but the sentiment is the same: both idealize women for their productive, reproductive, and altruistic qualities.[4]

The significance of Veblen's social theory to *Jennie Gerhardt* becomes clear once we consider the grounds of Dreiser's valorization of Jennie. Consider the narrator's attempt to distill her personality:

> The spirit of Jennie — who shall express it? This daughter of poverty . . . was a creature of a mellowness. . . . There are natures. . . . [which] see a conformable and perfect world. Trees, flowers, the world of sound and the world of color. These are the valued inheritance of their state. If no one said to them "Mine," they would wander radiantly forth, singing the song which all the earth may some day hope to hear. It is the song of goodness.
> Caged in the world of the material, however, such a nature is almost invariably an anomaly. (16)

In contrast to Dreiser's other major characters, Jennie is prelapsarian — not necessarily better than Carrie or Clyde but linked to the natural world and untainted by the values of capitalism. The terms of Jennie's unfallenness —

called integrity or wholeness by her admirers and mushiness or sentimentality by her detractors—correspond exactly to Veblen's golden age of peaceable savagery. Jennie's character resists contamination by the possessive
"mine" of ownership. She is industrious and cooperative rather than materialistic or invidious. On a more mundane level, she is an ideal worker and
mother.

Dreiser and Veblen honor the same serviceable instincts, despite (or
perhaps because of) the exclusion of upper-class women from "all effectual
work" by the "canons of good repute" (*Leisure* 357). As Veblen voices the
familiar sentiment, "It grates painfully on our nerves to contemplate the
necessity of any well-bred woman's earning a livelihood by useful work. It is
not 'woman's sphere'" (*Leisure* 179). Lester operates from this principle
when he tries to restrain Jennie from doing her own housework: "She
would have done most things herself, had Lester not repeatedly cautioned
her not to. 'There's just one way to do this thing,' he insisted. 'Get someone
else to do it'" (268). Lester wants Jennie to confine herself to managing
the work of others, heightening her social status at the cost of her innate
serviceability.

Veblen's social theory becomes an especially helpful matrix for interpreting *Jennie Gerhardt* when social science merges with cultural criticism.
Veblen traces the origins of the invidious status system back to the early
distinction between men's and women's work. During the era of peaceable
savagery, women performed, for the benefit of the community, the agricul-
tural work and husbandry for which their workmanship and parental bent
fitted them (*Instinct* 78, 93–94). But with the advent of the barbaric era,
male "exploit" (self-serving activities such as competing in contests, fight-
ing battles, and capturing women) was valorized, and women's serviceable
work was redefined as "drudgery" (*Leisure* 10, 13; "Instinct" 94).[5] Humans
learned to consider work, low-status women's work, as "irksome," inferior,
and effeminate and to look up to men who own goods without producing
anything ("Instinct" 81, *Leisure* 36; cf. *Instinct* 174). Veblen finds traces
of the barbaric distinction between men's and women's work in the modern disdain for manual labor (making things), whereas business (making
money) commands respect (*Leisure* 5).[6] Such an invidious and, from Veblen's perspective, perverse opposition exemplifies his belief that in modern
America, "the dominant note appears to be a differential rating in respect of
aggressive self-assertion" (*Instinct* 180). The dominant note in Veblen is,
arguably, the exposure of hierarchical, differential ratings as corrupt ethics
and destructive praxis.

Such is precisely the logic of *Jennie Gerhardt*. Although Jennie's character stands as Dreiser's tribute, the novel's plot constitutes his cultural criticism. *Jennie Gerhardt* traces the inevitable conflicts between Jennie's "savage" instincts and those prized by "barbaric" capitalist communities. The narrator makes this point clearly:

> The world into which Jennie was thus unduly sent forth was that in which virtue has always struggled. . . . Virtue is that quality of generosity which offers itself willingly for service to others, and, being this, it is held by society to be nearly worthless. Sell yourself cheaply and you shall be used lightly and trampled under foot. Hold yourself dearly, however unworthily, and it will come about that you will be respected. . . . [Society's] one criterion is the opinion of others. Its one test, that of self-preservation. (87)

This popular method of calculating an individual's worth is what Veblen terms pecuniary valuation. As in Veblen's theory, an individual's actual "worth" in *Jennie Gerhardt* has nothing to do with the "respect" the world accords (or denies) her. "Self-preservation" commands status, but "service to others" draws contempt. Most of the characters surrounding Jennie employ the pecuniary valuation to determine human worth, but she calculates by a different arithmetic. Perhaps the best example is when Jennie decides it is "a wonderful thing to be a mother — even when the family was shunned" (95–96). Not only is she almost the only major Dreiser character whose child plays a significant role in her life, but she welcomes motherhood even at the cost of further ostracism. It is precisely because Jennie does not seek the world's approval, because she manifests integrity rather than invidiousness, that Dreiser admires her. Dreiser also exposes the perverse reasoning by which she is condemned: because virtue places the needs of others before those of the self, it is despised.

The logic of this equation and Dreiser's criticism of it correspond precisely to Veblen's analysis of the status system. According to Veblen, the distinguishing feature of modern *Homo sapiens* is not, as it is for Descartes, rational thought or, as Christianity tells us, the possession of an immortal soul. Instead it is the tendency to form invidious comparisons. Assigning one person to a low-status position makes another's seem higher. The ethical glue holding Veblen's social theory together is identical to Dreiser's sentiment in *Jennie*: modern humans value the unworthy and despise the worthy.

The sexual division of labor is again instructive. According to Veblen, women's "peaceable, industrial employments. . . . imply defective force,

incapacity for aggression or devastation, and are *therefore* not of good report" ("Instinct" 94, emphasis added). The responses of many characters in
Jennie to poor women's work illustrate Veblen's point but nowhere more
directly than when Lester's sister, Louise, discovers him living with Jennie
and retorts, "I should think . . . that you of all men would be above anything
like this — and that with a woman so obviously beneath you. Why I thought
she was — " she was going to add "your housekeeper" (227).

Guarding over male prestige and the status system, Louise acts like the
women whom Veblen describes so memorably in *Leisure Class*. According
to Veblen, an upper-class woman's vicarious life distances her from her
essential nature, for such a "woman's life is, and in theory must be, an
expression of the man's life at the second remove" (*Leisure* 356). Louise
manifests the "repugnance" of "the better class" for the "ceremonial un-
cleanness" of "menial service" (*Leisure* 37). Veblen's theory makes it easy to
demolish Louise's grounds for superiority: upper-class women are the functional equivalents of the servants they despise (*Leisure* 60, 182; "Beginnings" 48). What is more to the point is that Dreiser clearly condemns
Louise's invidious logic and sides with the woman she seeks to dispossess.
Even Lester can recognize that Jennie's true worth transcends pecuniary
calculation: "She was charming . . . not strong or able in any of the ways the
world measures ability, *but with something that was better*" (193, emphasis
added).

Veblen's comment describes Jennie well:

> So long as the woman's place is consistently that of a drudge, she is, in the
> average of cases, fairly contented with her lot. She not only has something
> tangible and purposeful to do, but she has also no time or thought to spare for
> a rebellious assertion of such human propensity to self-direction as she has
> inherited. (*Leisure* 358–59)

As is so often the case in Veblen's writings, the irony in this passage is self-
protective; its function is to conceal a forthright declaration of his values.
But peering out from behind the twentieth-century "drudge" is Veblen's
noble savage woman. Jennie, seen by the wealthy characters — though
never by Dreiser — as a drudge, is likewise contented with her lot. Because
of her workmanship and parental bent, she enjoys taking care of others,
even when self-interest would dictate otherwise.

In the same spirit that he brings to vindicating another group of socially marginal women, the well-heeled mistresses of his other novels such
as Aileen, Berenice, and Suzanne, Dreiser valorizes the workmanship and

service, along with the illicit sexuality, of Jennie Gerhardt. His vindication of female sexuality is both sincere and self-serving. Dreiser resented being made to feel like a pariah for his own "varietism," and he had a large personal stake in reclaiming individuals who had been consigned to the margins of respectability for their sexual license. The unfair punishment Jennie receives for her sexuality is doubled because she is also poor.

Jennie Gerhardt illustrates, in magnified form, the tendency of Dreiser's novels to commiserate with the underdog. Dreiser accomplishes here what Veblen does throughout his writings: he sympathizes with the despised, valorizes the marginal, and exposes the corrupt values of pecuniary civilization.[7] Where *Jennie* differs from the other novels is in the extent to which the title character stands apart from dominant cultural values. Jennie's serviceable instinct of workmanship and parental bent distinguish her from the "marvelously warped" and "radically wrong" values of her society (92, 93). Although Jennie gains some material comforts and financial security, these are never what motivate her, for "money was not the point at issue with her" (390). Nor does Jennie ever "lose her judgement of life or her sense of perspective or proportion" (167). Although Lester deserts Jennie, her "natural industry" never does, and she meets the many crises of her life hoping to render "some little service" to the people she loves (197, 212). Jennie is simply disposed "against idleness" (389). She cannot even pretend to be a leisure-class bride.

Jennie maintains what Veblen might call her "savage" integrity through the poverty of her childhood, the relative wealth of her years with Lester, and her middle-class comfort after Lester's defection because of her grounding in workmanship. According to Veblen, the decisive factor "is a question not so much of possessions as of employments; not of relative wealth, but of work. It is a question of work because it is a question of habits of thought, and work shapes the habits of thought" (*Business* 348). At one point Lester contemplates his lover's habit of thought: "It appealed to him as a big, decent way to take life, even if it did eliminate aggressiveness and the ability to gather material things" (195). Jennie's nonparticipation in the predatory and materialistic games that Dreiser and Veblen associate with early twentieth-century America means that she will not win any competitions. But like Faulkner's Dilsey, Jennie endures. Dreiser leaves Jennie living peacefully with two adopted children: "She believed in giving," he tells us. "She had no desire for investment or for the devious ways of trade. The care of flowers, the care of children, the looking after and maintaining the order of a home were more in her province" (397).

I should not want to glamorize Jennie's existence, nor to gloss over the tragedies of her life, but in a novel so marked by deaths, her very survival is suggestive. Even in a pecuniary culture, says Veblen, the instinct of workmanship endures. Although frequently eclipsed by invidious instincts, the staying power of workmanship is considerable. According to Veblen, the instinct of workmanship, in men and especially in women, is too basic a component of human nature to be extinguished (*Instinct* 86–87). It crops up, often along with the attendant parental bent, in even the most barbaric human communities.

Notes

1. Jennie's innate goodness, self-sacrificing tendency, and love of serviceable work may also make some readers uncomfortable because these qualities fail to correspond to textbook definitions of naturalist characterization. Yet Jennie is not alone in the naturalistic wilderness; Frank Norris's Hilma Tree in *The Octopus* shares many of her qualities.

My point is not that Dreiser always presents women in this way—Carrie, Roberta, and Aileen run counter to the stereotypical feminine role in various ways. Nor does Dreiser categorically deny men Jennie's altruistic and self-sacrificing tendencies. Some of the men Dreiser sketches in *Twelve Men* (1919) manifest traits similar to Jennie's. For instance, Charlie Potter—who is widely criticized for excessive generosity—maintains, like Jennie, the creed of "personal service" ("Doer" 68). Yet Dreiser does not tie the serviceable instincts of his Good Samaritans in *Twelve Men* to their gender as he does with Jennie Gerhardt.

2. "Women work longer and harder than most men," says Gilman. "It has been amusing . . . how this least desirable of labors [cleaning] has been so innocently held to be woman's natural duty. . . . All that is basest and foulest she in the last instance must handle and remove. Grease, ashes, dust, foul linen, and sooty ironware,— among these her days must pass" (20, 246–47).

3. Bringing Veblen into the American literature classroom can be difficult because his ideas span most, if not all, of his books. *The Theory of the Leisure Class,* his most famous book, remains for many readers the most accessible; students investigating literary realism and naturalism can profit immensely from the book or selections from it. Several of Veblen's essays can stand on their own and work well with early twentieth-century American literature. "The Economic Theory of Women's Dress" masterfully combines satire with social analysis into a "theory" of fashion which is still relevant; this essay illuminates countless realist and naturalist novels— *Sister Carrie* and Edith Wharton's *The House of Mirth,* for example. The Veblen essays that have the greatest bearing on my argument regarding *Jennie Gerhardt* are "The Beginnings of Ownership," "The Barbarian Status of Women," and "The Instinct of Workmanship and the Irksomeness of Labor."

4. For further discussion of Veblen and gender, see Diggins, Miller, Waddoups and Tilman, Ryan, and Eby.

5. Veblen is not one for precise dating, but at one point he cites the early Neolithic as the era of transition from peaceable savagery to predatory barbarism (*Instinct* 149).

6. The distinction between business and industry, a cornerstone of Veblen's social theory, is most clearly explained in *The Theory of Business Enterprise*. What is possibly Veblen's most notorious suggestion, that engineers (who make things) should be given control of business (which, to date, only makes money), rests on the distinction between industry and business.

7. The Cowperwood trilogy by no means presents an underdog, but Dreiser certainly romanticizes the financier's outsider status. The same is true of *The "Genius."*

Bibliography

Diggins, John P. "The Barbarian Status of Women." In *The Bard of Savagery: Thorstein Veblen and Modern Social Theory*, 141–68. New York: Seabury Press, 1978.

Dreiser, Theodore. "A Doer of the Word." In *Twelve Men*, 53–75. New York: Boni and Liveright, 1919.

———. *Jennie Gerhardt*. Edited by James L. W. West III. Philadelphia: University of Pennsylvania Press, 1992.

———. *Letters of Theodore Dreiser*. Edited by Robert H. Elias. Vol. 2. Philadelphia: University of Pennsylvania Press, 1959.

———. "Neurotic America and the Sex Impulse." In *Hey, Rub-a-Dub-Dub*, 126–41. New York: Boni and Liveright, 1920.

———. *Theodore Dreiser: The American Diaries, 1902–1926*. Edited by Thomas P. Riggio, James L. W. West III, and Neda M. Westlake. Philadelphia: University of Pennsylvania Press, 1982.

Dreiser-Mencken Letters: The Correspondence of Theodore Dreiser and H. L. Mencken. Edited by Thomas P. Riggio. Vol. 1. Philadelphia: University of Pennsylvania Press, 1986.

Eby, Clare Virginia. "Veblen's Anti-Anti-Feminism." *Canadian Review of American Studies* (1992 special issue, pt. 2): 215–38.

Gilman, Charlotte Perkins. *Women and Economics: A Study of the Economic Relation Between Men and Woman as a Factor in Social Evolution*. 1898. Reprint. Boston: Source Book Press, 1970.

Hapke, Laura. *Tales of the Working Girl: Wage-Earning Women in American Literature, 1890–1925*. New York: Twayne, 1992.

Hussman, Laurence. *Dreiser and His Fiction: A Twentieth-Century Quest*. Philadelphia: University of Pennsylvania Press, 1983.

Marcus, Mordecai. "Loneliness, Death, and Fulfillment in *Jennie Gerhardt*." *Studies in American Fiction* 7 (Spring 1979): 61–73.

Miller, Edythe. "Veblen and Woman's Lib: A Parallel." *Journal of Economic Issues* 6:2 and 6:3 (September 1972): 75–86.

Pizer, Donald. *The Novels of Theodore Dreiser: A Critical Study*. Minneapolis: University of Minnesota Press, 1976.

Ryan, Barbara E. "Thorstein Veblen: A New Perspective." *Mid-American Review of Sociology* 7 (1982): 29–47.

Veblen, Thorstein. "The Barbarian Status of Women." Reprinted in *Essays in Our Changing Order*, edited by Leon Ardzrooni, 50–64. New York, 1934.

———. "The Beginnings of Ownership." Reprinted in *Essays in Our Changing Order*, 32–49.

———. "The Economic Theory of Woman's Dress." Reprinted in *Essays in Our Changing Order*, 65–77.

———. *The Instinct of Workmanship and the State of the Industrial Arts*. 1914. Reprint. New York: Norton, 1941.

———. "The Instinct of Workmanship and the Irksomeness of Labor." Reprinted in *Essays in Our Changing Order*, 78–96.

———. *The Theory of Business Enterprise*. 1904. Reprint. New Brunswick, N.J.: Transaction Books, 1978.

———. *The Theory of the Leisure Class*. 1899. Reprint. New York: Modern Library, 1934.

Waddoups, Jeffrey, and Rick Tilman. "Thorstein Veblen and the Feminism of Institutional Economists." *International Review of Sociology* (Rome) 3(1992): 182–204.

Wadlington, Warwick. "Pathos and Dreiser." Reprinted in *Critical Essays on Theodore Dreiser*, edited by Donald Pizer, 213–27. Boston: G. K. Hall & Co., 1981.

Ward, Lester. *Pure Sociology*. 2d. ed. New York: Macmillan, 1907.

Warren, Robert Penn. "Vital Statistics." In *Homage to Dreiser*, 5–7. New York: Random House, 1971.

10
Labor and Capital in *Jennie Gerhardt*

CHRISTOPHER P. WILSON

AS IS THE CASE IN MANY OF DREISER'S business chronicles, the design of *Jennie Gerhardt* works by making the dominant features of individual personalities coextensive with forms of social organization. Particularly in the Kane family, which represents the novel's corporate sector, matters of personal temperament and even physical stature find their embodiment in the forms of capital. Lester Kane's "fixed and determined" quality as a "bearman," for instance, finds itself naturally incarnated in the corporate organization—in Dreiser's view, the corporate organism—he comes to inhabit. "It was natural," Dreiser writes, "that a temperament of this kind should have its solid, material manifestation at every point"—meaning, in Lester's case, "his financial affairs well in hand, most of his holding being shares of tremendous companies, where boards of solemn directors merely approved the strenuous efforts of ambitious executives to 'make good'" (404). And if Lester creates a kind of den of "commercial self-sufficiency" (234), the declining William Gerhardt implements a class ethic seemingly derived from bodily form and even biology. The novel describes Jennie's father as having inherited an "honesty of intention" from his ancestors, an unreasoning faith from "sturdy German artisans" that "came into his veins undiminished" (50). In Dreiser's natural class metaphysics, the social and the biological seem interchangeable and class affiliation therefore instinctual.

Beyond this parallel, however, labor and capital might seem to have little else to do with each other in this novel. Indeed, Dreiser's attitude toward this relationship is difficult to fathom, despite the obviously autobiographical relevance of the meditations above. In a portrait long recognized as derived from the example of Dreiser's own father, Johann Paul Dreiser,[1] William Gerhardt often seems little more than an anachronism, a man clinging futilely to his old world religious beliefs; meanwhile, Lester's more

The author would like to thank John Heineman, Richard Schrader, and Jim Smith for their advice and assistance.

predatory brother, Robert (described as "Spartan" [273], "hard" [137], with "eagle nose" [137]), occasionally is described in positive terms, identified as the very "spirit of business energy and integrity embodied" (234). (So much for instinctual class loyalty.) The *working* worlds of the Gerhardts and Kanes, although linked socially by Jennie herself, barely, if at all, intersect. Lester's and Jennie's "natural affinity" (124) is like a vertical attraction that cuts across what are, in Dreiser's view, horizontally aligned "planes" or "circles" (129, 235) of class existence. "We all run in classes" (405), Lester's "executive" (394) wife, Letty, declares, and before long, class norms reassert themselves and Lester returns to his circle. *Jennie Gerhardt* itself, pausing to explain where "the comfortable reader" needs filling in, clearly identifies the social plane on which Dreiser constructs his own fiction (107).²

Yet labor suffers an even deeper silence in *Jennie Gerhardt.* If the opening chapters briefly sketch the domestic employment of Jennie and her mother, there is virtually no subsequent detailing, for instance, of William Gerhardt's working day. (Even the close reader can have difficulty keeping track of where it is Jennie's father actually works.³) More centrally, the corporate wars of the Kane brothers — in particular, Robert's plan to establish a holding company in the wagon and carriage industry — seem essentially horizontal themselves, that is, a matter merely of internecine financial, marketing, and pooling schemes among otherwise fraternal business elites. It was true, of course, that the Kanes' home city of Cincinnati had led the United States in the carriage trade throughout the end of the nineteenth century; likewise, a Carriage Builders' National Association had in fact formed in 1872, mainly to seek protection from competitive imports. Nevertheless, the main spur to industrial growth had not been commercial consolidation, but reduced labor costs — specifically the introduction of machine tooling, interchangeable parts, and mass production in the 1870s, enabling factories to assemble inexpensive carriages for a world market.⁴ Dreiser certainly recognized, as he so amply documents in *An Amateur Laborer,* that industrial fortunes were extracted from scientifically routinized tasks in the workplace, from managerial spies, and from the recurrent threat of layoffs and lockouts (cf. Dudden); nevertheless, there are but two mentions of labor costs in Robert Kane's calculations (322, 332). Indeed, Dreiser may have intended *Jennie Gerhardt* to emphasize how easily labor was forgotten. While toiling himself during the novel's composition years, he had found himself asking of the well-to-do: "And what did they care for me. Here they were speeding along this country road in their automobiles, and driving by in their carriages. I was nothing to them. They did not see me"

(*Amateur Laborer* 172). Lester Kane, both maker of and rider in carriages, is virtually indifferent to the glass-blower Gerhardt; beyond a mild curiosity, "he had thought nothing of him, one way or the other" (348).[5]

Nevertheless, there *is* an underground economy between labor and capital in *Jennie Gerhardt,* and recovering it begins by turning to recent historiography on late nineteenth-century artisan culture. Indeed, this recent scholarship allows us not only to revise our understanding of the novel, but to arrive at a more precise picture of Dreiser's own father. To date, literary scholars—distracted in part by the generalities of Dreiser's own success columns and by what Thomas Riggio aptly calls "the [paternal] image of the defeated religious fanatic Dreiser felt compelled to project" (6) —have persisted in seeing Paul Dreiser's social status in ahistorical terms: either as a "proletarian" scarred by poverty or as a failed entrepreneur and "businessman." In actuality, Paul Dreiser's life has all the signs of a journeyman (and eventual master) artisan, one of thousands of German-American workers who populated everything from furniture making to coopering to shoe making to tailoring in the mid-nineteenth century, particularly in midwestern cities. The clustering of German Americans in the skilled trades, in fact, was the single most uniform occupational feature of their migration, as well as their attachment to the crafts most threatened by mechanization (Faires 48). In the 1840s, emigrating heads of families and single men from William Gerhardt's region of Saxony had been disproportionately artisans and masters (Köllmann and Marschalck 531).

As his occupational strategy, Dreiser's father—not "peasant"-like or "premodern," as is often said, but economically prudent and rigorously work-centered—rooted his new American identity in his extensive knowledge of the wool crafts. At first locally successful, he was soon called from city to city for his expertise, his reputation even used by mill owners in advertisements opening new businesses. Over time, he moved up from journeyman to master craftsman, to manager, and even to part owner, all the while exhibiting a versatility, as Riggio shows, that allowed him to rebound from early setbacks. Paul Dreiser's mobile social status was not wholly unusual. As Herbert Gutman has shown, particularly in small, new industrial cities, many manufacturers had themselves been artisans or "mechanics." Numbered among the artisans who went on to establish carriage factories in Cincinnati, for example, were German-American craftsmen who had imported their skills in wood or iron work.[6]

Before advanced mechanization, the power of these master artisans— who, because of their vertical mobility, came to understand the entire pro-

duction process in a given trade — translated itself into considerable community status. They stood as symbols of both individual self-improvement
and civic responsibility. As one historian described this artisan republicanism,

> the crafts themselves reputedly respected individual abilities but also stressed
> virtuous mutuality and cooperation. Each competent master appeared, in his
> workshop relations, as the quintessence of independence, free to exert his
> virtue uncorrupted; the dependence of journeymen and apprentices — in prin-
> ciple a temporary condition — was tempered by their possession of a skill and
> graced with the affection and respect of their masters, in . . . a web of "recipro-
> cal" obligation.[7]

As late as 1878, the superintendent of Cincinnati's Chamber of Commerce — pointing to the carriage trade, which still averaged only fifteen
workers per shop — could affirm this producer ideology as the key to the
city's future. The men, he said, "who are managing our industrial establishments" were "mechanics themselves" who had started at the "bottom." Men
who had once been "small producers who have grown up by degrees," artisans therefore provided social stability by avoiding speculation and diversi-
fying commerce. They were akin to "oaks, whose great spreading branches
now shelter so many families of workingmen."[8]

Naturally, by Theodore's youth, Paul Dreiser's life seemed the last leaf
of such a society. Indeed, the competing individualist and mutualist ethics
within artisan culture itself had already begun to split apart. As the industrial revolution proceeded to de-skill craft production, Paul Dreiser's life
registered not just the humiliations of poverty but the ignominy of being
culturally displaced: wedded to a trade declining regionally, trying desper-
ately to apprentice his sons and daughters to his craft but finding them
uninterested (Lingeman 34–35; *Dawn* 25). Even when Theodore's autobiography *Dawn* is examined closely, it is not shame over his father's worth
but Paul's unwillingness to *apply* his artisan skills that often generated the
young boy's ire. Seeing his father as a "beaten" man, Dreiser nevertheless
recounted proudly that no one "knew more about wool and its manufacture"; he could "qualify as a manager of a woolen mill or a buyer. . . . and
lastly, if least, as a master machinist . . . since he could set up and operate
every machine used. And why it was he lacked the courage of his own value,
I to this day fail to understand" (164–65). Even what has been regarded as
Paul Dreiser's disastrous "investment in machinery" (W. A. Swanberg's
phrase) in Sullivan may have been the result of the common tactic among

German-American artisans to retain tool ownership, literally reserving part of the means of production, well into the industrial phase.[9]

More important than the historical fidelity of Dreiser's paternal portraiture, however, is how *Jennie Gerhardt* works to reconstruct this older, artisan-based universe — and, in turn, how it uses that world to critique Lester and Robert Kane. Even the patriarch Archibald Kane's origins are implicitly anchored in that world. Although initially set in the modernizing 1880s, *Jennie Gerhardt* also looks back to the antebellum era, when carriage and wagon building had been local trades, organized in eastern and midwestern municipalities by skilled artisans and immigrants. In these days, as when Archibald was a first-generation Irishman and relatively poor (138) himself, trade was conducted not on a cash basis but on a barter (or "dicker") system. Modest fortunes were certainly made on the heels of the antebellum transportation revolution, but commercial practice and integrity were, where possible, defined by republican mutuality. This context compares intriguingly with Dreiser's explanation that Archibald rose to success with complete "honesty," simply fulfilling a social demand:

> He had built a tremendous fortune, not by grabbing and browbeating and threatening, but by seeing a big need and filling it. Early in life he had realized that America was a growing country. There was going to be a big demand for vehicles — wagons, carriages, drays — and he knew that someone would have to supply them. . . . he made good wagons, and he sold them at a good profit. It was his theory that most men were honest, that at bottom they wanted honest things. (137)

Although Dreiser might appear merely to be praising commercial foresight, this passage also honors things well made, the physical embodiments of Kane's republican notion that "truth" was the "basis of real worth" (293). Moreover, Kane's conception of honesty and community relations extended to benevolence toward his own workers. In his will, Dreiser notes with emphasis, Archibald leaves small tokens to his employees first (295), before proceeding to pressure Lester. Contrary to the norms of his current social circle, Archibald even goes to the funeral of his former yard watchman, a gesture his sons cannot understand.

In essence, Dreiser's novel transforms mutualism into a kind of paternalism. This transmutation, in turn, has its reciprocal counterpart in William Gerhardt, himself a watchman who has built his trade, as Paul Dreiser had, on the patronage of an individual manufacturer. Gerhardt, Dreiser explains, had relocated from the East to the Midwest, following a glass manufacturer named Hammond, who necessarily had come to depend on him (50).[10] In short, Gerhardt's and Archibald's worlds are mirror images of each other; indeed, these men might be seen as split, competing patriarchs of Dreiser's historical imagination. Yet Dreiser describes the bond between Gerhardt and his employer with decided ambivalence, as a class relation characterized by "integrity," a vexed word in this novel, yet also naive faith and risky dependence on William's part:

> Gerhardt felt, rather than reasoned. . . . A slap on the back, accompanied by enthusiastic protestations of affection or regard, was always worth more to him than mere cold propositions concerning his own individual advancement. . . .
>   "William," his employer used to say to him, "I want you because I can trust you," and this, to him, was more than silver and gold. (50)

Although elsewhere Dreiser laments the passing of Archibald's honesty, its place taken by the cold calculations of Robert, here he casts doubt on Gerhardt's nostalgic clutching to a preindustrial notion of "economy," as if money consciousness would have suited him better. In his final days working for Lester, Gerhardt is even reduced back to unpaid labor (265) — to Dreiser, an appropriate fate.

Meanwhile, if Dreiser sees the imagined past shared by Archibald and William less as mutualism and more as paternalism — from capital's vantage point a sign of beneficence, from labor's an instance of risky faith — he also has little patience for the traditions of artisanal republicanism, which once gave the master artisan sovereign family and local authority.[11] Even though *Jennie Gerhardt* chronicles the historical justification for William's communal power, Dreiser casts that authority merely as remnant of outmoded immigrant ways, old-fashioned neighborhood surveillance. Possessed of what Dreiser calls a "Calvin" face (82), Gerhardt is portrayed as unthinkingly applying neighborhood norms, a "genial clannishness" combined "with a desire to regulate the conduct of his fellows" (54). Significantly, Dreiser dismisses not merely Gerhardt's Lutheran moral rigidity but in particular the "narrow eye" (53) with which he applies it, an eye Dreiser associates with the corporate body of German artisanship, rooted long ago in face-to-face relations (the precise thing the dawning world of this novel lacks). Appropriate to the decay of this legacy, Gerhardt degenerates into a night watchman, sleeping by day, his actual craft having been erased in the novel, its place taken by a job that underscores his dependent status. Describing Gerhardt's "eyrie" (100), Dreiser positions the watchful eye against a background of futile economizing:

Every week he laid by five dollars out of his salary, which he sent in the form of a postal order to his wife. Three dollars he paid over for board, without room, and fifty cents he kept for spending money, church dues, a little tobacco and occasionally a glass of beer. A dollar and fifty cents he put in a little iron bank. . . . His room was a corner in the topmost loft of the mill where he worked, he having been permitted to stay there after becoming acquainted with the proprietor, who respected his honesty as well as his value as a watchman. To this he would ascend, after sitting alone on the doorstep of the mill in this lonely, forsaken neighborhood until nine o'clock of an evening; and here, amid the odor of machinery wafted up from the floor below, by the light of a single tallow candle, he would conclude his solitary day, reading his German paper. (99–100)

Holed up in a factory, isolated from where workers live (typically, workers retired to their own districts), Gerhardt now has no family and no neighborhood over which to watch. Later, Dreiser associates Gerhardt's role not with the reciprocity due a fellow artisan but with a "trick" the old man has played on his foreman's misplaced "trust" (241).

The rise of the second-generation Kanes is thus the result of a consolidation struggle, a sibling rivalry easily resolved because of weak resistance from below. The Kanes erect a "trust" whose very existence depends on Dreiser's lack of investment in the realm Gerhardt represents. Dreiser's remarks on Robert's foresight follow suit. Consistent with Dreiser's rather sentimental nostalgia for Archibald Kane's "honesty" — two of the antebellum needs for wagons and carriages, by way of contrast, had been for slave owners on southern and Caribbean plantations[12] — or his inconsistently high regard for commercial "integrity," the novel's descriptions of Robert's successful pooling scheme repeatedly note his passion and vision at the expense of Lester's laggardness (305). As is true in *The Financier*, the descriptions of Robert's scheme for the carriage trust seem consistent with the recipes of contemporary success literature — anything but hard-edged (189, 300, 322).

And yet this is only half of Dreiser's split story. *Jennie Gerhardt* also seems uneasy with Robert's severance from the class relations Archibald once represented. If Lester's sentiments run in the direction of employee pensions, Robert breaks with his father's paternalism (170), with the older man's regard for loyal office subordinates (223), and with clients his father had formerly cultivated (187). Robert is even willing to let his own family's factory stand moribund to make the new pooling scheme succeed (322). Lester himself never feels more declassé than when he realizes that Robert has, in essence, made him into an "employé" (302). And although it might seem that Archibald's resolve to sever Lester from Jennie stems merely from a sense of social propriety, the patriarch's reasoning is actually laced with commercial considerations for Lester's corporate personality. Archibald advises:

> "I used to think, when I was much younger, that my sons' matrimonial ventures would never concern me, but I changed my views on that score when I got a little farther along. I began to see, through my business connections, how much the right sort of a marriage helps a man. . . . The scandal has reached down here [to Cincinnati]. What it is in Chicago I don't know, but it can't be a secret. That can't help the house in business there. . . . The whole thing has gone on so long that you have injured your prospects all around, and yet you continue." (274–75)

Jennie Gerhardt's power is registered most of all, I think, in the way the vocabulary of capital concerns has come to inhabit the class norms Lester accedes to. Once lacking Robert's "ruthlessness" (305), Lester is rather unsentimentally educated, through the plot, to "a number" of things Dreiser lists as "equally ruthless": to abandon Jenny, "marry Mrs. Gerald," become a "director in the United Carriage Association," "appear as a controlling factor" in other companies (366). Concerned now with "policy" (279) and worried over "bad business" (237), Lester drifts into treating Jennie as an employee, transferring her to another locale (190), then laying her off: "I thought it good business to leave you," he says (392). She is thus granted a fate not unlike the one that loomed over all of her class; Lester, however, is momentarily rejuvenated (367). And given William Gerhardt's injury, decline, and death and the perpetuation of the Kanes' trust, the novel might easily be read as seeing capital's victory as final. Indeed, Dreiser's business dream-work has, in recent criticism, been largely read in this way — as imagining a corporate organism that is, in essence, immortal precisely as its employees are not (Michaels 54–55).

Nevertheless, Robert's and Lester's victories are severely tempered, in part because Dreiser cannot seem to fully abandon the mutualist traditions *Jennie Gerhardt* often seems so intent on burying. For, of course, it is the very enclosure and interdependence of Lester's and Robert's new worlds that provide an ironic echo of the watchful eye that Jennie (and Dreiser himself) had so wanted to escape. If William Gerhardt has no workers (and no children) over whom to watch, Dreiser recognizes that a new kind of surveillance is *built in* to the consolidation scheme that the Kanes' business class erects. Robert's pooling scheme, bringing together previously rival carriage manufacturers, secures a class ground and makes the social organism or circle all the more interdependent; as his father says, it makes local gossip a regional matter. Returning to his analogy of the body and society, as Lester himself drifts toward his demise, Dreiser observes:

> [Lester] could not make out what [life] was all about. In distant ages a queer thing had come to pass. There had started on its way, in the form of evolution, a minute cellular organism which had apparently reproduced itself by division, had early learned to combine itself with others, to organize itself into bodies . . . and had finally learned to organize itself into man. Man, on his part, composed as he was of self-organizing cells, was pushing himself forward into comfort, and different aspects of existence, by means of union and organization with other men. (395)

Although one certainly pauses over the word "union," of course it is Lester's own desire, out of a need for comfort, to recombine with his "brother" (end his Cain exile) that dooms his relationship with Jennie. If comfort is the carrot that entices Lester back to the norms of his family and class, the "integrity" that holds their "company" together—in truth, nothing like integrity, but brute force and mutual greed—has been the stick. Thus, it is appropriate that the carriage itself, as in Dreiser's memory in *An Amateur Laborer*, becomes a sign of severe contradiction. Manipulated in the novel to represent the privatization of the Kanes' world, the carriage is one of Dreiser's symbols of "fortune": both an object of economic affluence and a deadly sign of fate. Carriages are used for Jennie and Lester's secret rendezvous (131), by Lester and Letty to escape the wedding to their private car (383), and, finally, by Lester's family to take his body to the train depot (415). Dreiser's memory of the well-to-do, quoted earlier, also mentions the automobile, the vehicle that would render the carriage trade itself extinct within a few decades.

Whether Dreiser foresaw this particular irony is beside the point; in fact, he seems to have envisioned the replacement of the horse, not the carriage itself ("Horseless Age"). What matters is that Dreiser's moral critique, at times despite his intentions, was formed by residual traces of a day when class circles followed a different design. What also matters is that, in the personal trajectories of William Gerhardt and Lester Kane, *Jennie Gerhardt* shows larger social bodies evolving. In this way, Dreiser's craft acknowledged its patrimony.

Notes

1. Johann Paul Dreiser's death was, in Lingeman's estimate, the catalyst (306) for Dreiser's start on *Jennie Gerhardt;* perhaps more precisely, the struggle to

generate (and complete) *Jennie* was tied to Dreiser's coming to terms with his father's death. See also the possible models of the German workers in *An Amateur Laborer* (143, 147).

2. On the possible relevance of "working-girl" story paper conventions to *Jennie*, see Hapke (81–83), who argues that Dreiser satirizes these formulas. Notably, by also ridiculing the clichéd Sunday newspaper plots that circulate around Jennie and Lester's affair (286), Dreiser distances *Jennie Gerhardt* from story paper *audiences* and their class. Lester says he will "welcome less attention from the proletariat and from the newspapers in the future" (288). Cf. *Dawn* 125.

3. Gerhardt is identified, of course, as a glass-blower "by trade" (4). But when Bass runs into trouble with the law, William suddenly announces he is a watchman at a furniture factory (67). Later, however, Jennie tells Lester her father is a glass-blower (133), the job in which he will be injured (148). After this point, he returns to "hunt up another job as a watchman" (174). It may be, of course, that he holds both jobs at once.

4. Historians emphasize the rapidity and completeness of the mechanization process in the 1880s. In 1865 every step in making a classic American buggy was done by hand, the skills necessary for this work being replaced nearly entirely in fifteen years; labor cost had been reduced from $45.67 in 1865 to $8.10 thirty years later (Duggan 310–12). By 1880, more than 61 percent of laborers worked in establishments with more than one hundred employees (Ross 105).

Among business elites, perhaps the most significant arrangements were carried out by local pools, such as the Cincinnati Carriage-Makers Club, which established agreements against destructive competition and worked to replace worker-based apprenticeship traditions with technical schooling (Duggan 317–18, Thomas 520).

5. Dreiser's own ambivalence about manual labor, of course, is well known; Lester's denial may partly reflect Dreiser's. In *An Amateur Laborer,* Dreiser characterizes himself as a "man of the world" now separated by a gulf from those, like his father, born and reared to hard labor, which, he says, they do "with ease and grace" (160). Cf. Lingeman 39.

6. One of the city's "first genuinely successful cheap buggy builder[s]" was a German immigrant named John Aeul, who "learned the wood-working trade in his own country," then worked in furniture and body work before forming a partnership in 1859 "with a blacksmith named Sohn"; iron work was done by a neighbor named August Bode. Another German, B. Veerkamp, started up in 1887 (*Carriage Monthly* 108, 111).

7. Wilentz 94. Cf. also Montgomery (204) on the strain of "self-advancement" in producer ideology.

8. Maxwell 11. This civic rhetoric in Cincinnati had, since antebellum times, elevated the skilled artisan to heroic status. By the 1880s, Ross reports, the artisan was made nearly invisible in public speeches that praised instead technological progress and business foresight (233–35).

9. Contrast Swanberg 5 with Jentz 69–70. Jentz also reports a similar fire destroying the tools, worth several thousand dollars, of German-American furniture workers (70), an episode that prompted unions to oppose vehemently what they regarded as this outmoded practice.

10. One historian of Terre Haute, Indiana (Salvatore 11–12), has emphasized the deference to business leaders implicit in community affairs; cf. also Dreiser's memory of his siblings going to the president of a local lumber company for charity (*Dawn* 24).

11. For a recent article in the new labor history sharing Dreiser's skepticism, see McDonnell.

12. Dreiser's formulation might be compared to the bland mystification of Chauncey Thomas describing the antebellum triangle trade: "These carriages were shipped by the sugar and molasses merchants of the northern cities to the planters of the West Indies, in commercial exchange for their product, which was speedily converted into rum, then in great demand at home and abroad. Thus the carriage-maker played his part in the interchange of commodities, and trade flourished" (519).

Bibliography

Carriage Monthly. Fortieth Anniversary Historical Number. 40(April 1904).

Dreiser, Theodore. *An Amateur Laborer*. Edited by Richard W. Dowell, James L. W. West III, and Neda M. Westlake. Philadelphia: University of Pennsylvania Press, 1983.

——. *Dawn: A History of Myself*. New York: Horace Liveright, 1931.

——. "The Horseless Age." In *Selected Magazine Articles of Theodore Dreiser*. 2 vols. Edited by Yoshinobu Hakutani, 152–60. Rutherford, NJ: Fairleigh Dickinson University Press, 1987.

——. *Jennie Gerhardt*. Edited by James L. W. West III. Philadelphia: University of Pennsylvania Press, 1992.

Dudden, Faye. "Small Town Knights: The Knights of Labor in Homer, New York." *Journal of Labor History* 28(1987): 307–27.

Duggan, Edward P. "Machines, Markets, and Labor: The Carriage and Wagon Industry in Late Nineteenth-Century Cincinnati." *Business History Review* 51(Autumn 1977): 308–25.

Faires, Nora. "Occupational Patterns of German-Americans in Nineteenth Century Cities." In *German Workers in Industrial Chicago, 1850–1910: A Comparative Perspective*, edited by Hartmut Keil and John P. Jentz, 37–51. Dekalb: Northern Illinois University Press, 1983.

Gutman, Herbert G. "The Reality of the Rags-to-Riches 'Myth,'" and "Class, Status, and Community Power in Nineteenth-Century American Industrial Cities." In *Work, Culture and Society in Industrializing America*. New York: Knopf, 1976.

Hapke, Laura. *Tales of the Working-Girl: Wage-Earning Women in American Literature, 1890–1925*. New York: Twayne, 1992.

Hegel, Richard. *Carriages from New Haven: New Haven's Nineteenth Century Carriage Industry*. Hamden, CT: Archon Books, 1974.

Jentz, John B. "Artisan Culture and the Organization of Chicago's German Workers in the Gilded Age, 1860 to 1890." In *German Workers' Culture in the United States, 1850 to 1920,* edited by Hartmut Keil, 59–80. Washington, DC: Smithsonian Institution Press, 1988.

Köllmann, Wolfgang, and Peter Marschalck. "German Immigration to the United States." Translated by Thomas C. Childers. *Perspectives in American History* 8(1973): 497–554.

Lingeman, Richard. *Theodore Dreiser: At the Gates of the City, 1871–1907.* Vol. 1. New York: G. P. Putnam's Sons, 1986.

McDonnell, Lawrence W. "'You Are Too Sentimental': Problems and Suggestions for a New Labor History." *Journal of Social History* 17(Summer 1984): 629–54.

Maxwell, Sidney D. "The Manufacturers of Cincinnati and Their Relation to the Future Progress of the City." Cincinnati: Robert Clark & Co., 1878.

Michaels, Walter Benn. *The Gold Standard and the Logic of Naturalism.* Berkeley: University of California Press, 1987.

Montgomery, David. *Beyond Equality: Labor and the Radical Republican, 1862–1872.* New York: Vintage Books, 1967.

Riggio, Thomas P. "The Dreisers in Sullivan: A Biographical Revision." *Dreiser Newsletter* 10(Fall 1979): 1–12.

Ross, Steven J. *Workers on the Edge: Work, Leisure, and Politics in Industrializing Cincinnati, 1788–1890.* New York: Columbia University Press, 1985.

Salvatore, Nick. *Eugene V. Debs: Citizen and Socialist.* Urbana: University of Illinois Press, 1982.

Schwartz, Carol A. "*Jennie Gerhardt:* Fairy Tale as Social Criticism." *American Literary Realism* 19(Winter 1987): 16–29.

Swanberg, W. A. *Dreiser.* New York: Charles Scribner's Sons, 1965.

Thomas, Chauncey. "American Carriage and Wagon Works." In *One Hundred Years of American Commerce,* edited by Chauncey Depew. Vol. 2, 516–20. New York: D. O. Haynes & Co., 1895.

Wilentz, Sean. *Chants Democratic: New York City and the Rise of the American Working Class, 1788–1850.* New York: Oxford University Press, 1984.

I I
Dreiser and the Genteel Tradition

FEW LITERARY ENCOUNTERS WOULD SEEM to have been so destined for trouble as the one between Theodore Dreiser and the leading lights of what has come to be known as the Genteel Tradition in arts and letters. A loose confederation of writers, editors, publishers, professional critics, and patrons of culture, the Genteel Tradition valued all that Dreiser despised. On the central questions of literary value and purpose, the two sides stood poles apart. Whereas Dreiser emphasized elemental drives and passions, genteel commentators insisted on the superiority of refinement and cultivation. Whereas Dreiser's sensibility was fundamentally tragic, that of the genteel custodians of culture was cheerily, if not blindly, optimistic. Whereas Dreiser understood his duty to reveal, regardless of the consequences, the crude forces at the center of American life, genteel publishers and editors saw their task as guiding and uplifting their readers.

Certainly Dreiser himself felt only contempt for the dominant cultural currents of his day. He condemned the basic genteel axiom that art should be the highest expression of "the Good, the True, and the Beautiful" as responsible for a literature that he regarded as timid, complacent, and false. Genteel authors, he thought, were so dedicated to reaffirming continuously that life really consisted of noble characters who sacrificed for others and honored their marriage vows that they could not accept the all-too-obvious existence of self-centered struggle. Even the concession that men had both higher and lower impulses (a concession never made in the case of women), Dreiser alleged, strained the intelligentsia. "If a man did an evil thing it was due to his lower nature, which had nothing to do with higher." The literary elite might have sustained a belief in their own goodness in the face of visible evidence to the contrary, Dreiser concluded, but their legacy amounted to "literary and social snobbery" (Dreiser 413).

For their part, genteel critics returned the animosity in kind. Dreiser's fiction was labeled crude, depressing, sensational, and, above all, immoral.

Editors either rejected the work as unfit for publication or demanded severe revisions before they would publish it. By concentrating on the least lovely aspects of life, many genteel commentators contended, Dreiser pandered to the coarsest taste. Even worse by genteel standards than his breach of taste was his failure to condemn the degradation that he depicted. This failure was, genteel critics maintained, equivalent to an endorsement of degeneration. A. Schade Van Westrum's complaint about *Sister Carrie* in the March 1901 *Book Buyer* was typical. "All . . . happens automatically, by physical processes alone; if these bodies have souls and minds, the author knows and tells us nothing of them" (Salzman xviii).

As real and significant as the clashes between Dreiser and his genteel antagonists were, not all of the exchanges were uniformly hostile. Each party was attracted to the other. For his part, Dreiser aspired to the literary and financial success that the genteel establishment could confer. Even after the *Sister Carrie* fiasco, he wrote Ripley Hitchcock, the editor who was to supervise the rewriting of *Jennie Gerhardt,* asking him to manage his career. Genteel editors, publishers, and critics, for their part, were considerably more complicated than their reputations as prudes and censors allowed. Hitchcock had shown interest in recruiting Dreiser since 1901 and had solicited *Jennie* for A. S. Barnes in 1905 before accepting it for Harper & Brothers in 1911. The properly genteel critic Hamilton Wright Mabie approved *Jennie Gerhardt* for publication, a book that was still much bolder than the sort of literature he usually celebrated. Understanding the *Jennie* saga requires as much attention to the less obvious pull the novel had for those who published it as to the all-too-evident disagreements.

Long viewed as an artistic credo that provided a cover of respectability for a rapacious ruling class, the Genteel Tradition in fact owed much to the growing autonomy of arts and letters in the nineteenth century. Before 1820, the literary arts were almost exclusively the province of the gentry of the eastern seaboard, who were the primary producers and consumers of a form of elegant expression known as belles lettres. Their dominance of the practice of literature was reflected in the meaning of the concept of culture. During the colonial and early republican periods, the term denoted "refined behavior" and "mental and emotional growth," meanings consistent with the patrician understanding that writing well was one of a number of activities that the elite mastered as a matter of course.

After 1820, however, all of this changed significantly. As the book market first gained stability and then preeminence, the gentry lost much of their direct control of literary conditions. For one thing, the growing importance of the sale of the written word to an impersonal and diverse public expanded the ranks of authorship, making it a career open to talent irrespective of birth. In addition, the literary marketplace by its very nature catered to a variety of tastes. As a result, previously shunned genres like the novel gained new repute. This fundamental transformation also brought about a change in the meaning of culture. By midcentury, the word signified the realm of imaginative thinking, distinct from "polity," where power was exercised, and "society," where the satisfaction of needs was pursued.

The Genteel Tradition originated in its adherents' preoccupation with the meaning and uses of this newly "discovered" realm of culture. The most frequently cited definition of the term came from Matthew Arnold, who regarded culture as "the best that was thought and said in the world." As Arnold and his American followers saw the matter, "the best" was a unique combination of beauty and truth—"sweetness and light" in Arnold's lexicon. The Arnoldian definition conferred on art a privileged role in the construction of culture. Great art, the theory went, was great because it represented the ultimate fruits of the human experience. Great art was powerful because it transmitted this experience to the viewer, listener, or reader, whose entire being would be infused with a new sense of human possibilities. Although genteel writers followed antebellum romantics in their stress on the imagination, their version was neither wild nor untamed. According to genteel writers on the subject, culture would indeed become instinctive, but, as Hamilton Wright Mabie assured his readers, the action that resulted was "by no means irresponsible; it may be directed and controlled; it may be turned, by such control, into a Pactolian stream, enriching us while we rest and ennobling us while we play" (*Books* 42).

For the men and women of the Genteel Tradition, then, "culture" linked aesthetic experience and self-control. This unification of self-expression and self-discipline was, genteel writers agreed, of the utmost importance in a world torn asunder by class conflict, materialism, the ugliness of industrial life, and ethnic pluralism. Although later critics accused the genteel figures of acquiescing in the triumph of industrial capitalism by indulging in the fruitless hope that evil and ugliness in the world would disappear if never mentioned in polite company, genteel authors thought that culture was inherently activist. Genteel theorists were fond of citing Arnold's contention that culture was to provide "a fresh stream of thought" that would contest "stock notions." Only culture, they held, could establish a set of values that embodied the general good rather than justified the dominance of any particular class. Culture was uniquely suited to combat the materialism of the age, they argued, because it was concerned with the things of the spirit and flexible enough to counter mechanistic thinking in which efficient means were valued over just ends. Here, in short, was the tool that genteel writers believed was capable of disciplining both society and politics.

The reputation of the Genteel Tradition as reactionary has obscured its origins as a reform movement that aimed to eliminate the self-absorption, parochialism, and lack of discrimination that its adherents discerned in antebellum culture. By genteel reckoning, neither transcendentalism nor evangelicalism possessed the discipline or the vision to respond to social ills. Genteel reform gained momentum with the Civil War, which centralized economic and social power and discredited both individualistic reform and particularistic loyalties. Even Ralph Waldo Emerson emerged from the conflict with a new understanding of culture less as the divine, inner spark realized through action and meditation than as a social phenomenon created in and disseminated by established institutions. By capturing existing institutions like universities and creating a whole network of publishing houses, magazines, and literary societies, genteel reformers easily outpaced their rivals for postbellum prominence by 1870.

Like many other comparable movements, the Genteel Tradition in power lost much of its reformist edge. Although many of its spokespersons warned against such an outcome, genteel publicists, critics, and teachers often reduced culture to a prescribed body of knowledge that was taken to be eternally true. Much as Dreiser and other like-minded critics complained, the genteel notion of beauty was frequently nothing more than mere ethereal prettiness. Similarly, the genteel claim that all political and social decisions had a moral component repeatedly resulted in the substitution of rigid moral judgments for causal explanation. The near genteel monopoly of the institutions of artistic expression enabled the promulgation of a truncated, elitist culture rather than, as some hoped, one that created a common set of symbols and values through which all Americans could democratically transact their collective affairs.

For some cultural custodians "elevation," a favored genteel keyword, was a privileged position that was available to only a select few. E. L. Godkin, the acerbic editor of the *Nation,* complained bitterly about the existence of a pseudoculture in which everyone felt that a smattering of education was a qualification for making pronouncements on all issues. "A society of ignoramuses who know they are ignoramuses might lead a tolerably happy and useful existence, but a society of ignoramuses each of whom thinks he is a Solon would be an approach to Bedlam let loose." Even when the tone of genteel declarations was considerably less strident and more sympathetic than Godkin's, the conservative implications of refinement, morality, and discipline were often inescapable. The author and essayist Charles Dudley Warner scolded the cultivated young for retreating from the world of work and for failing to spread culture, but he could envision the transaction only as a gift from the blessed to the needy: "Unless the culture of the age finds means to diffuse itself, working downward and reconciling antagonisms by a commonness of thought and feeling and aim in life, society must more and more separate itself into jarring classes, with mutual misunderstandings and hatred and war" (477).

Not everyone who subscribed to genteel definitions of culture or who believed that the unity of beauty and truth could form the basis of criticism of existing institutions had elitist or escapist goals in mind. Some actually celebrated democratic life, albeit in a restrained form that did not pass muster with later critics. When Arnold himself had launched a dyspeptic lament over the absence of beauty and distinction in the United States, the realist novelist and critic William Dean Howells responded by proclaiming that the average and the common constituted America's true distinction and a source of beauty that Arnold did not comprehend. The Scribner editor and critic William Crary Brownell surprisingly went Howells one better. Brownell was the foremost explicator of Arnold in the United States and had responded to the literary upheaval of the 1910s by penning *Standards* (1917), an intemperate defense of eternal verities that excoriated artistic relativists for their abandonment of civilization and morality. A decade later, however, he wrote *Democratic Distinction in America,* which contended that American democracy and popular culture were vigorous and even beautiful. Without abandoning his Arnoldian principles, Brownell even praised the movies — a form for which Randolph Bourne, the self-styled literary rebel against the Genteel Tradition in the 1910s, could marshal little enthusiasm.

Beauty may have been a genteel keyword, but its meaning was far from fixed. During the 1880s literary men and women debated whether aesthetic pleasure was best understood as deriving from celestial or earthly sources. This so-called realist war ended with a victory for those who were committed to a literature that portrayed life as lived. Literary realists such as Howells contended that what was true was inherently beautiful and attempts to celebrate the ideal were tantamount to lying. Their attempt to portray "natural" conditions led realists to posit a "natural" morality, which often conflicted with the propriety dictated by the rigid codes that other genteel proponents saw as simply embodying transcendent truths. Sympathy for a broader notion of morality was behind Brander Matthews's early and ardent support for Mark Twain. A professor of French drama at Columbia, Matthews was one of the most prolific critics of his day. Dismissed by Bourne as a "man who knew everyone and felt nothing," Matthews was more adventurous than his genteel autobiography made him appear. He passed along to his friend Theodore Roosevelt the books of such colleagues as the ethicist Felix Adler, the historian Charles Beard, the anthropologist and cultural relativist Franz Boas, the philosopher John Dewey, and the economist Charles E. R. A. Seligman, author of the *Economic Interpretation of History*. Seligman's influence on Matthews was apparent in Matthews's own "Economic Interpretation of Literary History," which he delivered to the Modern Language Association in 1910.

The genteel willingness to confront the existing social order was on display in Edward Bellamy's famous *Looking Backward*. The novel clearly derived its cultural criticism of the disorder of industrial capitalism from the genteel notion that the beautiful was harmony incarnate. In his discussion of civic planning, Bellamy often returned to the genteel principles of unity and morality. Compared with Leninism and the anarchism of the Industrial Workers of the World, Bellamy's socialism looks tepid, but both the radical economist Thorstein Veblen and the anarchist Elizabeth Gurley Flynn, neither of whom could be called genteel, credited *Looking Backward* with turning them to political engagement.

Nor does an elitist retreat to the antiseptic arena of culture provide the best interpretation of the work of John Jay Chapman. Chapman's was an eclectic career, ranging from scathing satires of political corruption in New York City to an attempt to recapture the relevance of the artistic life of the Greeks for a reinvigoration of civic life. Chapman's work was never fully free from the mugwumpish, elitist disdain for the aspirations of the masses; later in his life, it took on an increasing anti-Semitic and anti-immigrant cast. Yet it was never void of Chapman's commitment to building a cultural life that would guarantee republican liberty. In the absence of a common culture, he contended during his best moments, only a cacophony of competing interests, not meaningful debate or true moral knowledge, would prevail.

For all the debt the Genteel Tradition owed Matthew Arnold, he did not escape genteel criticism. Genteel critics rejected both Arnold's dismissal of American institutions as rough-hewn and his championing of what he called "the saving remnant," the cultivated elite whom he would have rule.

If not always democratic in practice, genteel writers paid tribute to American democracy in their writing. But other commentary concentrated on the limitations of his premises. The latter tack was that of Lewis Gates, who spent his life teaching creative writing at Harvard, where he taught, among others, Frank Norris and Gertrude Stein. Gates owed a great deal to Arnold, praising culture as the vital knowledge necessary to refashion the world and criticizing utilitarianism and philistinism for its rank materialism. Yet he was not beyond terming Arnold a latter-day Puritan. Arnold, Gates charged, was unable to justify art unless it provided moral uplift. Arnold lacked full appreciation of artistic form, Gates insisted, because he could never treat works of art "as self-justified integrations of beauty and truth" (180). Men and women, he concluded, needed to suspend the moralistic impulse to interpret rightly the power and charm of art.

Although Dreiser was reluctant to admit it, he encountered both sides of the Genteel Tradition during the *Jennie Gerhardt* period. As the recent University of Pennsylvania edition of the novel proves, Harper & Brothers cut more than 16,000 words before publishing the novel. Dreiser was not the most elegant writer, and his infelicities abounded. A survey of the changes leads one to conclude that the editing team under the direction of Ripley Hitchcock bowdlerized the text and removed a good deal of Dreiser's social and philosophical commentary. The moralistic and complacent editing took from the novel much of its grim naturalism. By excising Jennie's sexual urges, the editors produced a touching love story merely set against a social background.

But Dreiser also encountered a more flexible and open side of the Genteel Tradition. Given the moral scandal and financial failure of *Sister Carrie,* the rawness of the submitted manuscript of *Jennie,* and Dreiser's well-earned reputation for being a difficult author with whom to work, the genteel editors of Harpers would have sent him a polite yet chilly rejection letter had they been all that prissy. Even when Dreiser heaped abuse on them in the most ungenteel terms for their duplicity in editing and advertising and for backing off from their obligation to re-issue *Carrie* — a charge that was rendered false in 1912 when the firm heavily promoted the novel — the Harpers team stayed the course.

The edited *Jennie Gerhardt* was, for all the damage done, hardly a "tragedy of the broken teacup," to use Norris's curt dismissal of Howellsian realism. The novel still implied more than enough for a significant number of squeamish reviewers to be offended. No reader could miss Senator Brander's responsibility for an illegitimate child, the oppressive poverty of the Gerhardts and the contrasting leisure of the Kanes, or, despite the sentimentality of the portrayal of Jennie, the nihilism of the final paragraph in which Jennie's life was pointedly without future or redemption. "There were those two orphan children to raise. They would marry and leave after a while, and then what? Days and days in endless reiteration, and then—?" All this was too much for the *Philadelphia Press,* which termed the novel "sordid," an example of "Schopenhauer's doctrine to the effect that nothing is positive but pain"; the *New York Press,* which called it "shabby"; and the *New York Daily News,* which complained of Dreiser's "lack of style and proportion, baldness and commonplaceness of diction" (Salzman 79, 82, xxiv).

The condemnation by genteel reviewers of a novel edited to genteel specifications was indicative of the contested nature of the tradition. Throughout its period of dominance in American arts and letters, those who saw culture as a prescription were challenged by those who saw it as a resource with which to confront a changing world. The former had a firm notion of what was good, true, and beautiful; the latter, while continuing to believe art should indeed advance those principles, rejected any attempt to fix them permanently. Those who wanted culture to be pliable and adaptable were more likely to accept the fact that culture did not always exist above market realities. Genteel theorists might have championed culture as a counterweight to materialism, but genteel publishing firms could not escape the logic of profit and loss and survive on "good" books alone. By the mid-1890s, publishers could no longer rely on the backlist, volumes with long active sales lives. As changes in the cost structure of the industry and the legal status of literary property made quick turnover essential, publishers placed new emphasis on novels that held the possibility of instant success. Even genteel firms like Harpers felt the pressure, especially after their bankruptcy and financial reorganization under the direction of the House of Morgan in the first decade of the twentieth century.

Ripley Hitchcock was one of a number of editors who personally benefited from this new dynamic. The son of a prominent Massachusetts physician and a Mount Holyoke Latin teacher and an 1877 graduate of Harvard, Hitchcock belonged to the most august clubs in New York City, was an early inductee into the National Institute of Arts and Letters, and edited Rudyard Kipling, Woodrow Wilson, and the genteel poet R. H. Stoddard. However genteel his personal tastes, Hitchcock was not averse to taking on commercial projects. He had successfully made Stephen Crane a literary sensation, publishing both *The Red Badge of Courage* and *Maggie: A*

Girl of the Streets. More impressive from a financial point of view was his salvaging of *David Harum,* a tale of various rural eccentrics in the neoromantic style, which became a runaway bestseller in 1898 after failing to get over the transom at more than thirty publishers before Hitchcock recognized what a judicious blue pencil could accomplish. Hitchcock may not have seen another *David Harum* or *Red Badge* in *Jennie,* but he was not unaware of lesser possibilities. Conscious that the reading public had extraordinarily varied tastes, he took care to keep the boldness that would attract those who made *Red Badge* and Harold Frederic's *The Damnation of Theron Ware* into best sellers in the 1890s while soothing the polite sensibilities of fans of *David Harum.*

It was not the lure of large sales alone that prompted the Harpers team to seek out and stay with Dreiser. Despite its problematic character, *Jennie* had ideological appeal. Ever since 1890, the Genteel Tradition had been under attack. The economic depression of 1893–97, the challenge at the ballot box by the populists (whose agrarian program and, to genteel eyes, crude demeanor and rabid talk ran counter to the genteel project of refined civilization), the influx of immigrants from eastern and southern Europe, and the rise of naturalist literature all had taken their toll on genteel confidence. If culture was to be a real force in the world, genteel writers implied, then the less beautiful and less moral aspects of life had to be acknowledged, if only to be overcome. For those who viewed culture as a resource, a manuscript such as Dreiser's could hardly be dismissed. Rewritten as a tale with an object lesson suitable for moral uplift and shorn of its hints of philosophical nihilism and condemnation of hypocrisy, *Jennie* could serve the Genteel Tradition far better than treacly fiction that denied the existence of sexual desires and class injustice, reinvigorating moral precepts all the more by demonstrating their truthfulness and power in the face of degradation.

Hamilton Wright Mabie would seem an unlikely figure to effect a détente with naturalist fiction. An editor of the *Outlook* (formerly the *Christian Union*), he had earned his critical stripes as a guide to the perplexed in search of a dose of Arnoldian culture. He had made his name in the 1880s when he criticized Howells's *Rise of Silas Lapham* for letting observation do the work of imagination. It was his reputation for moral probity that had led Harper Vice President Frederick Duneka to request he vet *Jennie Gerhardt* for improprieties. Duneka probably did not have to inform Mabie of the unpleasant theme or the suggestiveness of presentation or note that it was "a fair question whether any really good end is subserved" (Dreiser, *Jennie Gerhardt,* 453). Having devoted his entire career to the proposition that art served moral purposes, Mabie shared Duneka's concerns about the consequences of a literature that was so promiscuous in its portrayal of the lower side of humanity.

But by 1911, however, Mabie's understanding of the power of culture in the Arnoldian sense had widened; *Jennie* clearly met the standards of acceptable art. Warning Duneka that he thought the theme of a fallen woman should not be done too frequently and should always be handled with reserve, he nonetheless praised what he took to be Dreiser's "reverential" treatment. One, he even went so far as to write, had "no sense of moral dirt, except with regard to the men" (Dreiser, *Jennie Gerhardt,* 453). Mabie's letter to Duneka was not the only time he commended Dreiser. In an 1912 review of books for the *Outlook,* he singled out both *Sister Carrie* and *Jennie Gerhardt* as "sincere studies of a side of life of which the world of sheltered women needs to know more. . . . It is not pleasant to look at the diseases of society, but it is wholesome and necessary, and Mr. Dreiser's stories are free alike from a moralization which the facts supply and from any coloring of relations which inevitably turn into a shabby drab as time goes on" (Mabie, "A Few Books," 644).

To late twentieth-century tastes, Mabie's analysis of Dreiser is inaccurate. Interpreting Dreiser as a moralist of the genteel type runs counter not only to Dreiser's view of himself but also to the texts Dreiser produced. Dreiser was less free from moral considerations than he often pretended, but he did not set out to write a tale with a conventional object lesson. Mabie's praise might well have eased the reception of Dreiser's work among readers who still hewed to the old criterion that the ability to promote good was a necessary if not sufficient measure of the literary value of a novel. In claiming Dreiser for the Genteel Tradition, Mabie might have been attempting to domesticate a literary naturalism he and his fellows could no longer suppress. If containment was the genteel strategy, it failed miserably. Today not even the strongest defender of the traditional canon claims descent from the Genteel Tradition.

More was at stake than an effort to domesticate Dreiser. The *Jennie Gerhardt* incident was also part of an endeavor to open up the Genteel Tradition. The endorsement of the novel was part of a larger attempt to refurbish culture as a tool that could rebuild a changing world. Although Mabie and the editors never gave up their conviction that art should serve socially useful purposes, they did implicitly concede that culture was composed of more than canonical texts and devices. They were badly mistaken, however, in their belief that by subordinating aesthetic to moral concerns they could control social life. As it turned out, they would soon not even control cultural life.

Bibliography

Arnold, Matthew. *Civilization in the United States.* Boston: Cupples and Hurd, 1888.
——. *Culture and Anarchy and Other Writings.* 1867–69. Reprint. Cambridge: Cambridge University Press, 1993.
Bender, Thomas. *New York Intellect: A History of Intellectual Life in New York City, from 1750 to the Beginnings of Our Own Time.* Baltimore: Johns Hopkins University Press, 1987.
Bernstein, Melvin. *John Jay Chapman.* New Haven, CT: College & University Press, 1964.
Blake, Casey Nelson. *Beloved Community: The Cultural Criticism of Randolph Bourne, Van Wyck Brooks, Waldo Frank, & Lewis Mumford.* Chapel Hill: University of North Carolina Press, 1990.
Borus, Daniel H. *Writing Realism: Howells, James, and Norris in the Mass Market.* Chapel Hill: University of North Carolina Press, 1989.
Brownell, William Crary. *Democratic Distinction in America.* New York: Charles Scribner's Sons, 1927.
——. *Standards.* New York: Charles Scribner's Sons, 1917.
Cmiel, Kenneth. *Democratic Eloquence: The Fight over Popular Speech in Nineteenth-Century America.* New York: William Morrow, 1990.
Cowley, Malcolm, ed. *After the Genteel Tradition.* Carbondale: Southern Illinois University Press, 1964.
Dreiser, Theodore. *A Book About Myself.* 1922. Reprint. New York: Premier Books, 1965.
——. *Jennie Gerhardt.* Edited by James L. W. West III. Philadelphia: University of Pennsylvania Press, 1992.
Dreiser, Theodore. *American Diaries, 1902–1926.* Edited by Thomas P. Riggio, James L. W. West III, and Neda M. Westlake. Philadelphia: University of Pennsylvania Press, 1982.
Gates, Lewis. *Three Studies in Literature.* New York: Macmillan, 1899.
Godkin, Edward Lawrence. *Reflections and Comments, 1865–1895.* New York: Charles Scribner's Sons, 1895.
Howells, William Dean. *Criticism and Fiction.* 1891. Reprint. New York: Hill & Wang, 1967.
Jones, Howard Mumford. *The Age of Energy: Varieties of American Experience.* New York: Viking Press, 1971.
Lingeman, Richard. *Theodore Dreiser: At the Gates of the City, 1871–1907.* Vol. 1. New York: G. P. Putnam's Sons, 1986.
Mabie, Hamilton Wright. *Books and Culture.* New York: Dodd, Mead, and Company, 1896.
——. "A Few Books of Today." *Outlook* 102 (23 November 1912): 643–52.

Oliver, Lawrence J. *Brander Matthews, Theodore Roosevelt, and the Politics of American Literature, 1880–1920*. Knoxville: University of Tennessee Press, 1992.

Perry, Lewis. *Intellectual Life in America: A History*. New York: Franklin Watts, 1984.

Persons, Stow. *The Decline of American Gentility*. New York: Columbia University Press, 1973.

Rathburn, John W., and Harry M. Clark. *American Literary Criticism, 1860–1905*. Boston: Twayne Publishers, 1979.

Rubin, Joan Shelley. *The Making of Middlebrow Culture*. Chapel Hill: University of North Carolina Press, 1992.

Salzman, Jack, ed. *Theodore Dreiser: The Critical Reception*. New York: David Lewis, 1972.

Santayana, George. *The Genteel Tradition: Nine Essays*. Edited by Douglas L. Wilson. Cambridge, MA: Harvard University Press, 1967.

Tomsich, John. *A Genteel Endeavor: American Culture and Politics in the Gilded Age*. Stanford, CA: Stanford University Press, 1971.

Trachtenberg, Alan. *The Incorporation of America: Culture and Society in the Gilded Age*. New York: Hill & Wang, 1982.

Warner, Charles Dudley. "What Is Your Culture to Me?" *Scribner's Monthly* 4 (1872): 470–78.

West, James L. W. III. *American Authors and the Literary Marketplace since 1900*. Philadelphia: University of Pennsylvania Press, 1988.

12
"Housework Is Never Done": Domestic Labor in *Jennie Gerhardt*

NANCY WARNER BARRINEAU

ALMOST SINCE ITS PUBLICATION IN 1911, *Jennie Gerhardt,* Dreiser's second novel, has been beset by charges that it is among his most "sentimental" works, a novel that retreats from the realism of *Sister Carrie* and represents the American scene less accurately than Dreiser had in 1900. Dreiser himself encouraged such readings when he wrote disparagingly to B. W. Huebsch in 1918 that both novels "represent old-line conventional sentiment" (*Letters,* Vol. 1, 250). Read as an autonomous literary text, *Jennie Gerhardt* may indeed seem "sentimental and implausible" (Hussman 100), its protagonist "a sentimental heroine" (Schwartz 17).[1] But viewed as a novel very much engaged with its own times, *Jennie Gerhardt* becomes a different sort of book: one that illuminates how much sympathy Dreiser invested in the practical conflicts of turn-of-the-century American women. *Jennie Gerhardt* is, in fact, a much more radical and realistic novel than its predecessor, especially in its treatment of the means by which working-class women survived at the century's end. In his first novel Dreiser had allowed Carrie to leave the drudgery of the factory for the glitter of the stage; in his second, he writes more convincingly and realistically of the working careers of laboring class women, many of them domestics.

Like Dreiser's own family, the Gerhardts survive because of the domestic labor of the family women. Mrs. Gerhardt, who is based on his memories of his own mother, is Dreiser's best fictional representation of working-class women who do housework—unpaid in their own homes or badly paid in someone else's. Dreiser paints an immediate picture of a wife and mother who is "no weakling": she takes "in washing, what little she [can] get, devoting the intermediate hours to dressing the children, cooking,

The early work on this essay was made possible by a National Endowment for the Humanities Summer Stipend in 1992.

seeing that they got off to school, mending their clothes, waiting on her husband, and occasionally weeping" (5). Because of advances in technology, keeping house was probably becoming less physically difficult — although perhaps not less time consuming — for the middle-class American woman.[2] But this novel relentlessly uncovers the real nature of housework for women like Mrs. Gerhardt, who had lower incomes, higher birth rates, and fewer labor-saving conveniences than women of the middle class — and, of course, no servants. Dreiser's list is shorter but no less daunting than the exhaustive survey of household tasks made by Abby Diaz in an 1875 article titled, appropriately, "A Domestic Problem." Diaz's list included, among many other tasks,

> arranging furniture, dusting, and "picking up"; setting forth, at their due times and in due order, the three meals; washing the clothes; ironing, including doing up shirts and other "starched things"; taking care of the baby, night and day; washing and dressing children, and regulating their behavior, and making or getting made, their clothing, and seeing that the same is in good repair, in good taste, spotless from dirt, and suited both to the weather and the occasion; . . . nursing the sick; "letting down" and "letting out" to suit the growing ones; patching, darning, knitting, crocheting, braiding, quilting. . . . (Matthews 98–99)

In fact, *Jennie Gerhardt* is part of a lively debate that raged during Dreiser's day (and continues in our own) about the value of domestic labor. In 1800 the U.S. Census listed housewives as "productive workers," but by 1850 census takers asked only about the "profession, occupation, or trade of each male person over 15 years of age." Then, when the category of "breadwinner" was first included in the 1900 census, the definition left out wives and daughters who stayed at home and did unpaid housework. Instead they were classified as "dependents," along with those too young, too old, or too sick to hold down regular jobs. In short, because the growing market economy had no category for housework, which earned no income, labor for one's family ceased to be considered "real" work. The domestic jobs with which poor and working-class women supplemented the family income were excluded as well, for census surveys of gainful employment made no mention of women who took in boarders, helped with the money-earning work of a family business, or did factory piece work at home (Folbre 464, 475–78). Consequently, despite indisputable evidence of arduous labor in and out of their own homes, when women such as those in Dreiser's fiction were interviewed in the 1890s, they insisted they had not "worked very much" during the Progressive Era (Cameron 56).

Scattered voices did raise the concerns of millions of American housewives. Conventionally, the 1885 Massachusetts census excluded housewives yet found it necessary to explain somewhat nervously:

> To be sure, [housewives] receive no stated salary or wage, but their work is surely worth what it would cost to have it done, supposing that the housewife, as such, did no work at all. There were 372,612 housewives in Massachusetts in 1885, and only 300,999 women engaged in all other branches of industry. If a housewife were not expected nor required to work, then for the labor of 372,612 women paid service would have to be substituted. Such a demand for labor could not be supplied by the inhabitants of the State itself. Consequently, as the labor of the housewives was absolutely necessary to allow society to exist in its present form, the housewife is certainly "in industry." (Folbre 480)

Feminists argued more assertively that housework was real, backbreaking work and that the failure to recognize or reward it exploited women. In 1878 the Association for the Advancement of Women petitioned Congress to hire "intelligent women" as census takers, since they might be expected to ask the right questions of the right people; but the petition was rejected (Folbre 477, 483–84). Thirty years later the magazine *Socialist Woman* proclaimed that "the lowest paid worker [is] the average housewife. She works the longest hours and gets the lowest remuneration. . . . In spite of the fact that she is the real maintainer of the race, our greatest economists have proclaimed her labor nonproductive, just because it never had a market value" (Malkiel 210–11).

It is precisely because Mrs. Gerhardt's work is unpaid (and because her husband cannot support the family) that as the novel opens she and Jennie hire themselves out to do the only work they can: more of the same domestic work for others. As scrubwomen at the Columbus House, the city's biggest hotel, they earn three dollars together for three days of strenuous and demeaning work each week. They are in fact like the immigrant families in Lawrence, Massachusetts, of which the *New York Call* wrote in 1912, "all the family must work if the family is to live" (Cameron 59).

Jennie's first job ends as the result of her seduction by Senator Brander, her pregnancy (which coincides with Brander's death), and her expulsion from the family home by her father. So she moves to Cleveland to look for work in, first, the department stores and then the factories; but the job market is glutted with cheap immigrant labor, and she is "always met by a rebuff" (103). Then, the narrator tells us, "as a last resource she turned to housework, although she had hoped to avoid that"—readily finding a job as a lady's maid earning four dollars per week (103–4). However, the earliest extant typescript suggests a different Jennie who has no such qualms: it reads "Housework, of course, was her aim."[3]

Like Carrie, Jennie is eighteen as her story begins; and (also like Carrie, we might infer) she has "not as yet been taught any special work" (4). But at this point in *Jennie Gerhardt* the work histories of Dreiser's two heroines diverge sharply. Realistically, Carrie, who has middle-class aspirations, never considers hiring herself out as a paid domestic. (Later she is also dissatisfied playing housewife for both Drouet and Hurstwood.) Increasingly, in fact, native-born American women were refusing to work as domestics in someone else's home, preferring even the drudgery and poor working conditions of factories. Most of the domestic workers represented by an 1890 census — including maids, chambermaids, housekeepers, cooks, and office cleaners — were young, unmarried, live-in employees. Immigrants and daughters of immigrants made up half their number, and one-fourth of them were African American. Their average wages were two to five dollars per week, their hours half again as long as the typical factory worker's (Wertheimer 209–12).

The complaints of domestic workers themselves indicate that they considered household work in many ways the most demanding and debasing kind of labor available. Based on her survey of household help published in 1897, historian Lucy Maynard Salmon concluded that American girls were loath to become domestics because of the small likelihood of promotion; the lack of challenge in mastering the job; the endless nature of the task (for, as they said, "housework is never done"); the long and irregular working hours, which reduced their independence; and the high probability of working alongside immigrants and women of color (419–22). By 1902 a woman could write confidently in the *Independent,* "there is no need to say to any one in this country that housework is the last occupation the intelligent American working girl will seek" (Trueblood 156).

A growing body of "'servant crisis' literature" also documents the problems middle-class women had finding, training, and keeping household help (Berch 345). When the Boston Women's Educational and Industrial Union offered in 1897 to retrain factory workers and fit them for domestic jobs to fill the servant shortage, its members were shocked to find "only one taker" (Schneider 25). Thus the number of American families employing full-time servants dropped sharply after 1900. In 1900, one million Americans, out of a total population of 75 million, were domestic servants; ten percent of all American families had full-time, live-in servants, and many others employed "help" by the day for tasks such as laundry.

However, by 1920, the middle class generally accepted the notion that servants were a thing of the past — except in the southwest and the southeast, where Chicana and African-American women still provided ample numbers of domestic laborers (Schneider 24–26).

The Long Day: The Story of a New York Working Girl as Told by Herself, a popular memoir of a single working girl published anonymously in 1906, provides an interesting parallel text to both *Jennie Gerhardt* and *Sister Carrie.* After she is orphaned at 18, left (like Carrie and Jennie) "unskilled, friendless, almost penniless," the author begins searching for a suitable job. She is naive in her hope that she will find " 'lady-like' employment": she gets no response when she answers ads for "ladies' companions; young women to read aloud to blind gentlemen and to invalids; assistants in doctors' and dentists' offices, and for the reception room of photograph galleries." Instead she becomes a badly paid factory worker who makes — at one factory after another — flowers, underwear, boxes, and jewelry cases. At one point, when her lodging house burns, she is left with nothing but the clothes she is wearing. But she insists that even then she could not "go into service," which she calls "the definite bond of servitude" (16–17, 57). Finally, by the time she writes her memoir, she has become a stenographer and typist earning twenty dollars a week.

For Jennie — more closely tied than Carrie to a not quite assimilated immigrant family barely holding on to its working-class status — domestic work is an almost instinctive choice. Without a doubt she is her mother's daughter; and she turns the one training she has had — years spent watching and helping her mother run the household — into a marketable skill. Jennie is far luckier than the author of *The Long Day.* She is pretty and graceful and thus can land a domestic job that is not typical of those filled by most of her real-life contemporaries but is instead almost " 'lady-like' employment."

Certainly the work Jennie is hired to do is *not* like the work she has trained for at home. Her new employer, Mrs. Bracebridge, "a rather chill but prepossessing brunette of the conventionally fashionable type," offers her the meager sum of four dollars a week (plus a place to sleep, which Jennie declines) to work as her maid from morning until eight or ten o'clock at night. But despite the long hours and the contempt with which she is treated, Jennie marvels at the light domestic duties she is expected to perform: in "a dainty cap and apron. . . . to wait on her mistress, to brush her hair, help her dress, answer the bell if need be, wait on the table if need be (although there was a servant for that), and do any other errand which her mistress indicated" (104). The job description, in fact, is the wealthy woman's parody of the work women of Jennie's class are brought up to do. It is clear from her expectations that Mrs. Bracebridge is a woman with little to do and that for her Jennie is a status symbol, paid to be a graceful and beautiful ornament.

To underscore the bogus nature of this manufactured labor, Dreiser juxtaposes the description with another portrayal of Mrs. Gerhardt's domestic plight. Now keeping house in Cincinnati with Bass, George, Jennie, and baby Vesta while the rest of the family remain in Columbus, Mrs. Gerhardt "worked like a servant and received absolutely no compensation either in clothes, amusements or anything else." She gets up while everyone else sleeps to build a fire; she cooks their meals, cleans the house, washes their clothes, and takes care of the baby while the rest work for wages. The mother-martyr, she insists that "she needed neither clothes nor shoes so long as one of the children would run errands for her" (108).

Meanwhile, Jennie's position at the Bracebridge house, like that of her first job, illustrates the causal link between the worlds of work and sex. Working girls like Jennie, especially domestic servants, were expected to be sexual adventurers who would, if not closely watched, initiate sexual liaisons with sons and husbands. Because they were thought to be sexually experienced and promiscuous, "a source of moral contagion" (Rosenberg 143), these women were often harassed as a matter of course. Thus, Jennie receives plenty of unwelcome attention from guests at the Bracebridge house, men who regularly accost her "with a view to luring her into some unlicensed relationship" (119). After she is propositioned several times, she begins to doubt herself, reflecting that "men seemed to think she would do these things." She wonders, "Was she innately bad and wrong herself?" (120). Unfortunately, she does not question the right of upper-class men to stereotype her and make assumptions about her sexual availability.

Lester arrives on the scene as merely a more interesting version of this kind of man. He *is* "greatly smitten with her"; but he also feels "as if somehow there were some way in which she could be quickly reached — why, he could not have said. She did not bear any outward marks of her previous experience. There were no evidences of coquetry about her, but still he 'felt that he might'" (121–22). Realistically, given the social context, he assumes that a young working woman, especially a domestic servant, is fair game for the "browsing" of the upper crust (122). He concludes that Jennie is his for the taking, and because of her circumstances she is. Eventually Lester insists that she quit her job and allow him to support her and to provide a "nice home" for her family. He tells her, "You're not suited for the kind of work you're doing. There's no chance of your ever accomplishing anything that way" (157). They both overlook the fact that she has in fact once again found a job that takes advantage of her domestic skills, although this one pays far higher wages: she keeps house for Lester and is available for nurturing, companionship, and sex when he wants them.

Later, when it is clear that he will never marry her, Jennie begins looking for a way to earn the five or six dollars a week that she calculates (quite conservatively) she will need to support herself and her child. Lester wastes no time in pointing out again that the jobs she could get would only be dead ends. Exasperated, Lester asks, "Well, what can you do, Jennie, different from what you ever have done? You wouldn't expect to be a lady's maid again, would you? Or clerk in a store?" She replies weakly, "I thought I might get some place as a housekeeper now" (247). But they both know it is unlikely she can earn enough money to be truly self-sufficient; although she is more polished now, she is still essentially a domestic worker.

What her first experiences with the world of domestic labor have taught Jennie is that she cannot afford to be the "innocent working-girl" that she is labeled at the outset of the novel (9). Like Carrie, she has learned to rely instead on a social contract in which men give women gifts and money to support themselves and their families; and women, with or without a marriage contract, give men sexual favors and provide domestic order.

Despite her material (and perhaps intellectual) rise during the course of her novel, Jennie's ending is far bleaker — and much more realistic — than Carrie's. She has no way of escape from the world in which she lives — a world which insists that, for women like her, domestic labor may be the only viable option. Jennie has not trained for another job, nor has she found a way to be economically self-sufficient. Rather, she relies on Lester financially, even after his death. As the novel ends Jennie worries about what to do when the orphans she has adopted grow up and leave her.

Jennie Gerhardt is not a sentimental period piece. Instead, it is rich social realism with subtexts that should be as disturbing to readers now as they were then. And when it is reunited with its necessary context — the lives of real working-class women at the turn of the century — it is also a novel that speaks to issues still lively eighty years after its publication. After all, it was 1993, not 1911, when Zoe Baird and Kimba Wood lost their bids for the position of U.S. Attorney General because of concerns about how the privileged classes in America treat household workers (Myers).[4] Dreiser's *Jennie Gerhardt* is fiction; but, as Jean Cocteau maintained, "Fiction is a lie that tells the truth" (Davidson 254).

Notes

1. Three such readings (among many) are by Hussman, Schwartz, and Dance. Virtually all the critics who label *Jennie Gerhardt* "sentimental" use the word not descriptively but in its traditional pejorative sense: overemotional, nonrational and antirealistic.

2. Several U.S. women's historians have deflated the traditional notion that technology brought real improvement for even the middle-class American housewife. Instead, they argue, "labor-saving" devices gave women new chores to do and raised the standards used to measure their achievements. Glenna Matthews, for instance, argues that despite the proliferation of refrigeration, electrification, and water systems, "in 1900 housework was still hard work for both the [middle-class] housewife and her maid" (100–3). Dorothy Schneider and Carl J. Schneider contend that the typical middle-class housewife worked the same number of hours in 1920 as she had in 1900; she merely spent her hours differently (30).

3. The typescript is among the Dreiser papers in the University of Pennsylvania Dreiser collection. I am grateful to the editor of this volume for calling this reading to my attention.

4. These episodes raised other disturbing questions about gender equity since both disqualified candidates were women, the first ever, by the White House's admission, to be questioned about the payment of Social Security for household employees. Other federal appointees who were male (among them Ron Brown and Bobby Ray Inman) were not similarly sanctioned when they admitted to breaking the same law. See Myers for the complete transcripts of White House press releases and briefings.

Bibliography

Berch, Bettina. "The Development of Housework." *International Journal of Women's Studies* 1(1978): 336–48.

Cameron, Ardis. "Landscapes of Subterfuge: Working-Class Neighborhoods and Immigrant Women." In *Gender, Class, Race, and Reform in the Progressive Era,* edited by Noralee Frankel and Nancy S. Dye, 56–72. Lexington: University Press of Kentucky, 1991.

Dance, Daryl C. "Sentimentalism in Dreiser's Heroines Carrie and Jennie." *CLA Journal* 14(December 1970): 127–42.

Davidson, Cathy N. *Revolution and the Word: The Rise of the Novel in America.* New York: Oxford University Press, 1986.

Dreiser, Theodore. *Jennie Gerhardt.* Edited by James L. W. West III. Philadelphia: University of Pennsylvania Press, 1992.

———. *Letters of Theodore Dreiser.* Vol. I. Edited by Robert H. Elias. Philadelphia: University of Pennsylvania Press, 1959.

Folbre, Nancy. "The Unproductive Housewife: Her Evolution in Nineteenth-Century Economic Thought." *Signs: Journal of Women in Culture and Society* 16(1991): 463–84.

Hussman, Lawrence E. "The Fate of the Fallen Woman in *Maggie* and *Sister Carrie*." In *The Image of the Prostitute in Modern Literature,* edited by Pierre L. Horn and Mary Beth Pringle, 91–100. New York: Frederick Ungar, 1984.

The Long Day: The Story of a New York Working Girl as Told by Herself. New York: Century, 1906.

Malkiel, Theresa. "The Lowest Paid Workers." *Socialist Woman* 2(September 1908). Reprinted in *America's Working Women,* edited by Rosalyn Baxandall, Linda Gordon, and Susan Reverby, 210–11. New York: Vintage Books, 1976.

Matthews, Glenna. *"Just a Housewife": The Rise and Fall of Domesticity in America.* New York: Oxford University Press, 1987.

Myers, Dee Dee. Press Briefing. Internet File Server, Electronic Government Information Service (EGIS), White House Information (January 1993).

Rosenberg, Charles. "Sexuality, Class and Role in 19th-Century America." *American Quarterly* 25(May 1973): 131–53.

Salmon, Lucy Maynard. *Domestic Service.* New York: Macmillan, 1897. Reprinted as "Objections to Domestic Service." In *Early American Women: A Documentary History 1600–1900,* edited by Nancy Woloch, 419–23. Belmont, CA: Wadsworth, 1992.

Schneider, Dorothy, and Carl J. Schneider. *American Women in the Progressive Era, 1900–1920.* New York: Facts on File, 1993.

Schwartz, Carol A. "*Jennie Gerhardt*: Fairy Tale as Social Criticism." *American Literary Realism* 19(1987): 16–29.

Trueblood, Mary. "Housework vs. Shop and Factories." *Independent* 54(November 13, 1902). Reprinted in *America's Working Women,* edited by Rosalyn Baxandall, Linda Gordon, and Susan Reverby, 156. New York: Vintage Books, 1976.

Wertheimer, Barbara Mayer. *We Were There: The Story of Working Women in America.* New York: Pantheon Books, 1977.

13
Self-Sacrifice and Shame in
Jennie Gerhardt

MIRIAM GOGOL

THE NEW, EXPANDED EDITION OF *Jennie Gerhardt* is powerful in its realism and pioneering in its disclosures about the life of the working class, particularly the plight of women domestic workers. In his depiction of Jennie Gerhardt, a washerwoman's daughter, Theodore Dreiser portrays the sensibility of a female worker of the 1880s without condescension as well as the perception of upper-class men of her sexual availability. He creates a family headed by an immigrant father unfamiliar with the ways of this country, a lost family with too many children and too little money in too hard times. A story often lived, *Jennie Gerhardt* was nonetheless a story that had never before entered the mainstream of American fiction.

The one ostensible flaw in this historically groundbreaking novel is the characterization of the heroine herself: Jennie Gerhardt. She has been seen by critics as too good, too patient, too long-suffering — in other words, a young woman sentimentalized and idealized by a middle-aged narrator.[1] The critic Richard Lehan says as much in his description of Jennie as a "fantasy character, an ideal woman, one who will remain faithful to a man without making any demands upon him" (87). Charles Shapiro describes her as "all suffering, almost too fudgy in her passivity" (16). Other critics imply that her sentimentalized portraiture diminishes the novel's overall quality. To James Lundquist the novel "is simply less interesting [than *Sister Carrie*], verging too closely upon a kind of sentimentality that threatens to turn the novel into a tear-jerker" (48). Lawrence Hussman sums up this point of view by comparing the novel to the film adaptation: "Even Holly-

I am especially grateful to Florian Stuber for his editorial suggestions and to Joseph Browne for his theoretical assistance. I also wish to thank Madelyn Larsen, Zanvel A. Liff, and Carol Holly for criticism, comments, and conversations that helped shape my thinking about Dreiser in this essay.

wood's legendary sentimentality couldn't easily equal the simpering emotion of this novel, Dreiser's weakest."[2]

This essay is a response to these criticisms. It examines the characterization of Jennie Gerhardt from another perspective, one that explains Jennie's character within the context of her family's dynamics. I suggest that both Dreiser's fictional and personal families are bound in the dynamics of shame and that by analyzing these dynamics in the context of shame psychology, a branch of family systems theory, the reader can see Jennie as psychologically authentic, thus removing—or at least explaining—a flaw critics see as central to the novel.[3]

Shame is the novelistic keynote of *Jennie Gerhardt*: scenes of shame open and close the volume. In the last pages, Jennie, the person closest to Lester Kane, has to hide her face behind a veil to appear at his funeral, for to the bitter end she is an outsider who fears detection and is reduced to secretly staring in at her lover's corpse. In the first few pages, a telling scene unfolds in which Jennie's brother Bass feels "mortification" at the thought that his cronies might see his sister and his mother cleaning floors in the Columbus House Hotel.[4] He is so concerned that he suggests to them that they take in laundry instead, thus sparing him the public exposure of his family's extreme poverty. Bass repeatedly cautions his sister: "Don't you ever speak to me if you meet me around there. . . . Don't you let on that you know me . . . you know why" (12). As Bass had indicated before, he did not want to be disgraced by being associated with those who looked so poor, even if they were members of his own family. Such an atmosphere of embarrassment exists in the family that members meet each other without acknowledgment.

Such memorable scenes of shame permeate the novel. In the first chapter, we see both Jennie and her mother on their hands and knees, cleaning the floors of the hotel lobby, "steel[ing] themselves" against "so public an exposure" (7). Two chapters later, Jennie runs away at the sight of her soon-to-be first lover, Senator Brander, when he catches her stealing coal. Again, Jennie hides herself in the back room of her home the first time the senator comes to visit. Her fear is to be seen, her wish is to cover up. Her problem is that she is ensnared in her family's shame-filled dynamics—dynamics that cripple all of its members.

Virtually every major scene in the novel involves shame, embarrassment, or mortification.[5] In fact, the word "shame" and many variations of it—"shamefaced," "shamefully," "shamelessness," "basic shame," "flood of shame," "ashamed" — appear repeatedly in the text, almost always to describe the members of the Gerhardt household. Indeed, we have two houses in the novel, representing the two opposing families that dominate it: the house of shame, represented by the Gerhardts, and the house of pride, personified by the Kanes. "Pride" or a variation of it — "proud," "proudly," "family pride" — is nearly always used to describe the Kanes. Lester is a "centralized authority" (230), a "personage" (168), an "important business personage" (168), a "big" man (168). He knew "how life was organized" (194).

Shame psychologists Merle Fossum and Marilyn Mason define pride as the underside of shame. They maintain that "pride is related to a fantasy of oneself rather than to one's actual behavior." Whereas shame is the inner experience of being looked down on by the social group, "pride is maintaining the fantasy, the delusion of grandeur, the fantasy of being the envy of other people" (vii). Perhaps Dreiser did idealize Jennie as an altruistic self-sacrificial saint, but the converse could be argued about Lester, who is idealized as "pride," or self-sufficiency, as someone entirely able to take care of himself. "Lester was not afraid of anything," notes the narrator. "He felt that he knew how to live and to die" (404).

Interestingly, Lester and the other prideful characters are not fleshed out. Dreiser is unable to give them the dimensionality that leads to the fuller characterization he is able to provide for shame-filled figures. Perhaps this is because Dreiser's personal family too held a legacy of shame, as Dreiser himself realized and as his biographers have been quick to note. Dreiser repeatedly wrote in his candid autobiography *Dawn* that he was enormously ashamed of his own family. Describing how his sister Sylvia brought home her illegitimate child (as Jennie does in the fictional account), Dreiser comments: "To me, the whole local situation during the time that this was happening was most unsatisfactory. Whenever I thought of it, I was unhappy, not because my own spirit was moralistically inclined, but because I hated to be looked down on — to be a member of a family that was locally a scandal. True to my mother's fears, the facts as to S —— did come out, and we were very largely shunned because of our moral difficulties" (xerox of transcript, 416, chap. 45). Dreiser's shame, we see, was felt even as he wrote *Dawn* as evidenced in his writing "S ——" instead of the name of Sylvia, his sister, to protect her from the shame of her own circumstances. Scandals such as this one traumatized the young Dreiser, who pondered "what people might be thinking of us" and whether we were "already a shame and a scandal, and also env[ied] those families who because of wealth or cleverness . . . were respected and looked up to" (*Dawn* 232, chap. 43). In light of such biographical parallels, it is not surprising that Dreiser imposes many of these same dynamics on his most powerfully rendered fictional families.

Those dynamics of shame have been the focus of much current research by family systems theorists. Family systems theory departs from previous theories of human emotional functioning by conceptualizing the family as an emotional unit and by viewing the individual as a part of that unit rather than as an autonomous psychological entity (Kerr 35). As family systems analyst Carl Whitaker states: "I don't believe . . . in individuals anymore; I think they're only fragments of a family" (xxi). In other words, we are all part of a larger system and play only a part in its history. To understand the part that anyone plays, it is both helpful and necessary to analyze the individual in the context of a larger family system. Perhaps this is why family theory potentially holds greater appeal for literary scholars than for psychoanalysts, particularly the "psyche" aspect as interpreted by Freudians, Kleinians, object-relations theorists, and Winnicottian interpreters. It accords more closely with "analysis" as interpreted by Lacan and with the philosophy of Foucault (see Skura 349–73).

Family systems theory posits that the functioning of any individual in a family can be understood only in the social context of the family and in relation to the other people closely involved with the individual. When the founder of family systems theory, Murray Bowen, defined the emotional unit of the family as an "undifferentiated ego mass," he helped to explain how the troubled people that he encountered as a clinical psychiatrist derived their behavior from their family systems (*Family Therapy* 472).[6] Families who develop an "undifferentiated ego mass" establish vague or tenuous emotional boundaries among family members. They encourage members to become emotionally entangled or enmeshed with one another and accordingly (and in some instances unconsciously) block attempts by an individual to differentiate himself or herself emotionally from other family members. Children in such families become entangled in the "family relationship process" as soon as they are born; their self-images are formed in "reaction to the anxieties and emotional neediness of others," of parents in particular, and family members tend to define children through their own "emotionally distorted perceptions" (Kerr 41).

A self-sustaining emotional field that is currently receiving much attention is shame (see Bowen, Kerr, and Fossum and Mason). According to contemporary psychologists, shame can be understood as the self judging the self; shame results from an internalized monitoring system that chastises the self[7] for not living up to the image it desires to project.[8] Experienced over a lifetime, shame is the ongoing feeling "that one is fundamentally bad, inadequate, defective, unworthy, . . . not fully valid as a human being" (Fossum and Mason 5). Experienced within the family as a whole, shame is the powerful and pervasive, yet often hidden, force that cultivates feelings of inadequacy within all of its members and gives rise, often over many generations, to various kinds of addictions or dysfunctional behaviors. A shame-bound family, say psychologists

> is a family with a self-sustaining, multigenerational system of interaction with a cast of characters who are (or were in their lifetime) loyal to a set of rules and injunctions demanding control, perfectionism, blame and denial. The pattern inhibits or defeats the development of authentic intimate relationships, promotes secrets and vague personal boundaries, unconsciously instills shame in the [individual] family members, as well as chaos in their lives, and binds them to perpetuate the shame in themselves and in their kin. (8)

From Dreiser's autobiographies, we know that he viewed his father as a fanatically religious tyrant, a man who upheld ideals that were impractical in this world. Dreiser wrote in *Dawn* that he had "never . . . known a man more obsessed by a religious belief" (*Dawn* 5–6, chap. 1) or one more driven by the "insane desire" (36) to pay dollar for dollar for each debt incurred, while his family suffered in extreme poverty. Such self-destructiveness "almost wrecked my father financially" not to mention the family (*Dawn*, xerox of first typescript, 2, chap. 1). Although Dreiser's father is particularly important in understanding *Jennie Gerhardt*, I should point out that he was not the only parent engaged in shame dynamics. Dreiser's mother, about whom Dreiser had richly ambivalent feelings, contributed her share of shame, not only with her threats to abandon the children but also with her real rejections and abandonments through "silent treatment" and relationship cutoffs.

Although Dreiser clearly idealized her (as we see in his unpublished essay that bears her maiden name — Sarah Schänab), he also felt manipulated and abandoned by her. In her frustration with her husband, their poverty, and raising ten children, she often threatened to leave. Her other children would cry, but Dreiser would faint. He said of her: "I thought it was little short of criminal in her to even pretend to desert us. . . . I looked on it as cruel, and the thought of her possible absence was always sufficient to produce an instant depression and the most dissolving emotions" (*Dawn*, typescript, 216, chap. xxix).

According to Dreiser biographer Richard Lingeman, the fictional father of Jennie is a carbon copy of Dreiser's father (337).[9] They share characteristics of devout orthodoxy, self-righteousness, perfectionism, blame, and denial—all descriptive metaphors of the controlling figure in a shame-bound family. Like Johann Paul, Sr., old Gerhardt too was a controlling figure; Gerhardt's overzealous attachment was to the Lutheran church, which he perceived as a "perfect institution" (51). He believed literally in the Beatitudes, was honest to a fault, and prided himself on his perfectionism (51).

> Oh, if he could only be so honest and upright . . . that the Lord would have no excuse for ruling him out. He trembled not only for himself, but for his wife and children. Would he not some day be held responsible for them? Would not his own laxity and lack of system in inculcating the laws of eternal life to them end in his and their damnation? He pictured to himself the torments of hell, and wondered how it would be with him and his in the final hour. (52–53)[10]

According to shame psychologists, the church is often internalized and used by control figures within the family system as a rule maker and supporter to justify an impossible set of injunctions (Fossum and Mason 88).

Old Gerhardt's "domineering orthodoxy" (51) often took the form of an inverted perfectionism—not so much doing what is right as not doing what is not right: not dancing, not playing cards, not going to theatres, and certainly not having premarital sex. As a result, he was very stern with his wife and his children. He expected them to live up to the standards of the pulpit: "Hell was yawning for those who disobeyed his injunctions" (51). When his children did not obey, they were cut off. Gerhardt labels Jennie a "street-walker" (84) and kicks her out of the house in the dead of night when he discovers that she is pregnant with Brander's child. Later when he is forced to live with her and her child, he ignores her, and when he moves out he does so without saying good-bye. Cutting people off is a mainstay of the shame-bound family. Without communication and with the need to blame, members are punished severely for violating the codes. Unable to measure up, they live with the hounds of shame in hot pursuit (Fossum and Mason 94).

And so it is with the Gerhardt children, particularly Jennie. As the oldest daughter of six siblings, she bears the brunt of her father's perfectionist attentions. Her role in the family is that of a codependent, meaning someone who maintains the family system and actually reinforces the family's codes. She does so through denial (of her own deeds, the illegitimacy

of her child, the fact that she is unmarried), protection (as chief safeguarder
of the family's secrets and provider of financial support), and minimization
(she intervenes and reduces the effects of each new family crisis).

The price Jennie pays as a codependent is great. Unable to distinguish
her needs from those of others, she gives herself away — emotionally, physically, and even sexually — to accommodate others' needs. Her desire to be
accepted and liked is so strong that she attempts to please others by agreeing with their thoughts, feelings, and behavior, regardless of her own response — which is for the most part imperceptible. Such sacrifice involves a
split from the self, for Jennie has needs too and to disregard them requires a
violation of her own self. According to family theorists, such a violation
ultimately results in self-hatred, a manifestation of which is low self-esteem,
for without proper nourishment the self cannot survive intact. To cope with
the pain of this low self-esteem, the codependent may erect defensive bar-
riers, which, particularly in women, can take the form of exaggerated help-
fulness, martyrdom, and timidity (Fossum and Mason 145), a description
that epitomizes Jennie and one that, as we know, has been seized on repeatedly by critics as the fatal flaw in her characterization.

Jennie's much-criticized martyrdom presents itself in the form of her
self "sacrifice" (87, 147, 380): She is a "sacrificial implement" (94), "serviceable" (180), a "helpless victim" (94). Each "dishonorable" deed that
she performs is not for her own sake but for the sake of others. When she is
seduced by Senator Brander, it is to obtain ten dollars to release her brother
from prison; she herself characterizes this sexual act as a "sacrifice" of "herself" for the sake of Bass (147). Again, when she is "doomed to a second
sacrifice" (149) in the form of her seduction by Kane, it is to aid her
desperate family when her father severely burns both of his hands. For
Jennie, "service" (87, 199) has a sexual aspect, as Lester intuits immediately
when he first sets eyes on her: "He had the rather well-founded idea that
Jennie would yield to him physically. . . . All her attitude toward sex was
bound up with love, tenderness, service" (136). She is indeed the "help-
mate" (264) and "handmaiden" (279) to Lester, "her lord" (364). She is
kept in the background to satisfy his desires.

As one of the most extreme female self-abnegators in modern American fiction, Jennie organizes her entire life around Lester, yet it is she who
insists that he leave her. She argues that he needs money and social opportunity and thus he needs another woman, in this case Letty Pace, whom he
ultimately marries. This self-sacrifice is the equivalent of death, as Jennie
herself acknowledges. Without Lester, she "wishe[s] she might die" (318).

Indeed, she thinks that it might be best for everyone: "It would be so much easier for him, for everybody, if she could just die" (318). Such a pattern of self-defeating behavior is part of the shame-bound process, many of the actions of which originate from self-loathing.[11]

Perhaps the most fascinating aspect of Jennie's shame is manifest in her double life: one "on the record" (as dutiful wife, mother, and daughter) and the other secretive and duplicitous (as mother of an illegitimate daughter and lover of two men). The central drama involves Jennie's keeping these two intertwined "foundation secrets" unrevealed: keeping Lester from knowing about her illegitimate daughter ("this stigma" [182], "this blotch" [182–83]) and keeping old Gerhardt and the children from finding out that she is not really married.

What makes this drama so absorbing is Jennie's need to keep the duplicity alive. Shame psychologists argue that shame begets shame, that metashame provides a renewed charge, for each new secret provides a "secret release" that is even more compelling (Fossum and Mason 105). It is a vicious cycle: the shame and fear Jennie feels from hiding Vesta intensifies her fervor. Her secrecy fuels her saintliness. One enforces the other to challenge Jennie to reach new heights of perfection. And she does. She becomes the perfect "wife," mother, and caretaker. She manages to be both saint and sinner—meeting the paradoxical demands of the shame system by being the perfect daughter of her exacting father and the fraudulent self denounced by the judging public.[2]

The dynamics of shame, as described by family systems theorists, help us perceive the portrayal of Jennie as the most searing in the novel. Her depiction is psychologically accurate and realistically rendered. The sacrosanct goodness that critics complain of is in fact compelled by Jennie's inner shame-filled dynamics. They demand that she sacrifice her own needs for the sake of others. And yet those who detect a flaw in her characterization may not be altogether wrong. Although Dreiser's imagination was able to depict her as psychologically true, he did not provide either the interior monologue or the external narrative description that indicated why she acted as she did. With the help of family systems theory, we can see the wholeness of Jennie and thus recognize the artistic triumph of the novel.

Notes

    1. Much of the time we seem to be in the mind of a middle-aged male narrator who endlessly debates the advantages and disadvantages of Lester Kane's

marrying Jennie. At times the narrator seems to be Dreiser himself in a midlife crisis (he had just turned forty when he finished writing the novel) trying to resolve an intrapsychic conflict over a conventional versus an unconventional "bachelor" life. In his prideful state, Lester believed that somehow he "could compel public acceptance of a clandestine situation" (299), but he eventually learns by bitter experience, as does Dreiser, that a force greater than himself—convention—rules. Lester is "hurt in his pride" at this defeat (300).

2. These critics are, of course, responding to the edition of *Jennie Gerhardt* published by Harper Brothers in 1911. See Shapiro, Lehan, and Hussman ("Squandered Possibilities"). For a lively discussion and summation of different critics' views on Jennie's character, see Hussman.

3. *Jennie Gerhardt* is by no means Dreiser's only novel dominated by the emotion of shame. Consider particularly *An American Tragedy* and *The Bulwark*. See Gogol.

4. This word "mortification" (12) is one of the many added words in the University of Pennsylvania edition of *Jennie Gerhardt*. By restoring such words, this edition helps illuminate how focused Dreiser was on shame in its many manifestations.

5. In her pioneer study, Lewis makes discrete distinctions among the terms "shame," "embarrassment," "mortification," and "humiliation." According to Lewis, they are all variants of shame feelings. "Humiliation" and "mortification" can be contrasted with each other. "Humiliation" is not connected to a specific source, whereas "mortification" can be found in wounded pride (72). "Embarrassment" involves a total suspension of "self-possession" and temporarily results in a "loss of self" in the sense of a suspension of self-functioning (74–75). Another important distinction is between shame and guilt, terms often confused with each other. Shame involves more self-consciousness and more self-imaging than guilt. The experience of shame is directly about the self, which is the focus of evaluation. In guilt, the self is not the central object of negative evaluation, but rather the thing done or not done is the focus (for further explanation, see Lewis [30]).

6. Although Bowen asserts that individuals derive their behavior from their family systems (472), I do not categorically accept and agree with this position. There may be other factors that contribute to an individual's behavior outside the family system including genetic and environmental influences.

7. By "self," I mean both the self as an inner witness to events and the self as an inner agent with controlling and directing functions. William James points out in 1890 that these two aspects of the self might best be spoken of as the "me" and the "I," the "me" being the self known and the "I" being the knowing self, the self as subject.

8. Zanvel A. Liff, former President of the Division of Psychoanalysis at the American Psychological Association, personal interview, 29 July 1993.

9. Many critics and biographers have shared this insight. As early as 1969, Lehan describes Gerhardt as "an exact duplicate of Dreiser's father" (82).

10. Both Dreiser's father and old Gerhardt seemed to suffer from multigenerational family shame that was reinforced by the local community. The narrator in *Jennie Gerhardt* comments as follows: "The German from the old country combines

a genial clannishness with a desire to regulate the conduct of his fellows. Particularly is this true of fathers of families who are moderately successful. They combine charity toward their poorer neighbors with a grade of positive advice, which they are only too anxious to see enforced." Old Gerhardt was "lacerate[d]" by the neighbors' gossip about his daughter's involvement with the senator. "He would rather die than have his private affairs become a matter of public scorn" (54–55).

11. An overlapping aspect of Jennie's codependency is "needing to be needed." Because she grew up shutting down her feelings, her sense of self-worth is derived from taking care of others—her siblings, Lester, Vesta, and her dying father. Often she is subtly persuasive with others and has many others leaning on her, even her rejecting father who ultimately lives with her and Lester in the house he judged immoral.

12. Even Jennie, usually so unintrospective, questions her motives in keeping Vesta a secret, for it is a secret that must inevitably end in discovery and defeat. When Jennie and Lester are in the first throes of their relationship, when there is a chance for legitimacy of their union through marriage, Jennie inexplicably refuses to tell him of the existence of Vesta and thus lives a complicated double life, at one point having Vesta live under the same roof without Lester's knowledge.

Bibliography

Bowen, Murray. *Family Therapy in Clinical Practice*. New York: Jason Aronson, 1978.

Dreiser, Theodore. *An American Tragedy*. New York: Boni and Liveright, 1925.

———. *A Book About Myself*. New York: Boni and Liveright, 1922.

———. *Dawn*. New York: Horace Liveright, 1931.

———. *Dawn*. Unpublished typescript. Dreiser Collection. Van Pelt–Dietrich Library Center, University of Pennsylvania. Philadelphia.

———. *Dawn*. Unpublished reproduction of manuscript. Dreiser Collection. Van Pelt–Dietrich Library Center, University of Pennsylvania. Philadelphia.

———. *Jennie Gerhardt*. Edited by James L. W. West III. Philadelphia: University of Pennsylvania Press, 1992.

———. "Sarah Schanab." Unpublished manuscript. Dreiser Collection. Van Pelt–Dietrich Library Center, University of Pennsylvania. Philadelphia.

———. *Sister Carrie*. Edited by John C. Berkey, Alice M. Winters, James L. W. West III, and Neda M. Westlake. Philadelphia: University of Pennsylvania Press, 1981.

———. *A Book About Myself*. New York: Boni and Liveright, 1922.

Fossum, Merle and Marilyn Mason. *Facing Shame: Families in Recovery*. New York: Norton, 1986.

Gogol, Miriam. "That Oldest Boy Don't Wanta Be Here." In *Theodore Dreiser: Beyond Naturalism*, edited by Miriam Gogol. New York: New York University Press, in press.

Holly, Carol. "Understanding the Family: Jane Maher's *Biography of Broken Fortunes*." *Henry James Review* (Spring 1987): 209–20.

Hussman, Lawrence E., Jr. *Dreiser and His Fiction: A Twentieth-Century Quest.* Philadelphia: University of Pennsylvania Press, 1983.

——. "Squandered Possibilities: The Film Versions of Dreiser's Novels." In *Theodore Dreiser: Beyond Naturalism,* edited by Miriam Gogol. New York: New York University Press, in press.

James, William. *The Principles of Psychology.* Vol. 1. New York: Henry Holt and Co., 1890.

Kerr, Michael. "Chronic Anxiety and Defining a Self." *Atlantic Monthly* (September 1988): 35–58.

Lehan, Richard. *Theodore Dreiser: His World and His Novels.* Carbondale: Southern Illinois University Press, 1969.

Lewis, Helen Block. *Shame and Guilt in Neurosis.* New York: International Universities Press, 1971.

Lingeman, Richard. *Theodore Dreiser: At the Gates of the City 1871–1907.* Vol. 1. New York: G. P. Putnam's Sons, 1986.

Marcus, Mordecai. "Loneliness, Death, and Fulfillment in *Jennie Gerhardt.*" *Studies in American Fiction* 7 (Spring 1979): 61–73.

McGoldick, Monica and Randy Gerson. *Genograms in Family Assessment.* New York: Norton, 1985.

Minuchin, Salvatore. *Families and Family Therapy.* Cambridge, MA: Harvard University Press, 1974.

Minuchin, Salvador, Bernice L. Rosman, and Lester Baker. *Psychosomatic Families: Anorexia Nervosa in Context.* Cambridge, MA: Harvard University Press, 1978.

Petrie, Dennis W. *Ultimately Fiction: Design in Modern American Literary Biography.* West Lafayette, IN: Purdue University Press, 1981.

Shapiro, Charles. *Theodore Dreiser: Our Bitter Patriot.* Carbondale: Southern Illinois University Press, 1962.

Skura, Meredith. "Psychoanalytic Criticism." In *Redrawing the Boundaries,* edited by Stephen Greenblatt and Giles Gunn, 349–73. New York: Modern Language Association, 1992.

Whitaker, Carl and T. Malone. *The Roots of Psychotherapy.* New York: Brunner/Mazel, 1981.

14
Jennie, Maggie, and the City

YOSHINOBU HAKUTANI

I read Dreiser's *Jennie Gerhardt* and *Sister Carrie* and they revived in me a vivid sense of my mother's suffering; I was overwhelmed. I grew silent, wondering about the life around me. It would have been impossible for me to have told anyone what I derived from these novels, for it was nothing less than a sense of life itself. All my life had shaped me for the realism, the naturalism of the modern novel, and I could not read enough of them.

— Richard Wright, *Black Boy* (1945)

"FOR A VARIETY OF REASONS," Morton and Lucia White write in *The Intellectual versus the City*, "our most celebrated thinkers have expressed different degrees of ambivalence and animosity toward the city." Citing an antiurban sentiment in the American literary "pantheon" that included Jefferson, Emerson, Thoreau, Hawthorne, Poe, and Henry Adams, Morton and Lucia White believe there is nothing in American literature like "the Greek attachment to the *polis* or the French writer's affection for Paris." Reviewing a wide range of American writers who in their opinion make up "the core of our intellectual history," they argue: "It would be extremely difficult to cull from their writings a large anthology of poetry or social philosophy in celebration of American urban life" (1–3). Their argument sounds quite cogent insofar as the writers they consider are concerned, since a central theme in nineteenth-century American fiction was for a white man to leave his community in quest of pastoral peace of mind. Not only was he able to live in harmony with nature, but he would find a bosom friend in the stranger, a dark-skinned man from whom he learned the values of life he had not known before. Natty Bumppo in Cooper's Leatherstocking novels makes such friendship with Chingachgook and Hard-Heart, noble savages of the American wilderness. Ishmael in *Moby-Dick* is ritualistically wedded to Queequeg, a pagan from the South Seas. Huck Finn finds a father figure in Jim, a black man.

Toward the end of the nineteenth century, however, this antiurban drive in American literature was substantially reversed. Novelists such as Cooper, Melville, and Twain focused their attention on young men who tried to move away from the complexity and supposed corruption of cities toward idealized nonurban settings. An American realist such as Dreiser took pains to deal with young women in search of their happiness in the city. Just as an African-American man found the rural South a living hell and dreamed of escaping racial bigotry and exclusion and living in the northern city, Jennie Gerhardt suffered social ostracism and dreamed of a happier life in the city, where she faced less prejudice of class and gender. In contrast to Maggie Johnson in Stephen Crane's *Maggie: A Girl of the Streets,* to whom the "shutters of the tall buildings were closed like grim lips . . . the lights of the avenues glittered as if from an impossible distance" (183), Jennie found in Columbus, Cleveland, Chicago, and New York not only privacy but the gay, energetic spirit of life that freed her from stifling social conventions.

Ironically, Jennie's deliverance from the bondage of class and gender begins with her employment as a scrubwoman in a luxurious hotel in Columbus. Such a scene was commonplace toward the end of the nineteenth century as many European immigrants lived in northeastern and midwestern cities. Unlike the atmosphere of the Bowery district of New York, where Maggie and her family are confined, that of the prosperous hotel in Columbus gives Jennie joy and happiness. "The hotel," Dreiser comments, "was a rather remarkable specimen for the time and place." To Jennie and "those who had never seen anything better," the five-storied structure "seemed wondrously gay and inspiriting" (6). Concluding this scene, Dreiser underscores "the whole raft of indescribables, who, coming and going, make up the glow and stir of this kaleidoscopic world" (7). Although her employment at the hotel leads to pregnancy and her father brands her "a streetwalker" (84), the entire atmosphere of the hotel "touched the heart of the innocent working-girl with hope" (9).

Unlike Maggie and her family, who forever remain victims of the big-city slum environment, Jennie and her family are endowed with abilities to circumvent the situation. While Maggie is trapped and her movement is circular at best, Jennie moves from smaller cities to larger ones: from Columbus to Cleveland, to Chicago, and to New York. Unlike Maggie's brother Jimmie, who cares only about his own life, Jennie's brother Bass is not only concerned about his family's welfare but is also sympathetic to his sister's predicament. In an immigrant family, the oldest son, being young and most acculturated to the American way of life, served as the catalyst for the success of his family. It is Bass's action that saves Jennie from the gossip-infested small neighborhood in Columbus. Bass, working at a cigar store, sends for Jennie to move to Cleveland, and later the entire family except for the father follows. Not only does this family movement parallel what took place when most of the Dreiser family moved to Chicago, as Philip Gerber points out (80), but such a movement of immigrant families in search of employment was commonplace at the turn of the century.

Bass's challenge to his social environment is diametrically opposed to Jimmie's capitulation to social pressure. "Bass was no sooner in Cleveland," Dreiser remarks, "than the marvel of that growing city was sufficient to completely restore his equanimity of soul, and stir up new illusions as to the possibility of joy and rehabilitation for himself and the family" (98). Unlike Columbus, the state capital, which was then, as now, a conservative city, Cleveland, developed by John D. Rockefeller, was an industrial, commercial, and hence a progressive city. Dreiser thus describes Cleveland: "All was business, all activity. The very turning of the corner seemed to rid one of old times and crimes. It was as if a new world existed in every block" (98). Jimmie, however, is preoccupied with girls who can be impressed with his daring in the battles of Devil's Row. He is mildly concerned about his sister's affair with Pete but is oblivious of his own seduction of girls. Although he is an alienated, defiant youth, he succumbs easily to social forces. "In revenge," Crane observes, "he resolved never to move out of the way of anything, until formidable circumstances or a much larger man than himself forced him to it" (140).

The motive for the Gerhardt family's relocation to Cleveland is two-fold. It is easier for young people to find jobs there, as Bass has already demonstrated: George, his younger brother, secures a cashier's position, and Jennie is quickly hired as a maid by a wealthy family. The other motive, as Bass writes Jennie, is for the family to establish a new base of life in a big city like Cleveland instead of clinging to their old neighborhood in Columbus, where Jennie must suffer the ordeal of an unwed mother. In a letter sent home, moreover, Bass describes a delightful cityscape of Cleveland, which Columbus lacks: "There were theatres here, he said, and beautiful streets. Vessels from the lakes came into the heart of the city. It was a wonderful city and growing very fast" (98).

Bass's enthusiasm for Cleveland is contagious, and the urban freedom and excitement there relieve Jennie of her worries. Once she meets Lester at the home of her employer, the narrative point of view shifts from Bass's and Jennie's minds to Lester's as the city makes an impression on him. Dreiser thus comments:

> The tremendous and complicated development of our material civilization, the multiplicity and variety of our social forms, the depth, subtlety and sophistry of our mental cogitations, gathered, remultiplied and phantasmagorically disseminated as they are by these other agencies—the railroad, the express and post-office, the telegraph, telephone, the newspaper and, in short, the whole art of printing and distributing—have so combined as to produce . . . a dazzling and confusing showpiece which is much more apt to weary and undo than to enlighten and strengthen the observing mind. (125)

This condition of American culture at the turn of the century, based on Dreiser's own magazine articles in the late 1890s, influences Lester.[1] Although his is "a naturally observing mind, Rabelaisian in its strength and tendencies," Lester is "confused by the multiplicity of evidences of things, the vastness of the panorama of life, the glitter of its details, the unsubstantial nature of its forms, the uncertainty of their justification" (125–26). The confusion in his mind turns out to be a reflection of his ambivalent attitude toward Jennie near the end of the novel. He is indeed torn between his attachment to her and his compliance with social conventions. In sum, Dreiser reasons: "There is a fate in love and a fate in fight" (124).

From Jennie's vantage point, "the multiplicity of evidences of things, the vastness of the panorama of life" makes her quest for liberation from class oppression less painful. As she moves from Cleveland to Chicago, the multiple and panoramic vision of city life intensifies. "Yes, Chicago was best," Dreiser declares. "The very largeness and hustle of it" made the concealment of Lester's liaison with Jennie easy (173). Genuinely attracted to Lester, she cannot regard his statement, "You belong to me," as offensive. Though "horrified, stunned, like a bird in the grasp of a cat," she hears "through it all something terrific, inviting, urging" (123). In addition, the uplifting mood and the booming economy characteristic of Chicago intensify the admiration of Lester and Jennie for each other.

Jennie is an altruistic woman. Typical of a youth in an immigrant family, Jennie feels she has a moral obligation to her family. Although she is keenly aware of her social transgression, her sense of guilt is mitigated by a genuine concern for her family's welfare. The familial ties of the Gerhardts are thus stronger than those of the Johnsons in *Maggie*. Each member of Maggie's family lives for himself or herself; the alienation of the Johnson family is complete even before the story begins. Mrs. Gerhardt is a compassionate woman who consoles her daughter in distress. Mrs. Johnson, on the contrary, is a least sympathetic mother: she speaks to Jimmie, who concurs in her statement, "She had a bad heart, dat girl did, Jimmie. She was wicked t' d' heart an' we never knowed it. . . . We lived in d' same house wid her an' I brought her up, an' we never knowed how bad she was. . . . Wid a home like dis an' a mudder like me, she went teh d' bad" (168).

Given such a social environment, Crane's portrayal of Maggie's life becomes utterly predictable. Growing up in such a family, Maggie has little desire to leave the slum life or to better herself. Although she is described as "blossomed in a mud-puddle" and "a most rare and wonderful production of a tenement district, a pretty girl" (141), she is not endowed with any sense of autonomy or vision. Blindly dependent on Pete, she mistakes him for a knight who will rescue a distressed damsel. When she sees him the next time in a different suit, she is impressed with his "prodigious" wardrobe (146). When Pete takes her to see sentimental plays, she thinks they exhibit "transcendental realism" (153). Naive and innocent, she wonders "if the culture and refinement she had seen imitated, perhaps grotesquely, by the heroine on the stage, could be acquired by a girl who lived in a tenement house and worked in a shirt factory" (154).

Whereas Bowery life destroys any semblance of individuality in Maggie, city life liberates Jennie from rigid societal restrictions because it becomes, by degrees, an open world as she moves from one city to another. In New York Lester makes arrangements for Jennie to live in an exclusive apartment so that they can avoid his acquaintances. During the stay he "thought he would have inured Jennie to her new life" as her personal problems in Cleveland were solved. The atmosphere in New York "into which she was so quickly plunged was so wonderful, so illuminating," Dreiser emphasizes, "that she could scarcely believe this was the same world she had inhabited before" (166). In her ordeal the city becomes her savior, for living in a city not only separates her from the restrictive past dominated by class and gender prejudices but also gives her the fluid, indeterminate space in which to gain her new identity.

The spirit of freedom the city inspires in Jennie is also shared with Lester. Whether she succeeds in her search for liberation has a corollary to what happens to his life in Chicago. Even though he establishes his life there with her and Vesta and brings old Gerhardt from Cleveland to live with them, Lester faces a choice between marrying Jennie and forfeiting his fortune. After his interview with Robert, Lester reflects on the conditions in which his life exists: "He sat down . . . and gazed ruminatively out over the flourishing city. Yonder was spread out before him life, with its concomitant phases of energy, hope, prosperity and pleasure, and here he was suddenly struck by a wind of misfortune . . . his prospects and purposes enveloped in a haze" (236–37). In contrast to the action in *Maggie*, that in *Jennie Gerhardt* thrives on Dreiser's rendition of Lester's ambivalent attitude toward life. Although Maggie's fate is predictable, Jennie's is not, even at the end of the novel. As Dreiser observes that human life entails "a fate in love and a fate in fight" (124), Lester's dilemma of love and money sustains the reader's interest. This dilemma, then, underlies Dreiser's dialectics of the pursuit of happiness and the inalienable right to property, two of the quintessential ideals reflected in American life at the turn of the century.

Despite his passion for Jennie, Lester must leave her if he is to retain his fortune. In a metropolis such as Chicago in the 1890s, the public is fascinated not so much with the romance and marriage of a wealthy man and a poor working girl as with the economics that dictate such an affair. "The American public," as Dreiser writes in journalistic fashion, "likes gossip concerning the rich, or did at this time. It was inordinately interested in all that concerned the getting of money and the spending of it, for that was almost the sole and vital interest of the nation" (284). Swayed by the national sentiment, Lester becomes susceptible to the social and economic pressures of the period; and Jennie, who has been at his mercy all these years, acquiesces in his decision. "Love was not enough in this world — that was so plain," Dreiser emphasizes. "One needed education, wealth, training, the ability to fight and scheme. She did not want to do that. She could not" (366). As a social historian, Dreiser is making such an observation not only to interpret the story at hand but to reflect on the world of business and on an American public preoccupied with that world.[2]

The objection of his family and friends to his life with Jennie notwithstanding, Lester persists in his refusal to desert her. To protect her from social ostracism, he first finds a large house with trees and a lawn in South Hyde Park, a retreat from his apartment on a busy street.[3] The house gives them anonymity and privacy. When "one is content to lead a secluded life," Dreiser reasons, referring to the smaller house by the lake Lester rents for Jennie, "it is not necessary to say much of one's past" (379). Inevitably Lester leaves Jennie for Letty, a society woman, but such an action only accounts for the surface reality of the story. Underneath Dreiser stresses a genuine spiritual tie between Jennie and Lester, which continues unbroken.

Maggie, unlike Jennie, grows up in a family in which her father, an abusive alcoholic, is unconcerned about his children. Even though old Gerhardt is not sympathetic to Jennie, he comes around to understand her as he grows older. In the beginning he is described as a fanatic Lutheran, just as Dreiser's own father was a fanatic Catholic, but compared with the priest who could have saved Maggie from drowning herself, old Gerhardt becomes a respectable human being. As Crane describes the priest, "His beaming, chubby face was a picture of benevolence and kind-heartedness. His eyes shone good will. But as the girl timidly accosted him he made a convulsive movement and saved his respectability by a vigorous side-step" (181).

Although Crane's portrayal of city life in *Maggie* seems to conform to deterministic doctrine, the story also suggests that an individual must take moral and personal responsibility for his or her life. Crane might have tried to minimize such a responsibility on the part of Maggie to dramatize the consequences of social determinism, but the Bowery life he depicts, which is extremely confined, does not allow for the residents' mobility, let alone their travels.

In *Jennie Gerhardt,* by contrast, both the idea and the excitement of travel are expressed throughout the novel.[4] As the Gerhardt children walk to the railroad tracks to steal coal, they watch luxurious trains pass by. "Jennie, alone, kept silent," Dreiser remarks, "but the suggestion of travel and comfort was the most appealing to her of all" (28). Lester, however, grew up in a family in which his father, founding a small wagon factory, had an ambition to build it up into a large industry. Like George Pullman, the inventor and builder of the Pullman car, Archibald Kane realized that "America was a growing country," that there was to be "a big demand for vehicles — wagons, carriages, drays," and that it was his mission to supply the demand (137).[5] After his father's death, Lester decides to leave the Kane Company and departs on a European tour with Jennie. He later regrets having wasted his time because his father's ambition and legacy were not "built by travellers." Jennie, however, "was transported by what she saw and learned" (307).

This travel makes her realize how narrow-minded people around her at home really are and "how pointless are our minor difficulties after all — our minor beliefs" (307). Moreover, it is with a scene of travelers at the Chicago station after Lester's death that the novel ends. Looking at the coffin, she hears "with a desperate ache the description of a route which she and Lester had taken more than once, slowly and melodiously emphasized. 'Detroit, Toledo, Cleveland, Buffalo, and New York'" (416). At the same time Drei-

ser, as narrator, hears "the voice of a passing stranger, gay with the anticipation of coming pleasures. 'We're going to have a great time down there.
Remember Annie? Uncle Jim's coming and Aunt Ella'" (417–18). Jennie
does not hear such a voice—she has no real family now—but she will
cherish her memories of travel with Lester for the rest of her life.

Lester does leave Jennie to marry Letty, but his love for Jennie does not
change. Dreiser explains that Lester "is making a sacrifice of the virtues—
kindness, loyalty, affection,—to policy" (365). Because Lester's marriage
to Letty reflects this policy, it becomes a marriage of convenience. Lester
tries to conceal the fact that he does not need Letty; to be kind he pretends
"the necessity of her presence" (404). But she is dispensable in a way that
Jennie is not. Even though class oppression has separated Jennie from him,
his love for her has not diminished, nor has hers for him.[6]

At first glance, *Jennie Gerhardt* and *Maggie* both appear to be stories of
social determinism in which heroines fall victims to their economic en-
vironments. The two novels, however, differ in the treatment of character.
Although Lester is portrayed initially as an animalistic man, he is also "a
product of a combination of elements—religious, commercial, social—
modified by the overruling, circumambient atmosphere of liberty in our
national life which is productive of almost uncounted freedoms of thought
and action" (126). Despite her lack of education and experience, Jennie is
endowed with the same spirit of freedom that buttresses Lester. The city, in
effect, makes it possible for both to achieve the kind of freedom they have
not known before. Crane, by contrast, in conforming to naturalistic doctrine, does not reflect in *Maggie* the cultural climate that prevailed in the
American 1890s. Stylistically as well, Dreiser's writing is reportorial and
Crane's is impressionistic. Unlike *Maggie*, *Jennie Gerhardt* is a novel that is
based on history and in turn enlightens that history.

Notes

1. Between 1897 and 1900 Dreiser wrote more than 120 pieces, mostly magazine articles, on contemporary American culture. The late nineties was an important
turning point in American history. In response to what he calls in *Jennie Gerhardt*
the "tremendous and complicated development of our material civilization, the
multiplicity and variety of our social forms" (125), Dreiser wrote most of his magazine articles as a dispassionate chronicler of American culture. At the same time,
though, he dramatized the delights and tribulations of people individually and

collectively. This body of writing, constituting a rare, remarkably coherent piece of Americana, is reflected in the story of Jennie and Lester.

2. Dreiser's comment on the national interest in "the getting of money and the spending of it" (284) is based on the booming economy he witnessed in the late 1890s that followed the worst depression the nation had up until then experienced.

3. Lester's attempt to impress Jennie by providing a Hyde Park mansion is reminiscent of Drouet, who drives Carrie through a section of Chicago where multimillionaires, such as Philip Armour and George Pullman, lived.

4. In Richard Wright's fiction, the forms of transportation — train, plane, covered truck — are used to symbolize black people's freedom from racial oppression: Bigger Thomas in *Native Son* dreams of flying an airplane, Big Boy in *Uncle Tom's Children* escapes a lynching by being driven away in a covered truck, Dave Saunders in *Eight Men* leaves a white southerner's farm by jumping on a passing freight train, and Fishbelly Tucker in *The Long Dream* leaves Clintonville, Mississippi, for Paris by jet.

5. See Dreiser's magazine article "The Town of Pullman," *Ainslee's* 3 (March 1899):189–200. Between 1898 and 1900 Dreiser also wrote many articles on technological advances in methods of transportation and their effect on travel and industry, among them, "The Harlem River Speedway," "The Horseless Age," "From New York to Boston by Trolley," and "The Railroad and the People," all reprinted in *Magazine Articles*. See also "New York's Underground Railroad," *Pearson's* 9 (April 1900):375–84; and "Good Roads for Bad," *Pearson's* 9 (May 1900):387–95.

6. In accepting Letty's marriage proposal, Lester confesses that he made a mistake by living with Jennie but that he has found it hard to separate from her. After this confession, the 1992 Pennsylvania edition includes Lester's remark, "I'm sorry to state and I'm not sorry to state" (338). This line clearly suggests that he will not regret being emotionally involved with Jennie despite his marriage to Letty. Deleting such a statement makes Lester, in the 1911 Harpers edition, more compliant with the mores of the higher social classes and hence less rebellious against social conventions.

Bibliography

Crane, Stephen. *Great Short Works of Stephen Crane*. New York: Harper & Row, 1965.

Dreiser, Theodore. *Jennie Gerhardt*. 1911. Reprint. Cleveland: World, 1946.

——. *Jennie Gerhardt*. Edited by James L. W. West III. Philadelphia: University of Pennsylvania Press, 1992.

——. *Selected Magazine Articles of Theodore Dreiser: Life and Art in the American 1890s*. 2 vols. Edited by Yoshinobu Hakutani. Cranbury, NJ: Associated University Presses, 1985, 1987.

——. *Sister Carrie*. Edited by John C. Berkey, Alice M. Winters, James L. W. West III, and Neda M. Westlake. Philadelphia: University of Pennsylvania Press, 1981.

Gerber, Philip L. *Theodore Dreiser.* New Haven, CT: Twayne, 1964.
White, Morton and Lucia. *The Intellectual versus the City.* Cambridge, MA: Harvard
    University Press, 1962.
Wright, Richard. *Black Boy: A Record of Childhood and Youth.* 1945. Reprint. New
    York: Harper & Row, 1966.

15
Jennie Gerhardt and the Dream of the Pastoral

JOHN B. HUMMA

PASTORAL LITERATURE SUPPOSES AN *Aristos* (from the Greek, "the best"). From Theocritus through, say, D. H. Lawrence, the pastoral poem or novel offers — usually prescribes — a nature ethic, implicit within which are several defining conflicts or points of tension: most obviously, an urban-rural tension featuring on a personal level deeper conflicts, or contrasts, between simplicity and innocence on the one hand and sophistication and knowledge (in the ways of the world) on the other. Curiously, American literature bows to English literature in the representation of the pastoral. Nowhere is this more evident than in the novel. In English fiction one thinks of Eliot, Hardy, Forster, Lawrence; in American fiction, although one finds pastoral-like elements and moments in novels by such authors as Cooper, Melville, Clemens, and Hemingway, none really completes or satisfies the dimensions of the pastoral novel. Willa Cather perhaps comes closest, but the play of her novels does not immediately embrace the contrasts and the ethic central to the pastoral form (although the story "Neighbor Rosicky" squarely and beautifully does).[1] Indeed, there seem to be no fully realized pastoral novels in the first tier of American fiction. But oddly, America's foremost novelist of the city — the author of *Sister Carrie,* America's foremost novel of the city — perhaps comes closest in *Jennie Gerhardt* to writing America's true pastoral novel. For Jennie is the novel's *aristos,* the one major character in Theodore Dreiser's fiction whom Dreiser without qualification and with perfect sincerity approves. And what he approves in her are precisely those qualities that represent the pastoral ethic or ideal.

Jennie Gerhardt, like *Carrie* and like Dreiser's other novels, *is* an urban novel. On one level it is about the dream of escape from urban life and its materialistic values. In this sense, Lester Kane is a figure caught in suspension, with his Hamlet-like indisposition to choosing, and he is not delivered from his state of suspension until the last pages, when it is too late. Jennie embodies the pastoral virtues of innocence, simplicity, unsophistication, the natural.[2] The central action of the story is Lester's attempt to break free from the constraints of the conventional (which he sees through) and of material comfort and prosperity (which he partly sees through) and his constant drifting with the expedient flow of these forces to successively larger cities. Like *Sister Carrie,* this novel at times asks to be called by the name of its male protagonist. But it is, after all, appropriately titled. By giving Jennie's name to the book, Dreiser asserts the claim of her values and establishes that necessary balance between the urban ethic and the pastoral one. The city only appears to overwhelm the pastoral in the novel. Jennie's presence steadily asserts the pastoral ideal in the face of a meretricious commercial ethic and an unnatural puritanical sexual morality, which is, horribly, as Dreiser represents it, the *conventional* morality.

Who is Jennie, what is Jennie? She is, as Donald Pizer recognizes, Tess Durbeyfield reincarnated on American soil.[3] She may not be, as Tess is, a *milk*maid, but like Tess she is, or becomes, "maiden no more." And like Tess she bears a child. Most significant, though, is that both women, despite their despoilings, are "fresh and virginal daughters of nature" (Hardy 155). Clearly each author wants us to identify his heroine with nature, and Hardy and Dreiser both believe that nature establishes the superiority of the two women. As Tess puts it to Angel Clare, "I am a peasant by position, not by nature" (302). Although Jennie, who is usually self-effacing, would not be given to saying this about herself, Dreiser establishes her *aristos* character throughout the novel. Even in comparison with the estimable and largely sympathetic Letty Gerald, Jennie is, as Lester comes to recognize, the superior woman. For although "Jennie's ideas did not flow as fast as those of Mrs. Gerald," she nonetheless "had actually the deeper, more comprehensive, sympathetic, and emotional note in her nature" (313–14). Or, as Lester tells Letty, "She possesses a world of feeling and emotion. She's not educated in the sense in which we understand that word, but she has *natural* refinement" (emphasis mine, 338–39). Like Tess, she is instinct combined with nature.

Chapter II is the shortest chapter in the book, dramatically so at less than three pages. It is brief because essentially it is a poem. Its sole purpose is to establish Jennie as a child of nature and, accordingly, to hint at the pastoral dimensions that later chapters establish firmly. As a *poem,* it is not altogether successful, reading at times like bad romantic versifying. It has a subtext, however, which may or may not be intentional. I say this because I believe we are right to suspect the subtextual in Dreiser, and because when he is at his best, things subliminal rise up. Dreiser asks at the very beginning of the chapter, "The spirit of Jennie — who shall express it?" (16). The maid, as it were, of "this distinguished citizen [Senator Brander] of Columbus" is one of those "natures born to the inheritance of flesh that come without understanding, and that go again without seeming to have wondered why" (16). The later Jennie will develop the capacity to wonder why, but for the young Jennie, this description is perfectly apt, as are the following sentences:

> Life, as long as they endure it, is a true wonderland, a thing of infinite beauty, which could they but wander into it, wonderingly, would be heaven enough. Opening their eyes, they see a conformable and perfect world. Trees, flowers, the world of sound and the world of color. These are the valued inheritance of their state. (16)

The "material" is that other world: as the novel establishes it, it is the world both of material progress, epitomized in the city, and of "convention." But Jennie as a child of nature looks beyond the city: "When the days were fair, she looked out of her kitchen window and longed to go where the meadows were." And there "were times when she had gone with George and the others, leading them away to where a patch of hickory trees flourished, because there were open fields, with shade for comfort and a brook of living water" (17). It is the pastoral she longs for.

She likes to walk in the countryside "where the sunlight was warm" and to enter "with instinctive appreciation the holy corridors of the trees" (17). With George and Martha, she sits in "a natural swing of a wild grape-vine" and tries to answer questions about this Eden they seem to inhabit (17). She speaks "dreamily," "deeply feeling the poetry of it herself" (18). The wondering, dreamy nature of their exchanges goes on for the better part of a page, until she clenches "her fingers in an agony of poetic feeling" and "crystal tears of mellowness" break forth (examples of Dreiser's not very happy success with lyricism). This brings the reader to his framing, concluding sentence: "Of such was the spirit of Jennie" (18).

"Eden" was my word, not Dreiser's, but it seems to me fairly clear that he is describing, in this song of innocence, a paradise. This is to be sure a paradise that will not last or that only promises but does not grant happiness, or more than fleeting moments of it. Striking, though, is Dreiser's selection of Columbus as his setting for this part of the novel and for assigning the roles of companions to Jennie in the chapter to "George" and "Martha." Dreiser makes the pastoral contrast work in terms of an earlier

"Columbian" idealism of the promise of America, an ideal whose efficacy was still rich in Washington's time — that is, in the time of the father (and mother) of the fresh, young country about which Crèvecoeur had written so movingly while it was still a colony and whose agrarian ideal Jefferson did not tire of promoting in his own writings. Jefferson's real fear was the city, and thus Dreiser's irony in the chapter. Columbus, Ohio, in the latter decades of the nineteenth century was already becoming a city. General (and President) Washington has shrunk, as the city in America has grown, to mere Senator Brander, whose residence, appropriately, is the Columbus House. Jennie's and Lester's moves to Cleveland, then to Chicago, and Lester's eventual but inevitable move to New York (although he dies in Chicago) are symbolic.

What is this elusive if not furtive pastoral in *Jennie Gerhardt*? Though it never occupies stage center, it is nonetheless never far from Jennie's thoughts. And Jennie carries the pastoral ideal into Lester's life, for it is the ethic of the pastoral, at last embodied in Jennie, that he realizes he has lost. For Jennie the pastoral lives mainly as her dream, but this does not prevent her from actually embodying it for Lester in her innocence and unsophistication. In his purely material prosperity and business success, his brother, Robert, embodies the new, corrupt ideal of the American dream. Lester sees through all this rightly enough: his failure is that he cannot see all the way through to the meaning of "the spirit of Jennie."

Here is Ernst R. Curtius's description of the *locus amoenus:* it is "a beautiful shaded natural site whose minimum ingredients comprise a tree (or several trees), meadow, and a spring or brook" (195). This recalls in faultless parallel Jennie's "patch of hickory trees," "meadows" or "open fields, with shade for comfort," and "a brook of living water." (The "living" is a good touch on Dreiser's part.) There is more to the pastoral, though, than setting. A dynamics of action goes with it as well. In *Map of Arcadia,* Walter R. Davis writes, "The standard pastoral action consists . . . of disintegration in the turbulent outer circle, education in the pastoral circle, and rebirth at the sacred center" (38). For Lester, the "turbulent outer circle" consists of the family's carriage business (and its larger capitalist context) and of the glittering but artificial social world of his sister Louise. Lester is very much a part of both worlds. The education that takes place in "the pastoral circle" is all his, but it stops short of completion. For although he has a sense of Jennie's largely "Wordsworthian" nature, containing those pastoral qualities of mellowness and innocence and a natural freshness, he does not completely comprehend its meaning for *him*. Consequently the "rebirth at the sacred center" never takes place, either for Jennie or for Lester. And although at Sandwood Jennie at last has her fields and trees and water, she is not made whole. The absence of Lester leaves her lonely. Thus, the last dimension, the completing one, without which the others fail to cohere, is love. Throughout their relationship Lester's refusal, or inability, to commit himself to Jennie prevents the perfection of the relationship, of the pastoral ideal. It remains a dream.

Although Jennie's naturalness is essentially Wordsworthian, unlike Tess she does not wade in a Hardyan garden of "slug-slime" and "cuckoo-spittle" (179).[4] Yet Jennie, in Dreiser's economy anyway, is as much in nature as is Tess. One of the most interesting passages in the book is this one, which follows Jennie's banishment by her father:

> She did not know where to go or what to do. Her wide eyes were filled with vague wonder and pain. She was outside now. There was no one to tell her how.
> It is in such supreme moments that growth is greatest. . . . Flashes of inspiration come to guide the soul. In nature there is no outside. When cast from a group or a condition, we have still the companionship of all that is. Nature is not ungenerous. Its winds and stars are fellows with you. Let the soul be but gentle and receptive, this vast truth will come home; not in set phrases, perhaps, but as a feeling, a comfort, which, after all, is the last essence of knowledge. In the universe, peace is wisdom. (88)

The last part of this is a bit contrived, but the import of its implicit contrast (which we construct only later) is clear. Nature receives Jennie because she is outside the material and conventional world; it does not accept Lester, who never breaks with this world.

It is not my purpose to treat the sexual aspect of Jennie's naturalness. Pizer does this very well. Here, of course, is where Dreiser is most influenced by Hardy, where he is least Wordsworthian. Important to the matter at hand, though, is society's treatment of Jennie's breach of taboo and Dreiser's view of this society's unnatural embrace of proprieties:

> To those who cannot understand this attitude in one not sheltered by the conventions, not housed in comfort and protected by the love and care of a husband, it must be explained again that we are not dealing with the ordinary temperament. The latter — the customary small nature, even when buoyed by communal advice and assistance — is apt to see in a situation of this kind only terror and danger. Nature is unkind to permit the minor type of woman to bear a child at all. The larger natures in their maturity welcome motherhood, see in it the immense possibilities of racial fulfillment, find joy and satisfaction in being the handmaiden of so immense a purpose or direction. (95)

Convention is the artificial standard reared in opposition to the pastoral's natural one. "This attitude" is Jennie's courageous facing of life "in the natural innocence of the good heart," although she is urged all the while by the conventional voice of morality "to withdraw and hide away, to shun the piercing and scornful gaze of men" (94). Jennie's greater problem, after Vesta is born, is Lester. Although he cares little for the world's conventional morality, he nonetheless does pay attention to some of its forms: "He did care for her in a feral, Hyperborean way, but he was hedged about by the ideas of the conventional world in which he had been reared" (243). One of Dreiser's fullest statements of convention's pull on the individual is this one:

> To contravene the social conventions of your time, to fly in the face of what people consider to be right and proper and to present a determined and self-willed attitude toward the world in matters of desire is quite an interesting and striking thing to contemplate as a policy, and quite a difficult one to work out to a logical and successful conclusion. The conventions, in their way, appear to be as inexorable in their workings as the laws of gravitation and expansion. There is a drift to society as a whole which pushes on in a certain direction, careless of the individual, concerned only with the general result. (283)

Finally this is Lester's attitude. For all of his appreciation of Jennie's qualities, he is yet content to drift with society, "careless of the individual" who is Jennie.

Dreiser frames Lester's helplessness, or weakness, even more precisely later on. Although "Lester's world seemed solid and persistent and real enough to him," when "the winds of adversity" begin to blow and he has to face "the armed forces of convention," then he becomes aware that "he might be mistaken as to the value of his personality, and that his private desires and opinions were as nothing in the face of a public conviction that he was wrong." Lester is a social coward: that is, he is a moral coward in the face of society's conventions. Dreiser's point is that Lester is in large and good company: "The people of his time believed that some particular form of social arrangement was necessary" (368). If he cannot be blamed for his actions (this is not an existentialist novel), he can nonetheless suffer for them.

Again and again we find Jennie under attack by conventions. In league with conventions are what Dreiser calls "materialized forces" (125). Jennie is under seige from these as well. Most obviously, her family's poverty attests to defeat at the hands of these forces, but leagued with them again is

Lester: "Although on the face of things he appeared to be a hunter and destroyer of undefended virtue, he was yet a man of such a complicated and interesting turn of mind that those who are inclined to be radically intolerant of his personality had best suspend judgement until some further light can be thrown upon it" (125). This is quite a statement; perhaps it can be accounted for by speculating that Dreiser probably is describing himself as well as Lester Kane when he tells us of Lester's urge to seduce Jennie. Lester, to be sure, is no more to be blamed than Dreiser for the follies in his sexual life: "There are some minds, fairly endowed with the power to see into things, that are nevertheless overwhelmed by the evidences of life and are confused." The reason for this unfortunate state of being is that "we live in an age in which the impact of materialized forces is well-nigh irresistible; the spiritual nature is overwhelmed by the shock." Of such a nature is Jennie. Dreiser continues:

> The tremendous and complicated development of our material civilization, the multiplicity and variety of our social forms, the depth, subtlety and sophistry of our mental cogitations, gathered, remultiplied and phantasmagorically disseminated as they are by these other agencies . . . have so combined as to produce what may be termed a kaleidoscopic glitter, a dazzling and confusing showpiece which is much more apt to weary and undo than to enlighten and strengthen the observing mind. It produces a sort of intellectual fatigue by which we see the ranks of the victims of insomnia, melancholia and insanity recruited. Our modern brain-pan does not seem capable of receiving, sorting and storing the vast army of facts and impressions which present themselves daily. (125)

Jennie Gerhardt sets up those polar configurations of the rural-urban, natural-artificial, pastoral-conventional, and spiritual-material. These devolve, ultimately, into sanity-insanity, happiness-unhappiness (though one is never, without supreme qualification, really "happy"), and health-illness. It is not accidental that Lester dies from the repletion that results from his overmastering, "materialized" way of life after he leaves Jennie.

Standing against this insanity is the little residence in Sandwood, a name as simple and natural as Jennie herself. On the one hand the name may satirize the misleadingly bucolic naming of developments (we recall Lester's project of "Inwood"); on the other, though, it describes Jennie's qualities of down-to-earthness ("Earth-mother") and solidity. Where Jennie lives should be *inside* nature, as she herself is. After she is driven from home by her father, Dreiser writes, "Her wide eyes were filled with vague wonder and pain. She was outside now. There was no one to tell her how"

(88). But nature has no outside, and in Sandwood she is inside. Dreiser describes a village on the Illinois-Wisconsin line beside a bay of Lake Michigan. Its denizens, though not rustics, are nonetheless "not rich people" (361). There are "a number of trees — quite a grove of pines in fact." People settled there for the "quiet, natural beauty and the advantages of the lake" (361). Jennie, on a drive with Lester, shows a fondness for the place: "the surrounding trees, green for the entire year, gave [the cottages] a pleasing, summery appearance" (362). She admires "the look of a little white church steeple, set down among green trees, and the gentle rocking of the boats upon the summer water" (362). All of this is pastoral enough. To complete the ideal, though, Dreiser writes, "There she would have a little garden, say; some chickens perhaps; a tall pole with a pretty bird-house on it; and flowers and trees and green grass everywhere about." Here, in a little cottage with a view of the lake, "she could sit of a summer evening and sew. Vesta could play about or come home from school. She might have a few friends or" — she surely must be thinking of the "friends" in Hyde Park — "not any" (362). Although Jennie has neighbors, Sandwood is her Innisfree, an islanded place where she can be alone.

Here at Sandwood "goodness of heart" might find its free range. For "what else was there that was real?" (308). In these terms, the unreal is the city, with its "materiality" and society and social "conventions." The unreal is present-day America, the corrupted or fallen Eden-Columbia. In all pastorals, the residing virtues are rooted in the past. And Lester, who knows this but chooses the material present, also is unreal. Two extremely effective images dramatize the contrast. In the first, the apostrophizing author speaks of those "few sprigs of green that sometimes invade the barrenness of your materialism" (77); in the second, Dreiser is describing Jennie's slow but superior thought, "which usually transcended the common, more superficial method, much as the flow of a river might transcend in importance the hurry of an automobile" (258). Jennie is those alive "sprigs of green" invading Lester's barrenness, just as she is the vital flow of the river to Lester's hurrying (to what end?) automobile.

In the end, however, even before she loses Vesta, Sandwood is not enough for Jennie. For she lacks that last requisite to the pastoral ideal: romance, love between man and woman. Dreiser writes, "Her flowers and her lawn and her view of the lake, which was beautiful, seemed to require something more than just her love of them to make her happy. It was Lester, of course, but she kept thinking she ought to try to make herself happy without him" (384). But she cannot. Such is the tragic card that circumstance has dealt to Jennie. Instead of "rebirth at the sacred center," Jennie "drifts" along until the death of Vesta, while Lester, who cannot commit himself to the woman he actually loves and who needs his love, continues his drift along an unreal course toward death.

One might call *Jennie Gerhardt,* somewhat oxymoronically, a naturalistic-pastoral novel. The action of the pastoral is not completed, because what is supposed to happen finally at "the sacred center" does not happen — but that is Dreiser's point. The characters achieve only the dream of the pastoral. Although education does take place within the "pastoral circle" — Lester learns from Jennie's greatness of spirit what he should do — in the end he chooses the "turbulent outer circle" where he disintegrates. Or rather circumstances choose it for him. Dreiser's novel is interesting, among other reasons, for the way that it formally satisfies, perhaps more nearly than any other American novel, the dimensions of the pastoral and, further, for the way that it describes, through the tropes of the pastoral form, the disintegration of the American dream.

Notes

1. For discussion of pastoral elements in Cather's fiction, see Rosowski, especially chapter 4 on *O Pioneers!* Recently claims have been made for the fictions of women regionalist authors like Sarah Orne Jewett and Kate Chopin as pastorals. Thus, *Country of the Pointed Firs,* if one stretches the definition of the novel, is read as a pastoral novel. So too *The Awakening,* although it seems to me that one has to make immoderate adjustments, in conceptual boundaries, to make claims for it.

2. In her passive disposition, it is easy to see Jennie, as Carol A. Schwartz does, as both a fairy-tale princess and the heroine of a sentimental romance. But of course she has shadings that make her peculiarly herself. Dreiser has in mind a larger role for her to play than either of these.

3. See *Dreiser-Mencken Letters,* in which Mencken guesses at Hardy's influence (229) and Dreiser confirms the guess (234).

4. Hardy, unlike Dreiser, is intent on destroying Wordsworthian pieties about nature. Dreiser seems to have missed or to have been unconcerned about Hardy's quarrel with Wordsworth, although it squares well with his own thinking. Here is Hardy early in *Tess:* "Some people would like to know whence the poet whose philosophy is in these days deemed as profound and trustworthy as his song is breezy and pure, gets his authority for speaking of 'Nature's holy plan' " (61–62).

Bibliography

Curtius, Ernst H. *European Literature and the Middle Ages.* Princeton, NJ: Princeton University Press, 1965.

Davis, Walter R. *Map of Arcadia*. New Haven, CT: Yale University Press, 1965.

Dreiser, Theodore. *Jennie Gerhardt*. Edited by James L. W. West III. Philadelphia: University of Pennsylvania Press, 1992.

Dreiser-Mencken Letters: The Correspondence of Theodore Dreiser & H. L. Mencken. Edited by Thomas P. Riggio. 2 vols. Philadelphia: University of Pennsylvania Press, 1986.

Hardy, Thomas. *Tess of the d'Urbervilles*. New York: Penguin, 1981.

Pizer, Donald. *The Novels of Theodore Dreiser: A Critical Study*. Minneapolis: University of Minnesota Press, 1976.

Rosowski, Susan. *The Voyage Perilous: Willa Cather's Romanticism*. Lincoln: University of Nebraska Press, 1986.

Schwartz, Carol A. *"Jennie Gerhardt:* Fairy Tale as Social Criticism." *American Literary Realism: 1870–1910* 19(1987): 16–29.

16
How German Is *Jennie Gerhardt*?

ARTHUR D. CASCIATO

My ANSWER TO THE QUESTION ABOUT the "German" nature of *Jennie Gerhardt* is the same as Randolph Bourne's was in 1916 when he took up the issue in relation to all of Dreiser's writing: an unequivocal "not at all" (95). Of course Bourne's negative assessment—and the firmness with which he asserted it—was self-consciously pitched to respond to the nativist hysteria of the war years when the patriotism of all German-Americans was in question. By denying the Germanness of Dreiser's novels, Bourne not only attempted to head off suspicions about the author's loyalty but, more important, refused the terms of the debate as the warmongers and "real" Americans wished to set them. Unwilling to concede what specific personal or literary qualities constituted an American, Bourne nonetheless presented Dreiser as "thoroughly" so, "a true hyphenate, a product of that conglomerate Americanism, that springs from other roots than the English tradition" (95). Here, as he would argue more insistently in his essay "Trans-National America," Bourne undid the assumed privilege of Anglo-Saxons by naming them "English-American"—thus not the essence or measure of the New World but only the ruling class of an international nation of Old World hyphenates.

This was more or less the tactic that H. L. Mencken, that great harrumpher of all things Anglo-Saxon, would deploy a year later when he too attempted to shield his pal Dreiser (as well as himself) from the ravages of rampant anti-German prejudice—though, to be sure, Mencken's defense was more pointed and truculent than Bourne's. Mencken's target was Stuart P. Sherman, the Anglophilic midwestern English professor who, in the pages of the *Nation,* had famously disdained Dreiser's naturalism as "barbaric." Barely disguising his desire to expel Dreiser and the rest of the "'ethnic' element of our mixed population" from polite American society, Sherman gerryrigged himself a tidy little sausage grinder in which realism

My thanks to Dinah Brand for stirring up these issues.

was defined as a theory of human conduct and naturalism a theory of mere animal behavior (72). "Since a theory of animal behavior can never be an adequate basis for a representation of the life of man in contemporary society," argued Sherman, "such a representation is an artistic blunder" (80).

This binary logic — realism/naturalism, human/animal, civilized/barbaric, American/German — was tight if not irresistible, but the skeptical Mencken wasn't fooled by its artistic pretensions: "What offends [Sherman]," he wrote, "is not actually Dreiser's shortcomings as an artist, but Dreiser's shortcomings as a Christian and an American" (87). The "supposed" before each "shortcoming" could be taken for granted, so loudly and persistently had Mencken heralded his fellow German-American, and he went on to insist, like Bourne, that Dreiser was a "true American." By refusing the assumptions of a traditional melting-pot ethnicity — Old World immigrant assimilates to New World (read Anglo-Saxon) attitudes, behaviors, and values — Mencken was able to turn the rhetoric of early twentieth-century Americanism against itself. He and Bourne took the high ground, social and artistic, from those desperate turn-of-the-century Anglophiles who would claim it *only* for themselves.

Although Dreiser's reputation as a citizen is, so far as I know, no longer in jeopardy, my own "not at all" in response to the question of the ethnicity of *Jennie Gerhardt* is no less urgent than Bourne's, and my refusal of the melting pot as the warrant of my answer no less self-interested and tactical than Mencken's. I am writing on a quiet Sunday morning on which the local newspaper carries the terrible headline, "Sarajevo Suffers Bloodiest Day." And when, in the same issue of the paper, I come upon similar stories closer to home, always displayed less prominently and in language seemingly more objective, I discover that our federal government fires minority employees at more than twice the rate of white ones. This "policy," if not as obviously horrible as ethnic cleansing, is at least arguably related to it. I also write as an Italian-American member of a profession that is increasingly dominated by a liberal multiculturalism, which, even as it celebrates difference, continues to follow the melting-pot recipe — at least when it comes to those of us who have descended from southern and eastern European immigrants.[1] In their rush to power, multiculturalists of this stripe have reduced so-called white ethnics — Italian-Americans, Polish-Americans, Jewish-Americans, Irish-Americans — to a sodden Eurocentric lump, and this despite the obvious and rich differences between and among our various cultural heritages and experiences. To protest such treatment is not necessarily to lose sight of the fact that my ancestors did not suffer as much or in the same ways as the ancestors of African-, Native-, Mexican-, and Asian-Americans. But suffer they did, if not from a savage racism that licensed slavery, genocide, colonialization, and internment camps, then at the very least from an unreasonable prejudice that engendered shame, guilt, and anger. And if multiculturalism's revision of the canon and the curriculum is our measure, as might be expected in what is after all an argument among academics, then the discrimination against writers from my own and other European ethnic groups continues apace, even as that against writers from American racial minorities is rightfully and successfully being redressed.[2]

His German-American ancestry notwithstanding, Dreiser needs no such help—not because talent or genius somehow always will out but rather because he has already received it from Bourne, Mencken, and others who found the courage to resist Anglo-American cultural hegemony and the model of ethnicity that authorized and supported it. They simply refused to accept the prevailing notion, in a country in which no one except the American Indian could claim to be indigenous, that the cultural practices of a single immigrant people were more "American" than those of all the others. Thus, for Bourne, there was "a new American quality" in Dreiser's writing, "an authentic attempt to make something artistic out of the chaotic materials that lie around us in American life" (95). And for Mencken, more bluntly: "Dreiser, after all, is an American like the rest of us" (89).

Not all of Dreiser's supporters, however, have been able to follow Mencken's and Bourne's examples in rejecting the "American-immigrant" opposition that structures and limits much of our thinking about ethnicity. Most prominent among these is Robert Penn Warren, one of Dreiser's most sympathetic modern readers. "Theodore Dreiser was the immigrant," wrote Warren, "and though he himself had been born in America, his family was not of that world" (10). That this dizzying non sequitur appears at the start of *Homage to Theodore Dreiser* suggests that Warren's attempt to make Dreiser what he never was—an immigrant—should somehow honor the novelist. Or, read in the context of Mencken's and Bourne's more defensive intentions, that Dreiser's apparent (at least to Warren) Old World ethnicity must somehow answer the charge that bedevils all of the novelist's would-be champions: that Dreiser's writing style was coarse, plodding, and awkward. By relocating Dreiser on the wrong side of the hyphen, Warren collapses the question of style into the question of ethnicity: Dreiser writes like an immigrant because he is one. In using this tactic, Warren not only strains all the piquancy out of what Mencken memorably called "the Drei-ser bugaboo"—how could such an inept stylist write such powerful nov-els?—but also, much like today's liberal multiculturalists, forestalls any crit-icism of Dreiser's writing, because to question it is to attack his ethnic identity.

In making his claim about Dreiser's origin, Warren, like Sherman be-fore him, cannot rely on the facts but only on a series of metaphorical substitutions that he asserts are factual. Because Dreiser was an immigrant, contends Warren, "he was the outsider, the rejected, the yearner, and that fact [sic] conditions the basic emotions and the basic power of his work" (10). This line of reasoning also launches Thomas P. Riggio's essay "The-odore Dreiser: Hidden Ethnic," the only sustained treatment of the rela-tionship between the novelist's ethnicity and his writing. Quoting Warren's assertion approvingly at the start, Riggio describes Dreiser's prose as "heavy Germanic," and thus any contemporary "stress" on its "awkwardness" is "a hangover in literary circles of the early class and ethnic bias that shaped the original response to his writing" (57). This last charge might be true; however, in setting out to expose this bias, Riggio inadvertently reintro-duces it when he assumes the "German" nature of Dreiser's writing without bothering to explore or define what he means by this category of ethnicity.

Riggio's assumptions about what constitutes "ethnic" writing become more explicit in a footnote in which he takes pains to transport Dreiser back to the American side of the hyphen. "There is considerable value," argues Riggio, "in Dreiser's not having become a German-American Cahan, Di-Donato [sic], or whoever. His fictional portrayal of America was broader and deeper partly because it did not stop at the boundaries of an ethnic community" (63). What this statement assumes (if not quite enunciates) is that Dreiser's novels were broader and deeper than those by the Jewish-American Abraham Cahan and the Italian-American Pietro di Donato be-cause, unlike them, he wrote—at least in some of his novels—*purely* as an American. Riggio admits as much later: "Dreiser ultimately wrote with a feeling for the larger rhythms of tragedy in America, but his first books in this vein were shaped, in a muted way, around the polarities of native and ethnic identities" (62). Riggio refers here to *Sister Carrie* and *Jennie Ger-hardt,* books he has already named "hidden" and "open" ethnic texts respec-tively, thus adding surface/depth to the list of binaries—native/immigrant, inside/outside, accepted/rejected—that Warren has seen as organizing Dreiser's life and writing. This dyadic structure begins to totter, however, when Riggio's view of *Jennie Gerhardt* and *Sister Carrie* as ethnic texts comes into contact with his definition of American writing. If, as he asserts, American texts are broad, deep, and large, then by implication ethnic ones (including *Jennie Gerhardt* and *Sister Carrie*) must be narrow, superficial, and small. Thus, one finds Riggio employing such language as "muted," "subterranean," and "hidden" in an attempt to patch over the cracks in his argument so that two of Dreiser's major fictions might not fall through them (62, 53).

Riggio's phrase — "the polarities of native and ethnic identities" — nicely schematizes the binary model of ethnicity that sustains his, as well as Sherman's and Warren's, arguments. It is also the same polarized formulation that a certain academic multiculturalism depends on to authorize and maintain its movement from margin to center and the same opposition of "us" and "them" that bloodies our headlines. It is exactly this dichotomy, with its shifting assumptions about who is "American" and who is "ethnic," that I believe Dreiser resists and reimagines in *Jennie Gerhardt*, a book that, along with Bourne, I would say again is "not at all" German but is, like *Sister Carrie* and every other novel by that true hyphenate Dreiser, German-American.

The first time Dreiser attempts to figure the complexity of his own German-American ethnicity occurs shortly after Jennie Gerhardt, that "daughter of poverty," begins to visit George Brander, the junior senator from Ohio, at his elegant rooms in Columbus's most exclusive hotel. About the impoverished partner in this ill-matched relationship, Dreiser remarks:

> As for Jennie, she admired the conditions surrounding this man, and subconsciously the man himself, the most attractive she had ever known. Everything he had was fine, everything he did was gentle, distinguished, and considerate. From some far source, perhaps old German ancestors, she inherited an understanding and appreciation of this. Life ought to be lived as he lived it. One should have things of ornament and beauty about. (24)

Dreiser has earlier established his heroine's eye for ornamental beauty when, as the "tall, distinguished" Brander first passes her scrubbing the staircase of the Columbus House, she notices not, as her mother does, that he is a "fine-looking man" but that he carries a gold-headed cane (8). And again later, when they first enter Brander's chambers, "Mrs. Gerhardt looked principally at his handsome head, but Jennie studied the room," which she proclaims as "fine" (14, 16). At this point readers might comfortably understand the difference in the respective gazes of mother and daughter — Mrs. Gerhardt's is a communal one linking people, Jennie's a consumerist one desiring things — as marking something like the basic divide between ethnic and American perspectives that Warren and others assume. But the distinction is not so easy to maintain when Dreiser goes on to attribute Jennie's appreciation of fine things to "some far source, perhaps old German ancestors" (24). Dreiser's speculation suggests that the relationship between the Old and New Worlds is not simply polarized but is instead more complexly and usefully imagined as convergent.

The pivotal move in Dreiser's representation of a more confluent American ethnicity is his insistence on the word "fine" — fine-looking man, fine room, fine things. Whether spoken by Jennie or her mother, whether applied to an object or a person, Dreiser teaches us to read the word as always doubly inflected: "fine" in the older and more customary sense of displaying craftsmanship of great delicacy and care and "fine" in the newer consumerist sense of being expensive or indicative of wealth.[3] Which sense of the word is being accented more heavily in any given utterance is impossible to say. In these instances, the word "fine" functions as the point of convergence at which "German" and "American" come together or, if you will, as the hyphen in "German-American," now in Dreiser's usage a mark staking out not only a border or boundary but also a common ground. In Dreiser's re-visioning, ethnicity is not simply a set of attitudes, behaviors, and beliefs peculiar to a single national or racial group but also a shared condition that might bring together all (hyphenated) Americans. Like Bourne and Mencken, Dreiser is reminding us that we are all immigrants, or at least the descendants of them.

Dreiser again underscores the confluent aspect of our ethnicities when he describes the bitter Christmas season that the nearly destitute Gerhardts will likely endure. "The Germans love to make a great display at Christmas," explains Dreiser, accenting the Old World marking of the Gerhardts' hyphenated ethnicity to amplify the pathos of their New World economic deprivation (25). But we might also notice that Dreiser, despite being brought up in such a household himself, carefully avoids mentioning even a single detail of what would constitute "a great display" for a German immigrant family. Instead, he describes in only the most general terms the holiday celebration that he knows the Gerhardts would want but cannot afford:

> Warm in the appreciation of the joys of childhood, [the Germans] love to see the little ones have toys and games. Father Gerhardt, at his saw-buck during the weeks before Christmas, thought of this often. What would little Veronica not deserve after her long illness? How he would have liked to give each of the children a stout pair of shoes, the boys a warm cap, the girls a pretty hood. Toys and games and candy they had always had before. (25)

Having erased from the page every cultural specific that might be construed as German, Dreiser is free to bring together the Gerhardts' desires, however far beyond their present means, with the apparently endless bounties of an American consumer economy that rises up as if by magic to fulfill them: "The whole city was rife with the Christmas atmosphere. Grocery stores and meat markets were strung with holly. The toy-shops and candy-stores were radiant with fine displays of everything that a self-respecting Santa Claus should have about him" (26). Again we see the word "fine," by which Dreiser signals the conflation of the old and the new. Thus it comes as no surprise to the attentive reader that Santa Claus turns out to be not Kriss Kringle of German folk legend or even old Gerhardt himself but rather a U.S. senator of decidedly Anglo-Saxon extraction, assisted by an elfish Irish-American groceryman:

> "Manning," [Brander] said, "could I get you to undertake a little work for me this evening?"
> "Why certainly, Senator, certainly," said the groceryman.
> "I want you to get everything together that would make a nice Christmas for a family of eight—father and mother and six children—Christmas tree, groceries, toys—you know what I mean?"
> "Certainly, certainly, Senator," said Mr. Manning. (30)

So convergent are native and ethnic identities in Dreiser's representation that he allows this generous but nonetheless generic windfall to satisfy the Germans' love of "great display." So successful are the senator and the grocer that Mrs. Gerhardt is reduced to tears of joy, while the otherwise stern heart of her immigrant husband "melt[s] at the thought of the generosity of the unknown benefactor" (32).

There are, however, numerous passages in which the nationality before or after the hyphen is accented—sometimes literally so. The ones that are marked as *German*-American almost always concern old Gerhardt, and Dreiser often underscores this inflection by advising the reader that Gerhardt's words, though rendered in English, are spoken in his mother tongue. Even when this is not the case, as in a scene as ethnically convergent as the Christmas one, Dreiser insists that Gerhardt thinks and acts with "the simplicity of a German working-man" (32). For example, although Mrs. Gerhardt correctly suspects the source of the Christmas presents and Jennie knows "by instinct the author of it all," old Gerhardt is "inclined to lay it all to the goodness of a great local mill owner, who knew him and wished him well" (32). If, as Dreiser seems to suggest, Gerhardt is being obtuse when compared with Jennie and her mother, then it cannot be obtuseness about the mystery of the holiday munificence. After all, he has yet to learn of his wife's and especially his daughter's relationship with Senator Brander and thus is as acute as we might expect anyone to be when he reasons that the gifts probably came from a "local great" who wishes someone in the household well. Only the specific source and object of affection escape him. However, by setting Gerhardt's ethnicity against Jennie's "instinct," Dreiser points out the former's obtuseness in clinging to an Old World identity when the New World would seem to meet his needs and desires naturally — at least in this instance.

In the early sections of the novel the passages that are accented German-*American* usually focus on Jennie's brother, Sebastian, or, as his street buddies dub him, Bass. That this habit of reducing someone's given name to a brisk sobriquet (Bass likewise refers to his sister as "Jen") originates outside the family is perfectly consonant with Dreiser's depiction of the Gerhardt's oldest child as a profoundly American type — the young dandy on the make, moving up. Bass, Dreiser informs us, "was imbued with American color and energy":

> He knew all about ball-games and athletics, had heard that the state capital contained the high and mighty of the land, loved the theatre, with its suggestion of travel and advertisement, and was not unaware that to succeed one must do something — associate, or at least, seem to, with those who were foremost in the world of appearances. (11)

Bass draws on this devotion to appearances later when, confronted by one of the daily exigencies of poverty, he devises a theatrical scheme to get his family the coal that they must have for heat. Bass pretends to be what he clearly isn't — a gentleman — so that one of his waif-like sisters, herself pretending not to know her own brother, can beg him to throw down some coal from the railroad cars. As soon as this strange gentleman fills the childrens' various baskets and buckets, Dreiser tells us that there "came another gentleman, this time a real one, with high hat and distinguished cape-coat, whom Jennie immediately recognized" (29). The real gentleman turns out to be none other than Brander, and in giving Bass's scam this final twist, Dreiser cleverly foreshadows the Christmas scene in which the senator, himself pretending to be Kriss Kringle, will tend to the family's needs. In both masquerades, as elsewhere, Dreiser reminds us of the slipperiness and contingency of any category of identity in American culture.

Viewed with an interest in Dreiser's representation of ethnicity, the entire novel appears to be structured by and around this triangulation of

Jennie, old Gerhardt, and Bass, with the properly hyphenated daughter located between and above the extremes of her German father and her American brother. Even her name — poised between the ethnic Genevieve and the assimilated Jen — bespeaks this balance and convergence. The same organizing structure is mirrored, albeit distortedly, in the relationship that Lester Kane has with his father, Archibald, and his brother, Robert. Unlike Jennie, Lester seems unable to attain the kind of equilibrium that a hyphenated American ethnicity demands. "The trouble with Lester," Dreiser explains soon after this headstrong scion of a wealthy Cincinnati carriage builder strides into the novel, "was that the complicated and incisive nature of his mind, coupled with his very robust physique, as well as the social and somewhat unintellectual nature of his duties, tended to produce a rather unbalanced condition" (127). The lion's share of the imbalance in this "essentially animal man" Dreiser traces back to Lester's Irish ancestors "who, in his father's day, had worked on the railroad tracks, dug in the mines, picked and shoveled in the ditches, carried up bricks and mortar on the endless structures of a new land" (126). Here, in contrast to Jennie, whose consumerist vision converges so happily with a customary attention to craft, Lester's ethnic heritage struggles against his fortunate social circumstances and against an otherwise "vigorous, aggressive, and sound personality" to produce a mental condition that Dreiser diagnoses as "confused" and beleaguered by "uncertainty" (126, 125).

Lester's unbalanced condition, however, does not keep his father from taking this second son as his favorite. In fact, the closeness of their relationship seems based in large part on their shared ethnicity, although Dreiser's depiction of the Irishness of the senior Kane is far less explicit than was his portrait of the Germanness of the elder Gerhardt. Dreiser does have one of Archibald Kane's competitors tell us that he is a "fine" man, and he also burdens the successful industrialist with "an old Irish servitor," so stock and loyal a figure that he speaks in a kind of brogue and rubs his hands "much in the spirit that a dog might wag his tail" when the favored son returns from Columbus to the family mansion (137, 139). But Dreiser mainly characterizes Archibald in terms of his honesty, as someone who theorizes that "most men were honest, that at bottom they wanted honest things, and if you gave them these they would buy of you and come back and buy again and again until you were an influential and rich man" (127). Dreiser's ethical business idiom seamlessly brings together the demands of an Old World morality and the desire for a New World commercial success. This suggests that in the Kane family it is Archibald himself who most closely approximates the ethnic convergence that Jennie modeled for us earlier in the novel. Kane's honesty in making his fortune is impossible to disentangle from his honesty in dealing with his fellow citizens in general. Thus, as is the case with "fine," the word "honest" is always doubly inflected, serving as a kind of intersection between "Irish" and "American."

From his father, then, the otherwise confused Lester gets the idea of "the need of being honest," although, as the rest of the novel demonstrates, he must always struggle to realize the richness of this inheritance (126). Another quality that Lester shares with his father, to a likewise limited extent, is "bigness." Dreiser's use of this word — he applies it to Jennie as well — is idiosyncratic, implying something like breadth of vision or ability to grasp life in all its complexity and subtlety. In the context of the passages of the novel more obviously marked as ethnic, "bigness" might also be read in the more specific sense of the capability to contain and successfully balance the ancestral markers on either side of the hyphen. "He's a big man," announces the same competitor who pointed out Archibald Kane's fineness, and we might by now understand that what is being underscored here is the way in which Kane, "shrewd but honest," has managed to make the moral teachings of his Irish heritage pay off in America (137). When Lester comes on the scene, a friend of the Kanes (Mr. Bracebridge) similarly remarks, "He's the biggest one in that family." Bracebridge, however, immediately qualifies his praise by adding, "But he's too indifferent. He doesn't care enough" (120). Indifferent about what, Mr. Bracebridge never says exactly; but it becomes apparent through the course of the novel that in large part he is referring to Lester's relative indifference to the "American" half of his hyphenated ethnicity — specifically his lack of interest in maintaining his family's business success and the high standing in American social life that comes with it.

Lester's older brother, Robert, is much more concerned with what Dreiser calls "the money relationship." Because of his narrower vision, Robert "was his father's right-hand man from a financial point of view" (137). "He's got a Scotch Presbyterian conscience," Lester complains about Robert, the ethnic idiom nicely suggesting just how thoroughly assimilated this Irish-Catholic entrepreneur has become to Anglo-Saxon business practices (169). That Robert is devoted to the main chance becomes clear when he and Lester clash over the proper way to run their father's business. Although Lester argues that they should continue Archibald's older and more customary methods — "friendly relationships, concessions, personal contacts and favors" — to build up trade, Robert favors instead a total break

with the past (171). The Kane Carriage Manufacturing Company, he believes, should become streamlined for the kind of mass production that
Stuart and Elizabeth Ewen claim was one half of a "double prong of Ameri-
canization" (36). Not surprisingly, Dreiser has the elder Kane attempt to
maintain a mediate position between his two sons: although he agrees with
Robert's assessment of where the future of the business lies, he admires
Lester's kindliness and wishes "it could be worked out in connection with
the success of the company" (171).

Before Archibald's wish can be realized, however, the battle for control
of the carriage factory comes to a head when Robert proposes breaking off
from "an old and well-established paint company in New York" to reinvest
in a more modernized concern in Chicago (187). As usual, Lester opposes
such a move largely on the grounds of the "long and friendly relationship"
that the Kanes have enjoyed with the New York firm; but Robert answers,
in the most baldly "American" terms imaginable: "We can't go on forever
standing by old friends, just because Father here has dealt with them or you
like them," he argues. "We must have a change. The business must be hard
and strong" (188). To the cold, coming logic of the modern capitalist, the
elder Kane can only capitulate, at the last reducing his honesty to the recognition that, in American business life, self-interest is defined by and limited
to profit and loss.

To this defeat Lester feigns his characteristic indifference, but its shock
drives him farther away from his family and deeper into his entanglement
with Jennie. With him, the remainder of the novel now reconfigures itself
once again, this last time into its most important triangulation—the one
that connects Jennie with her own father and Lester. At the heart of this
final structuring we shouldn't be surprised to find another ethnic passage,
not a literal one to be sure but the very one that I believe preoccupies
Dreiser throughout the novel—the death of old Gerhardt.[4]

To anyone interested in fiction written by Americans of immigrant descent—which is really to say most of American literature—*Jennie Gerhardt*
might offer itself as a remarkable anticipation of and sequel to one of the
major texts in the up-from-the-ghetto tradition: Anzia Yezierska's novel,
Bread Givers. To assert that Dreiser's 1911 book anticipates Yezierska's 1925
one should not be surprising, because both narratives are centrally concerned with the progress of a youthful heroine from urban poverty to
middle-class security or at least, in Jennie's case, its appearances. No matter how vast their specific differences, ethnic and otherwise, both young

daughters must struggle against aging patriarchs to achieve their rise in social and economic status. That Dreiser's novel "continues" Yezierska's is perhaps a more surprising claim. For many contemporary critics and readers, the most troubling if not confounding part of *Bread Givers* is its ending, in which Yezierska's heroine, Sara Smolinsky, having at long last attained the petit bourgeois respectability that a Columbia University degree and a grade-school teaching position proclaim, reconciles with the rabbi father whose religious orthodoxy has hampered her upward mobility at every turn. After marrying the principal of her school and then taking in the ailing Reb Smolinsky, the usually hopeful and independent Sara concludes the novel on an ominous note: "But I felt the shadow still there, over me. It wasn't just my father, but the generations who made my father whose weight was still upon me" (297). What I think the second half of *Jennie Gerhardt* affords us is a chance to see how the introduction of an immigrant-inflected ethnicity into a modern American household might turn out and, more important, how Dreiser, himself a middle-class success, bears up under the weight of the generations who made his own father.

The refocusing of the plot of *Jennie Gerhardt* onto the figure of the father begins in earnest when, shortly before he finally loses his battle for control of the carriage business to his older brother, Lester meets old Gerhardt for the first time. The timing of their meeting is not fortuitous. Dreiser manages Lester's brief first impression of Jennie's father so deftly that it is impossible not to read it through the younger Kane's preoccupation with his own family's problems. Having paid little attention to either Gerhardt or his wife, Lester thinks, "The old German appeared to him to be merely commonplace. These were such people as his foreman hired" (173). In this way, Dreiser has Lester bring Gerhardt, if only imaginatively, into the family business, but at a most unpropitious moment since "the old German" cannot escape being seen as one of those aged employees that Robert, after Archibald's eventual surrender, will let go in his drive to run the company "on a hard and cold basis" (170). The full implications of this brief encounter can only be realized later when Lester, committed to a more customary course than his brother, takes in the injured and nearly homeless Gerhardt who, after his wife dies and his children abandon him, has been sleeping in the furniture plant at which he works as a night watchman. Lester is compensating here not only for the bad behavior of Jennie's siblings — "fine" children he calls them, this time with an unmistakably ironic cast — but also for Robert's sharp business practices and especially for his father's failure to be loyal to those "old fellows" who had helped him build the Kane Carriage Manufacturing Company (170). In acting toward old Gerhardt in a way that his father had once believed his employees deserved, Lester lives up to the need of being honest better than honest Archibald ever did. Thus he manages, at least in this one instance, to bring together into productive equilibrium both sides of his hyphenated identity.

Old Gerhardt is less successful at finding his balance. Despite Lester's example, he is still the same hard-headed German immigrant to whom Dreiser introduced us at the start. Gerhardt's vision of ethnicity remains to the end the most polarized of anyone's in the novel. He declares, for instance, that "in Germany they knew how to do these things right, but these shiftless Americans knew nothing" (254). Yet it is in the slightly goofy experiment in communal living that Lester, Jennie, and old Gerhardt set up on the far South Side of Chicago that Dreiser comes closest to suggesting a utopian possibility in *Jennie Gerhardt*. Against the backdrop of the fracturing of the Kane and Gerhardt families (and against his memory of the atomizing of his own German immigrant one), Dreiser imagines a household run according to an economy of abundance and cooperation. In doing so he finally manages to align the values, behaviors, and desires of the Old and New Worlds. This economy is most clearly realized in the relationship between old Gerhardt and Lester, both of whom begin to prosper in ways that the dominant economy of scarcity and competition had previously frustrated: Lester is able to realize the business ideals that his father finally could not; old Gerhardt is allowed to work and succeed according to the values of his proud German working-class heritage.

There is nothing exceptional about the contract to which Lester and old Gerhardt originally agree: in exchange for room and board in Lester's household, old Gerhardt will serve as a kind of hired man whose "steady job" is "running the furnace of a country house" (250). To this basic service, however, the simple German workingman willingly adds a whole host of "self-established duties" (342):

> Gerhardt was there, as has been indicated, to look after the details usually taken care of by a hired man, and he did so much more faithfully and effectively. In spite of his age, and he was very well along in years now — crotchety, fussy, inquiring — he was about the house and grounds, mornings and evenings, picking up sticks and pieces of paper that might have blown in, exchanging neighborly greetings with the stableman, the postman, the milkman, the newspaper peddler and whoever else happened to have any regular or passing business with the establishment. (265)

As Gerhardt sees them, his responsibilities also extend indoors, where he follows Lester, Jennie, and the servants about the house, "turning out the gas-jets or electric-light bulbs which might accidentally have been left burning, and complaining of extravagance" (265).

Within such an economy, even Gerhardt's idiosyncratic German thriftiness, so troublesome to his own assimilating children, can contribute meaningfully to the construction and maintenance of the only instance of "delightful" family life in the novel (264). And through his selflessness, the almost suicidally depressed Gerhardt is himself revitalized:

> From having sunk to the place where he had considered all life more or less a failure — his own in particular — and having wanted nothing so much as to die, he had risen to the place where he now felt that there were a few more years ahead of him, and that he would be able to do considerable work in the world. (265)

The household that Dreiser imagines is so ideal that Lester's characteristic American consumerist extravagance, no matter how irritating to the thrifty German, also pays off. Lester's profligacy with wooden matches, for instance, becomes a ready source of lighters for Gerhardt's own pipe and for the kindling he uses to fire the furnace he tends. The crowning achievement of this economy of abundance, however, is the old German's frugal recycling of Lester's regularly discarded clothing. Lester's garments, when cut down to his own size, not only supply Gerhardt with more work clothes than he will ever need, but also can be sold to secondhand clothes dealers for money to be donated to his beloved Lutheran church. What Dreiser has staged here is a situation in which neither Lester nor old Gerhardt need budge from their polarized positions as American capitalist and German workingman. Somehow they together produce a community so utopian that all of their needs and desires are met and nothing is wasted (266–67).

Dreiser, however, cannot long sustain his compensatory and wish-fulfilling fantasy of family life, and in this inability we feel most strongly the pressure that the novelist's own family history exerts on the text. Dreiser began to write *Jennie Gerhardt* on January 6, 1901, less than two weeks after his own father Johann Paul Dreiser passed away. At the time of his death, old Dreiser was living peacefully in the home of his daughter Mame and her husband, Austin Brennan, and, as Richard Lingeman has suggested, these circumstances — a father who has reconciled with a daughter whom he had earlier disowned because of her promiscuity — supplied Dreiser with the "seed of a novel" (306). Such a biographical reading, however, might prompt us to equate Jennie and Mame rather than, as I have been trying to suggest, Jennie and Dreiser himself. Both are examples of Bourne's "true hyphenates."

Although Jennie brings together her father and her lover into the novel's most balanced alignment, what inevitably conjoins these two men also contains the woman. The one thing that this otherwise ideal community cannot confer on Jennie, or on themselves as a community, is a sense of legitimacy, an incapacity figured by the marriage certificate that the old German badly wants to see and that Lester always wants to avoid discussing (250). More important, this fragile equilibrium between opposites demands that Jennie never speak of, let alone act on, her own desires. She must instead, like Dreiser, submit to fiction at every turn: for Gerhardt's sake she must appear to be a loving and dutiful wife, and for Lester's she must not press for the legal and social status that such a performance usually deserves. The cost of Dreiser's ethnic utopia, then, is silence and self-sacrifice.

The death of old Gerhardt, like the death of old Dreiser, frees the hyphenate child from the constraints involved in sustaining the tenuous union between the Old and New World ethnicities. But the death of the old German seems as well to propel the plot of the novel toward a whole series of losses that Jennie must endure: the loss of Lester to Letty Pace, the death of Vesta, and finally the death of Lester himself. In the end, it is Jennie herself who is left alone to embody and sustain the hyphenated ethnicity that Dreiser has imagined for her, one that entails a significantly diminished horizon, charged with a nostalgia for the economy of abundance and cooperation that she and her father and her lover realized only once, and then too briefly. After this series of deaths, Jennie learns to scale down her bigness, adapting to the province others considered appropriate for someone of her stature and resources. She gives up her dreams of social work and teaching and fashions an existence out of what remains available to her. She continues to "believe in giving," and to spend the remainder of her life (and Kane's trust fund) in a Gerhardt-like "care of flowers, the care of children, the looking after and maintaining the order of a home" (397). Dreiser, too, goes on to accommodate but also refashion the demands of what critics saw as legitimately American writing. *Jennie Gerhardt* might therefore be seen as the first and only immigrant fiction that Dreiser wrote, and certainly old Gerhardt is the last major character of Dreiser's to be openly marked as German. Still it must be said that all of Dreiser's novels, whatever their various emphases and concerns, imagine and negotiate a sometimes convergent, always complex hyphenated Americanness that resists being reduced to a simple — and thus potentially lifeless — opposition between so-called ethnic and native identities.

Notes

1. My notion of a liberal multiculturalism, and its emergence as dominant in the academy, is drawn from Spivak.
2. For a fuller discussion of this issue, see Oliver.
3. For a definition of "customary" in the sense that I am using it, see Ewen (224).
4. My use of the phrase "ethnic passage," as well as my reading of *Jennie Gerhardt,* is indebted to Ferraro.

Bibliography

Bourne, Randolph. "The Art of Theodore Dreiser." In *The History of a Literary Radical.* New York: B. W. Huebsch, 1920. Reprinted in Kazin, 92–95.
Ewen, Stuart and Elizabeth. *Channels of Desire: Mass Images and the Shaping of American Consciousness.* Minneapolis: University of Minnesota Press, 1992.
Ferraro, Thomas J. *Ethnic Passages: Literary Immigrants in Twentieth-Century America.* Chicago: University of Chicago Press, 1993.
Kazin, Alfred and Charles Shapiro, eds. *The Stature of Theodore Dreiser.* Bloomington: Indiana University Press, 1955.
Lingeman, Richard. *Theodore Dreiser: At the Gates of the City, 1871–1907.* Vol. 1. New York: G. P. Putnam's Sons, 1986.
Mencken, H. L. "The Dreiser Bugaboo." *The Seven Arts* (August 1917). Reprinted in Kazin, 84–91.
Oliver, Lawrence J. "Deconstruction or Affirmative Action: The Literary-Political Debate over the 'Ethnic Question.'" *American Literary History* 3 (Winter 1991): 792–808.
Riggio, Thomas P. "Theodore Dreiser: Hidden Ethnic." *MELUS* 11 (Spring 1984): 53–63.
Sherman, Stuart P. "The Barbaric Naturalism of Mr. Dreiser." *Nation,* 2 December 1915. Reprinted in Kazin, 71–80.
Spivak, Gayatari Chakravorty. "Teaching for the Times." *Journal of the Midwest Modern Language Association* 25 (Spring 1992): 3–22.
Warren, Robert Penn. *Homage to Theodore Dreiser.* New York: Random House, 1971.
Yezierska, Anzia. *Bread Givers.* New York: Persea Books, 1975.

Samuel E. [G]ross:
Dreiser's Real Estate Magnate

EMILY CLARK

THE IMPORTANCE OF HOME OWNERSHIP is a recurrent theme in *Jennie Gerhardt*. In the early sections of the novel, the Gerhardt family strives and hopes for a real home; in the later chapters, the period that Jennie and Lester spend in their home in Hyde Park is the time during which they are most like a true family. Near the end of their semi-idyllic life in Hyde Park, Lester goes into business with a real estate dealer, Samuel E. Ross, who is based on an actual Chicago real estate developer of the time, Samuel E. Gross. By examining the career of Gross, one can learn a good deal about the meaning of home ownership as Dreiser presents it in this novel.

Samuel Eberly Gross, who was active in the late nineteenth and early twentieth centuries, built more than twenty-one subdivisions and ten thousand homes, mostly for working- and middle-class citizens. After serving in the Civil War and earning a law degree, he embarked on a real estate career in Chicago in the late 1860s. His arrival in Chicago coincided with the post–Civil War building boom, and he eagerly joined the rush, purchasing property on which he began to build houses in 1867. Even at this early stage of his career, he was confident in his business acumen and welcomed the investment opportunities in the rapidly growing city. In 1868 he wrote to his mother, "What I invest in real estate is pretty sure of not being lost unless the city sinks" (Letter, February 13, 1868).

Chicago did not sink, but it was devastated by the Great Chicago Fire

Portions of this essay are based on research done for a Chicago Historical Society exhibition "The Merchant Prince of Cornville: S. E. Gross and His Subdivisions," and on an article, "The Merchant Prince of Cornville," *Chicago History* 21 (December 1992). I would like to acknowledge the contributions to that research of my cocurator and coauthor, Patrick Ashley. In addition, see my essay "Own Your Own Home: S. E. Gross, the Great Domestic Promoter," forthcoming in the proceedings of the 1992 Winterthur Museum conference, "The American Home: Material Culture, Domestic Space and Family Life." All illustrations in this chapter are from the collections of the Chicago Historical Society.

"[He] was a magnetic-looking person of about fifty years of age, tall, black-bearded after the Van Dyke pattern. . . ." (*Jennie Gerhardt* 327)

of 1871. To save his business, Gross gathered his papers and rowed them to a tugboat in the Chicago River. He was thus able to resume his business activities shortly after the disaster. The rebuilding of the city after the fire attracted architects and builders from across the nation, who flocked to Chicago to take advantage of new opportunities. The frantic pace of the city's reconstruction was checked by the nationwide depression of the mid to late 1870s, however, and Gross, like other developers, suffered. Building construction began to revive after the 1870s, and Gross's career again flourished. In the years between the fire and 1890, Chicago's population grew to roughly four times its prefire size. Through annexation, the city spread to outlying areas. As transportation methods improved, the working and middle classes were no longer compelled to live in the central city. "The man who for years was exposed to that grinding monopoly, the old Chicago boarding house or hotel, determined to look beyond the inside district for a home and build on the selected site a house for which he could call his own. The shrewd real-estate man saw his opportunity" (*Industrial Chicago* 278).

In the 1880s Gross began developing working-class subdivisions throughout the Chicago area. For instance, his New City development drew prospective residents from the workers in the meat-packing plants and related industries of the Union Stockyards, and his Gross Park area catered to German laborers and businessmen from the nearby brickyards and Deering Harvester works. In these developments, Gross tapped into the need for affordable single-family homes for the working classes, a demand not adequately met by other developers.

Gross's success in providing homes for the working classes can be tied to three factors: locating his developments on the outskirts of the city, connecting his subdivisions to the growing public transportation system, and employing advancements in building technology. The working classes appreciated the affordable homes that he provided, particularly as he allowed his customers to make only a small down payment and continue with low monthly payments.

Building in the outlying areas of the city was critical, as the city government had passed ordinances after the Great Chicago Fire that limited the construction of frame buildings within the city limits. Gross circumvented these ordinances by developing tracts that lay outside the fire limits. These areas were becoming increasingly manageable as residential sites: public transportation systems were being improved, and more industries were moving outside the central city. Gross shrewdly selected sites that were — or soon would be — accessible to the city by transportation lines.

South-east corner Dearborn and Randolph Sts.

"What was now far-out prairie property would soon — in the course of a few years — be well built-up suburban residence territory." (*Jennie Gerhardt* 332)

It is known through court records that Gross entered in 1887 into a partnership with Charles T. Yerkes, the traction magnate, to develop an addition to his Gross Park subdivision. (Yerkes was of course the inspiration for Dreiser's Frank Cowperwood in *The Financier, The Titan,* and *The Stoic.*) Yerkes sued Gross in 1899 for failing to subdivide, improve, and sell the lots; Gross argued, in turn, that Yerkes had not performed his own duties and had neglected "to procure the running of cars often enough to accommodate travel to and from the vicinity" (*Yerkes v. Gross,* 1899).

Gross kept construction costs down and homes affordable by purchasing mass-produced materials in bulk quantities and building from standardized plans. But building a successful subdivision involved more than selecting an advantageous site and erecting inexpensive homes. The land had to be surveyed and platted; sewer, gas, and water lines (none of which was standard on Chicago-area property at the time) and streetlights had to be installed; sidewalks and roads had to be laid; and trees needed to be planted. After these improvements were made — or often before — Gross set up a branch office at the subdivision and began his marketing campaign.

Once a lot was purchased, the new owner could build his own home or could contract with Gross to have a dwelling built from the more than four hundred house plans he had available. Sometimes less than a year elapsed between the time Gross purchased the land and the building of the first homes. He also added major improvements to some of his subdivisions, such as schools, train stations, and meeting halls. Gross was proud of his ability to quickly transform a wide expanse of virgin soil into a prosperous, bustling community of homes and commercial buildings.

What truly set Gross apart, however, was his mastery of promotion and marketing. Like Dreiser's character Ross in *Jennie Gerhardt,* Gross was more flamboyant in his techniques than were other Chicago real estate developers of the time. To advertise his subdivisions his office churned out colorful pamphlets, catalogs, and broadsides that were distributed freely to interested customers. Gross specifically targeted the immigrant population of Chicago by advertising extensively in German-, Swedish-, and Italian-language newspapers, in addition to papers targeted at labor unions and the Jewish population.

It was probably owing to the profusion of Gross's advertising that Dreiser became aware of him. Dreiser himself worked for a real estate developer while in Chicago as a young man in the early 1890s (Lingeman 80). Dreiser's employer was not especially successful and would not have traveled in Gross's circles, but at that point Gross was at the height of his

". . . his rather conspicuous offices . . . windows replete with gold lettering stating his name over and over." (*Jennie Gerhardt* 327)

career and his name was probably a household word to many Chicagoans — particularly to those who, like young Dreiser, were involved in the real estate business.

When Lester Kane is searching for a new means of making money, he encounters the real estate developer Ross at the Union Club (of which Gross was in fact a member). Lester trusts Ross because he has seen "his signs out on the prairie stretches, and . . . his ads in the daily papers" (331). To Lester this indicates a certain reality and integrity. Citizens of Chicago might have assumed the same inherent trustworthiness of Gross simply by virtue of the ubiquitousness of his advertisements. Ross described the special qualities he possessed that made him so successful — qualities that Gross also exhibited: "There was something in prestige, something in taste, something in psychic apprehension. . . . [He was] the presiding genius" (330). Ross convinces Lester of his reliability, and they form a partnership to develop an area on the south side of the city.

One example that Dreiser gives of Ross's taste and genius is his selection of the name for the subdivision that he and Lester are to develop. "It was given a rather attractive title — 'Inwood,' although . . . there was precious little wood anywhere around there" (333). Ross assures Lester that the name will attract people looking for a suburban home. "Seeing the notable efforts in tree-planting that had been made to provide for shade in the future, they would take the will for the deed" (333). This is quite similar to Gross's choice of names such as "Under the Linden" and "Brookdale" for his subdivisions and is reminiscent also of his inclusion of winding roads and tree plantings in his developments. By giving the illusion of bucolic surroundings, or "arcadia," Gross could make his areas seem more appealing to those living in the overcrowded city.

But in *Jennie Gerhardt* Ross is thwarted in his ambitions for his subdivision. It is rumored that a meat-packing plant is going to relocate into the vicinity, and buyers are alarmed:

> The mere suspicion that the packing company might invade the territory was sufficient to blight the prospects of any budding real-estate deal. . . . Ross was beside himself with rage. . . . He decided, after quick deliberation, that the best thing to do would be to boom the property heavily, by means of newspaper advertising, and see if it could not be disposed of before any additional damage was likely to be done to it. . . . The additional sum of $3,000 was spent in ten days, to make it appear that Inwood was an ideal residence section, equipped with every modern convenience for the home-lover, and destined to be one of the most exclusive and beautiful residence sections of the city. It was "no go" . . . from any point of view, save that of a foreign-population neighborhood, [and] the enterprise was a failure. (333–34)

In reality, Gross did not view proximity to the stockyards as a handicap to the development of a subdivision. In one advertisement for his "New City" subdivision he enticed customers with the following claim: "350 men now working the Packing Houses have bought homes from me. . . . Why shouldn't you?" (*Tenth Annual . . . Catalogue* 60). But Dreiser's take on the situation does bring up the question of how honest Gross's advertisements were. Did he put on the pressure of lavish ads, touting the desirable traits of his subdivisions, only when he was most desperate for sales? Or were these ads simply an extension of his genius? Was he truly sympathetic to the needs of the foreign born and working classes by targeting his *housing* to those

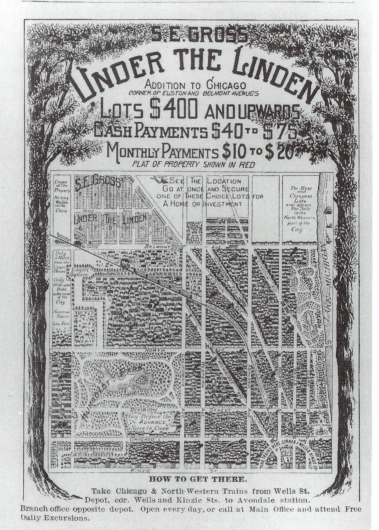

". . . the title was good business from a practical point of view, for Chicago, being as yet so largely treeless, and people looking for some section even partially equipped with trees, would be attracted by the name." (*Jennie Gerhardt* 333)

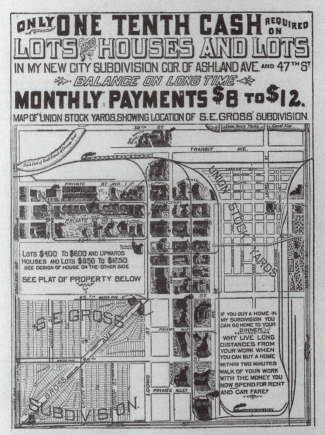

". . . the mere suspicion that the packing company might invade the territory was sufficient to blight the prospects of any budding real-estate deal." (*Jennie Gerhardt* 333)

groups? Or was he more mercenary by targeting his *advertisements* to those groups only when the ideal clients had not responded?

A recurrent theme that Gross cleverly manipulated in his advertising was the "cult of domesticity" that had become popular by the midnineteenth century. This middle-class movement idealized the home as the embodiment of stability, good citizenship, moral development, dedication to family, communion with nature, and protection from the vices of the city. Gross exploited these domestic images by emphasizing the superiority of home ownership in his publicity. A craving for this ideal of domesticity recurs throughout *Jennie Gerhardt* and is in many ways a direct cause of Jennie's liaisons with Senator Brander and Lester Kane. The Gerhardt family is destitute, and Jennie, more than anything, would like to provide her family with a home. When Lester offers Jennie just that, in return for her love and companionship, she is

> shocked and yet drawn by this siren song of aid, [and runs] along in thought to the full significance as far as her mother [is] concerned. All her life long Mrs. Gerhardt had been talking of this very thing, a nice home. If they could just have a nice home, a larger house with good furniture and a yard filled with trees, how happy she would be. In it they would be free of the care of rent, the commonplaceness of poor furniture, the wretchedness of poverty. (157)

Jennie obtains a home for her parents and eventually one for herself with Lester, although at a price. Late in her life she is finally able to make an independent, albeit humble home for herself; but she lives in it as a single mother, with only her two adopted children for company.

Running throughout Gross's advertisements and writings was his strong belief that a home was not simply a shelter from the elements but rather stood for something much more important. His attitude toward the home went beyond economic interest: to him it was a concrete, outward display of a person's drive for self-sufficiency and independence. A home was a visible sign of a person's achievements and position in life, a sign that was as valid and appropriate for the working man as it was for the middle- and upper-class breadwinner. Gross felt that all men should be able to afford homes of their own and that owning these dwellings made them better citizens, for they then had vested interests in their communities. None other than Henry Ward Beecher had stated the idea quite clearly: "A house is the shape which a man's thoughts take when he imagines how he should like to live. Its interior is the measure of his social and domestic nature; its exterior, of his aesthetic and artistic nature. It interprets, in material form, his ideas of home, of friendship, and of comfort" (104). It is true that Gross manipulated these themes in his advertisements, but it appears from his other writings, and from published interviews with him, that he did indeed have a genuine commitment to the idea of "The Home" and its social utility. Dreiser uses these ideas in *Jennie Gerhardt* to present Jennie, her family, and even Lester as sympathetic characters and to explain their motivations.

Jennie's willingness to undertake liaisons with Senator Brander and Lester Kane, without benefit of marriage, can be tied to her desire to provide a comfortable home for her family. Her mission throughout her life with Lester is to create and maintain a home for him. However, in the end his own desire for a home life that more appropriately befits his station in life contributes strongly to his decision to marry Letty. When he leaves Jennie, she does not demand exorbitant sums of money from him — only enough to allow her to maintain a modest cottage, the kind of home appropriate for her. It is also fitting that Lester should get involved with a real estate dealer who specializes in homes for the working classes, as Lester's sympathies lie with the workers in his dealings with his family's company.

Although Gross had a long career and was more successful than Dreiser's Ross, he too failed in the end. In April 1908 he declared bankruptcy. The cause of his failure at the time was given as "unwise speculation," but it was probably also influenced by the financial panic of 1907. Gross's fortunes had certainly fallen from his net worth of $5 million, as estimated at the peak of his career, but he was hardly destitute. At the time of his death on October 24, 1913, his estate was valued at $150,000.

Bibliography

Beecher, Henry Ward. "Building a House." *Star Papers.* New York: Derby & Jackson, 1859. Quoted in Clifford E. Clark, Jr., *The American Family Home, 1800–1960,* 104. Chapel Hill: University of North Carolina Press, 1986.

Charles T. Yerkes v. S. E. Gross, Circuit Court of Cook County (1899).

S. E. Gross to Elizabeth Gross, 13 February 1868. S. E. Gross Collection, Chicago Historical Society, Archives and Manuscripts Department.

Industrial Chicago. 6 vols. Chicago: Goodspeed Publishing Co., 1891, 1:278.

Tenth Annual Illustrated Catalogue of S. E. Gross' Famous City Subdivisions and Suburban Towns. Chicago: S. E. Gross, 1891.

18
The Hotel World in *Jennie Gerhardt*

JAMES L. W. WEST III

LIKE MANY AMERICANS OF HIS TIME, Theodore Dreiser was fascinated by the world of the hotel. He knew it from his days as a reporter and feature writer; some of his earliest journalistic efforts, in fact, were anecdotes and brief interviews gathered in the corridors and lobbies of major urban hostelries (*Journalism* 79–84). Dreiser was familiar with the elaborate culture of hotel life that had developed in the United States by the 1890s. This culture flourished in large American cities, where industrialists, politicians, entertainers, sports figures, and traveling businessmen patronized large and opulent establishments. Luxury hotels, and the separate worlds that they encompass, play important roles in several of Dreiser's novels — *Sister Carrie* and *An American Tragedy,* for example — but they are perhaps most evident and significant in *Jennie Gerhardt.* In this story about social pressure and convention, hotels are valuable refuges where rules can be suspended temporarily. They are arenas in which persons of various classes and occupations can come together, often moving temporarily up or down the social ladder; they are also protected spaces for people who wish to escape convention, to assume other identities for a time, or to mask their behavior from the larger society.

Hotels in turn-of-the-century America were often identified with particular cities. Usually they were located near downtown centers of shopping and commerce, and often they were marked by innovative or fanciful architecture (Raitz). The best-known ones were sources of much civic pride: New York and Chicago, for example, competed during the 1890s over

For her generosity in sharing materials and giving helpful advice, I wish to thank Molly W. Berger, a Ph.D. candidate and American Antiquarian Society Fellow, 1993–94, Department of History, Case Western Reserve University. Ms. Berger's thesis is entitled "The Modern Hotel in America, 1829–1929." I wish also to thank Debra Morris, a Ph.D. candidate in English at Pennsylvania State University, who at my suggestion undertook a term-paper project on the hotel in Dreiser's work in a 1987 seminar on the American novel. Ms. Morris kindly shared some source material and references with me.

which city had the largest and most stylish hotels, just as they would compete a few decades later over which city had the tallest skyscrapers (Boorstin). Major hotels were often marvels of engineering and technological innovation. Journalists of the time were fond of reporting how many tons of iron and steel, how many miles of wiring, how many acres of floor space, and how many square feet of plate glass were to be found in these enormous establishments.

In *Jennie Gerhardt* one finds mention of several actual American hotels: the Arlington Hotel in Washington, D.C.; the Southern Hotel in St. Louis; and the Grand Pacific, the Tremont House, and the Auditorium in Chicago. Famous international hotels also make appearances: the Savoy and Claridge's in London and Shepheard's in Cairo. One finds notice too of well-known resorts and mineral-water spas: Mt. Clemens in Michigan, West Baden Springs in Indiana, White Sulphur Springs in West Virginia, Saratoga Springs in New York, Baden-Baden in Germany, Carlsbad in Bohemia, and Scheveningen in the Netherlands. In part these upper-class hotels and resorts are present in the narrative to add realism and to alert readers to the fact that Lester Kane moves in circles of wealth and power. On a different level, though, these hotels provide settings for many important scenes in the novel — scenes of seduction, negotiation, confession, and death.

Jennie Gerhardt begins in a relatively modest hotel, the Columbus House, where Jennie and her mother go to find work. This hotel is a familiar place in their city; Bass, Jennie's oldest brother, likes to loiter there with his friends in the evenings. He and his cronies are attracted by the glow and shine of the hotel; they shed their backgrounds of poverty and toil, don their flashiest clothes, light up two-for-five-cent cigars, and eye the women who pass. For them the Columbus House is a place in which to take on a different identity for a few hours and observe the well-to-do classes.

Jennie and her mother are awed, initially at least, by the Columbus House. Some day Jennie will stay in much finer hotels, but for now this one represents luxury and privilege to her and her mother. Dreiser describes their first impressions of the hotel this way:

> The lobby was large, and had been recently redecorated. Both floor and wainscot were of white marble, kept shiny by frequent polishing. There was an imposing staircase with hand-rails of walnut and toe strips of brass. An inviting corner was devoted to a news and cigar stand. Where the staircase curved upward the clerk's desk and offices had been located, all done in hardwood and ornamented by novel gas fixtures. One could see through a door at one end of

the lobby to the barber-shop, with its chairs and array of shaving mugs. Outside were usually to be seen two or three buses, arriving or departing in accor-
dance with the movement of the trains. . . . Mother and daughter, brought into
this realm of brightness, saw only that which was far off and immensely superior. They went about too timid to touch anything, for fear of giving offense.
(6–7)

It is important that Jennie should first encounter Senator Brander on
the lobby staircase of the Columbus House. There is much symbolism in
the scene: the senator has just entered the hotel from the world outside; he
wears a "silk hat and loose military cape-coat," which mark him as "some
one of importance" (8). He mounts the front stairs on the way to his private chambers, and his eye is caught by Jennie, who has been scrubbing the
steps on her hands and knees. She stands to let him pass, and he notices her
beauty—"the high, white forehead, with its smoothly parted and plaited
hair," her "mouth and full cheeks," and her "well-rounded, graceful form"
(8). This encounter leads to a closer relationship in which Jennie and her
mother gain admittance to the senator's rooms so that they can pick up and
deliver his laundry. Jennie loves these rooms, with their expensive masculine knick-knacks, their comfortable furniture and green-shaded lamps,
their elegant carpeting, and their air of "mannish comfort" (14). They
represent a different world to her, offering glimpses of how a person of
wealth and influence lives.

Jennie comes to these same rooms on the night Bass is arrested for
stealing coal. She pleads with Senator Brander for help, which he provides,
and then loses her maidenhood to him later that same night when his
passion overcomes his judgment. For an hour or so in this hotel room he
forgets his elevated social position and yields to his desire for this pretty
daughter of poverty. Jennie's life changes in this hotel room, although she is
as yet unaware of it. The journey she is beginning is a long one; it will
eventually carry her up the staircases of many other fine hostelries and into
many other elegantly appointed hotel chambers.

One can learn a great deal about the world that Jennie is entering by
looking into the history of almost any one of the great caravansaries mentioned in *Jennie Gerhardt*. The Arlington Hotel in Washington, D.C., for
example, is Senator Brander's place of residence when Congress is in ses-
sion, and he dies there not long after Jennie has become pregnant by him.
Many readers of *Jennie Gerhardt* in 1911 would have recognized the Arlington Hotel as a famous institution: it stood at the corner of Vermont Avenue
and Lafayette Square, just opposite the White House, and many senators

and senior members of the House of Representatives lived there during the legislative season. The sitting rooms and smoking parlors were arenas for almost constant political negotiation and deal-making; members of the press regarded the Arlington as a secondary White House and haunted its corridors for information and scoops (Williamson 276–77). Because the Arlington was not especially large—its capacity was only 325 guests—it had an air of exclusiveness and privilege. It also had the best dining room in Washington. It was at the top of the pecking order of the city's hotels, followed in prestige by the Shoreham, the Ebbitt House, and Congress Hall (Townsend 180, 575). If Senator Brander is to be a man of power and influence, then the Arlington must be his hotel. His dying there is also appropriate: he has begun to think seriously of withdrawing from public life to marry Jennie and retire with her to some secluded place, but the public arena proves stronger in the end, ensnaring him and bringing death in a hotel whose name is synonymous with the world of politics.

Jennie gives birth to her child and then passes, by various shifts, into the employ of Mrs. Bracebridge in Cleveland. Here she meets Lester Kane, who pursues her. Jennie resists for a time, but after her father burns his hands and is rendered unfit for labor she enters into a negotiation with Lester over the terms under which she will become his mistress. It is agreed that he will support the Gerhardts; he will provide a house and furniture for her mother and money for the family's living expenses. Jennie, in turn, will be his kept woman, available for trips and vacations. It is significant that this negotiation takes place in the dining room of a Cleveland hotel, the Dornton, and that Jennie and Lester consummate their arrangement a short time later in a suite in "one of the more exclusive apartment hotels" in New York City, which Lester selects carefully in order "not to take chances" on being recognized (165–66). Such negotiations and arrangements are best concluded in the safe, anonymous settings provided by metropolitan hotels.

Jennie's life with Lester for some time thereafter is conducted in hotels, resorts, and spas. She continues to live with her family in Cleveland and joins him whenever he asks her to. She travels to other cities, where she poses as Lester's cousin, and she spends time with him in famous hotels and exclusive watering places. Much of Jennie's education and development occurs on these trips: Lester takes great pleasure in buying fine clothes and expensive luggage for her and in observing the transformation in her appearance when she dons her stylish dresses and new hats. Jennie, too, is pleased by these changes:

Could this be she, she asked herself, looking in the mirror of her boudoir at the figure of a girl clad in blue velvet, with yellow French lace at her throat and upon her arms? Could these be her feet, clad in soft, shapely shoes at ten dollars a pair, these her hands on which she was drawing gloves, which harmonized well with her dress? The hats he had purchased gave her face an archness of expression not dreamed of by her before. She, Jennie Gerhardt, the washer-woman's daughter. (166)

Jennie learns many lessons in the world of the hotel. Not long after she begins her liaison with Lester, for example, we see her being tutored in table manners at the Southern Hotel, a famous turn-of-the-century establishment in St. Louis (Williamson 102). And on a deeper level we observe her as she begins to think about her life in a sophisticated way during a period of travel a few years later. Her thoughts come to her while she and Lester are in Greece and Egypt after his father's death. "It is curious the effect of travel on a thinking mind," observes Dreiser (307); movement and leisure have always been stimuli for private thought and self-assessment, and so they prove to be for Jennie. She sees evidence of decayed and forgotten civilizations, "powerful, complex, complete," in which millions of people lived and died, all of them "believing in other gods, other forms of government, other details of existence" (307). Against this background Jennie sees that most of her transgressions have been slight. She comes to realize something of her own insignificance and develops the beginnings of a credo: "They would be dead after a little while, she and Lester and all these people. Did anything matter except goodness — goodness of heart? What else was there that was real?" (308).

Travel is a time for change, and during this same trip a negotiation occurs that will bring profound alteration to Jennie's and Lester's lives. This is the negotiation between Jennie and Letty Gerald over Lester's matrimonial future. These two women reach an unspoken understanding, and significantly they work it out in two well-known hotels — the Savoy in London and Shepheard's in Cairo. Their negotiations result eventually in Lester's leaving Jennie and marrying Letty, who is his social equal and a powerful ally in his economic rehabilitation. Jennie, who is prescient, recognizes Letty's advantages for Lester from the first time she meets her in the Savoy. "This was the kind of woman he should have had," she thinks. "This woman was suited to his station in life" (313). Later, when Lester and Jennie encounter Mrs. Gerald again in Cairo, Dreiser uses charged language to emphasize the negotiation that now takes place. "Well, at last I've found you!" says Letty to Lester, announcing her intentions when she encounters him at Shepheard's Hotel. Jennie, who is sitting with Lester, picks up on the point immediately, and when Letty invites Lester to dance a few moments later, Jennie's response is a studied capitulation. "You're welcome to him," she says. "He ought to dance" (316). When Lester and Letty depart, Jennie speaks these final lines: "You go," she says to Lester. "Take him, Mrs. Gerald" (316).

Shepheard's Hotel is an appropriate venue for such a negotiation. It was a favorite stopping place for westerners in Cairo and had a long and curious history as an institution. It had been erected on the site of the palace of Muhammad Bay al-Alfi, and part of the hotel had once housed the sheik's harem — a detail that was the subject of much badinage among the guests. Shepheard's was an arena in which members of two radically different cultures, eastern and western, came in contact with each other. It was especially well known for its long front verandah, which faced a busy thoroughfare (known as the Sharia Kamel) on which the passing show of Egyptian life was observed and mused upon by the European visitors (Ludy 276–77). Lester and Jennie are sitting on this verandah when Letty approaches Lester with her invitation to dance. Lester has been brooding over the history of Egypt and its civilization: "the thin, narrow strip of soil along either side of the Nile that had given these successive waves of population sustenance; the wonder of heat and tropic life; and this hotel with its modern conveniences and fashionable crowd set down among ancient, soul-weary, almost despairing conditions" (315). Such thoughts preface the scene in which he and Letty stroll together through the gardens of Shepheard's. The hotel was famous for its beautiful gardens, a fact apparently known to Dreiser, who mentions the "rich odours," which float in the air "from groves and gardens" (316). The scene between Lester and Letty in these fragrant, lantern-lit gardens is the beginning of his courtship of her and marks the start of his disengagement from Jennie (319).

The hotels in which Jennie stays surely calls forth peculiar thoughts from her. Perhaps it is not reading too much into this novel to imagine what she must think whenever she ascends a grand hotel staircase with Lester. Once, not so long ago, she scrubbed a hotel stairway on her hands and knees. Now she ascends such staircases on Lester's arm. One of the hotels in which they stay several times in Chicago was in fact famous for its main stairway: this was the Tremont House, which boasted a gorgeous curving front staircase of marble, ornamented by gilt statuary and stained glass (Figs. 1 and 2). What must Jennie think when she ascends these stairs? It is certain that she knows, better than Lester can, the kinds of labor it takes to

Figure 1. The Tremont House in Chicago, in which Jennie and Lester stay several times, and in which they have a rendezvous in Chapter LVII. Chicago Historical Society, ICHi:00774.

Figure 2. The lobby staircase at the Tremont House. Jennie and Lester would have ascended these stairs to their rooms. Chicago Historical Society, ICHi:24243.

keep a hotel such as the Tremont shiny and functioning. To him the clerks, bellboys, maids, laundresses, and scrubwomen are simply part of the apparatus of the establishment. To Jennie, by contrast, these are people of her own class. If not for the accidents of fate, she herself might still be scrubbing stairways and collecting laundry from hotel rooms.

Jennie comes to know the world of the hotel quite well during the course of this novel. She learns that one can assume a different identity in a hotel and can use hotels to mask one's private activities. Lester, for example, lives in Chicago with Jennie in an apartment on the North Side, but he hides this behavior by maintaining a suite at the Grand Pacific and conducting his business dealings at the Union Club. No questions are asked, and he continues in this way for several years. It is only bad luck that his sister Louise stumbles on his arrangement and sets in motion the machinery that alienates Lester from his family and deprives him for a time of his inheritance.

Except for their few years in this North Side apartment and the period later in the Hyde Park house, Jennie and Lester live together only in hotels. Their existence in these establishments is rootless and detached but reassuringly safe (Ward). Jennie comes to see that luxury hotels are really part of an extended subculture that exists independently of the cities in which they are found and that moves by its own set of rules. Hotels are busy, impersonal little towns, populated by quickly shifting groups of guests and transients. Exchanges are polite but superficial, and few inquiries are made about one's identity or private behavior. The activities and motives of the guests are not scrutinized too closely; what goes on in their rooms is their own business.

Hotels of this type constitute small communities, replete with restaurants, clothing shops, tobacco stores, gift shops, drinking saloons, ticket agencies, laundry services, billiard parlors, writing rooms, barber shops, steam baths, and on and on. One really need never leave such a hotel; everything necessary for daily sustenance is there if one has sufficient money to pay for it. These hotels are also showplaces for new technology—elevators, incandescent lights, mechanical annunciators, bell systems, and up-to-the-minute bathing facilities. Technology and conspicuous display divert the guests and encourage them to loosen their purse strings. Their morals and inhibitions tend to relax as well: denizens of the hotel world can live out their fantasies of wealth and consumption there, needing only to settle the bill at the front desk when it is time to reenter the larger society (Hayner 166–76).

The most frequently mentioned hotel in *Jennie Gerhardt* is just such an

Figure 3. One of the dining halls at the Auditorium, laid for a banquet. The arch, accented with incandescent lights, was one of the dominant architectural motifs throughout the hotel. Chicago Historical Society, ICHi:00583.

establishment. This is the Auditorium Hotel in Chicago, a vast and opulent building that housed under one roof a 400-room hotel, a seventeen-story office tower, a 4,000-seat opera house, a smaller recital theater, an enormous tenth-floor dining room with a view of Lake Michigan, and two separate banquet halls (Fig. 3). Here was a true town-within-a-city, furnished not only with contiguous shops and restaurants but with businesses and entertainments as well. The famous Chicago architect Louis Sullivan designed this complex; it was formally dedicated in December 1889 in a gala affair attended by President Benjamin Harrison, and it was expanded in the early 1890s by 400 rooms in anticipation of the World's Columbian Exposition of 1893 — which Dreiser attended, and which figures importantly in *Sister Carrie* (Miles Berger).

The Auditorium is Lester's preferred hotel in Chicago. When he ends his arrangement with Jennie and breaks up the Hyde Park home, he goes to live there. It is his base of operations just after he assumes his inheritance and reenters upper-crust Chicago society. Certainly Lester must find comfort and ease at the Auditorium: it was the first building in the world to be entirely wired for electricity, and it was full of modern conveniences and gadgets. The apparatus for which it was best known, and which figured most frequently in journalistic accounts of its attractions, was a mechanical dial mounted in each room with which the guest could summon a variety of goods and services — iced water, newspapers, stationery, bath towels, room service, and so forth (Fig. 4). Dreiser makes no mention of this device in *Jennie Gerhardt* — perhaps he did not even know of it — but one still cannot help but imagine what Lester would have thought whenever he operated this gadget. With this dial he can procure many items that Jennie once brought to him and can summon services that she once performed for him. Certainly this toy must be amusing to him, but after its novelty has worn off one imagines that he must miss Jennie's warm human presence, her concern for him, her genuine affection and love. A dial on the wall of a hotel room must seem a poor substitute.

It is in this same hotel, the Auditorium, that Lester dies. As with Senator Brander, this is an appropriate place for Lester to end his life, since he has chosen this world of wealth and display over the simpler sphere that Jennie inhabits. Lester has come from New York to Chicago on business, and he falls ill while he is there. He takes to his bed in the Auditorium and asks that Jennie visit him. She comes willingly: they have not been in contact for several years, but here in this hotel — a familiar setting to them both — they quickly resume their old roles. Jennie sits by Lester's bed, soothing him with her voice and performing small services. She has sat by such beds before and knows how to tend the dying. She has done so for her mother and father and most recently for her daughter. The novel now approaches its emotional climax — Lester's deathbed speech. Here in the Auditorium, in a scene that resembles a confessional or a rite of extreme unction, Jennie hears Lester's declaration of love. This is the culminating point of the story, and it occurs in a hotel. Lester could not have made his confession anywhere else.

The world of the hotel is almost the only one that Jennie and Lester ever know together. They are citizens of this demimonde; it welcomes them readily, with no questions asked, and it gives them privacy and anonymity. In the end it provides Lester with a place to die. He and Jennie attempt twice to live together as husband and wife in other lodgings, but both times

Figure 4. A wall dial similar to the ones found in the Auditorium in Chicago. This is an unusual specimen of the device; it is from the Elysée Palace in Paris, a hotel that catered to the American and British trade. The commands are in English, but the directions for operation are in French. (Reproduced from Watkin, David, et al. *Grand Hotel: The Golden Age of Palace Hotels, An Architectural and Social History.* New York and Paris: Vendome Press, 1984.)

they are found out and forced back to the hotel world. There they can escape the social pressures that bedevil them elsewhere; they are free to behave as they please and to take pleasure as they wish. They are really at home with each other only in hotels, where they can shed convention, assume other identities, and make a private world together.

Bibliography

"Auction Draws Final Curtain at Auditorium." *Chicago Daily News*, 8 July 1942.
Berger, Miles. "The Auditorium." In *They Built Chicago*, 93–100. Chicago: Bonus Books, 1992.
Berger, Molly W. "Leaving the Light On: The Modern Hotel in America." Unpublished paper presented to the Society for the History of Technology, Uppsala, Sweden, August 1992.
Boorstin, Daniel J. "'Palaces of the Public.'" In *The Americans: The National Experience*, 134–47. New York: Random House, 1965.
Davis, Stephen B. "'Of the Class Denominated Princely': The Tremont House Hotel." *Chicago History* 11 (Spring 1982): 26–36.
Dedmon, Edmund. "Chicago Builds Its Parthenon." In *Fabulous Chicago*, 171–77. New York: Atheneum, 1981.
Donzel, Catherine, et al. *Grand American Hotels*. New York and Paris: Vendôme Press, 1989.
Dorsey, Leslie and Janice Devine. *Fare Thee Well: A Backward Look at Two Centuries of Historic American Hostelries, Fashionable Spas and Seaside Resorts*. New York: Crown, 1964.
Dreiser, Theodore. *Journalism, Volume One: Newspaper Writings, 1892–1895*. Edited by T. D. Nostwich. Philadelphia: University of Pennsylvania Press, 1988.
Gastos, Gregory S. *History of the West Baden Springs Hotel*. French Lick, IN: Springs Valley Herald, 1989.
"The Grand Pacific Hotel. Completion of 100 New Rooms." *Daily National Hotel Reporter*, 11 February 1891.
"The Grand Pacific Hotel. A Review of Recent Improvements." *Daily National Hotel Reporter*, 5 November 1891.
"The Great Hotels. — The Grand Pacific." *Land Owner* 5 (July 1873): 125–26.
Hayner, Norman S. *Hotel Life*. Chapel Hill: University of North Carolina Press, 1936.
Hill, Thomas E. *Souvenir Guide to Chicago and the World's Fair*. Chicago: Laird and Lee, 1892.
"Hotels." *Unrivaled Chicago*, 82. New York: Rand McNally, 1986.
Ludy, Robert B. *Historic Hotels of the World*. Philadelphia: David McKay, 1927.
Raitz, Karl B. and John Paul Jones III. "The City Hotel as Landscape Artifact and Community Symbol." *Journal of Cultural Geography* 9 (Fall/Winter 1988): 17–36.

Townsend, George Alfred. *Washington Outside and Inside.* Hartford, CT and Chicago: James Betts & Co., 1874.

Ward, Joseph A. " 'The Amazing Hotel World' of James, Dreiser, and Wharton." In *Leon Edel and Literary Art,* edited by Lyall H. Powers, assisted by Clare Virginia Eby, 151–60. Ann Arbor, Mich.: UMI Research Press, 1988.

Watkin, David, et al. *Grand Hotel: The Golden Age of Palace Hotels, An Architectural and Social History.* New York and Paris: Vendôme Press, 1984.

Williams, Jesse Lynch. "A Great Hotel." *Scribner's Magazine* 21 (February 1897): 135–59.

Williamson, Jefferson. *The American Hotel: An Anecdotal History.* New York: Knopf, 1930.

Wilson, Richard Guy, ed. *Victorian Resorts and Hotels.* Philadelphia: Victorian Society in America, 1982.

19
Death and Dying in *Jennie Gerhardt*

JAMES M. HUTCHISSON

JENNIE GERHARDT IS TO A GREAT DEGREE concerned with the subject of death. To list the people who die in the novel is to list virtually every significant character except Jennie herself: Dreiser describes in full detail the deaths of Mrs. Gerhardt, old Gerhardt, Vesta, and Lester Kane; and several other characters die offstage — Senator Brander, Mrs. Kane, Mr. Kane, and Malcolm Gerald, Letty Gerald's first husband. These deaths serve Dreiser as plot devices, of course, but one still wonders why so many characters die. More specifically, why does Dreiser dwell on death and the act of dying so much in the novel? One answer is that the deaths of these various characters all affect Jennie's well-being — financial, emotional, and moral. In one way or another, she is dependent on almost every character who dies.

But Dreiser also uses death as a means of exploring one of the central dialectics of the novel — that of orthodox religion versus scientific naturalism. Put simply, the characters in the novel fear death because they are uncertain about the existence of an afterlife. We can best understand these feelings by understanding the culture of death in nineteenth-century America. For centuries, death had simply marked a passing from a transitory world to a permanent afterlife. But as evolutionary biology began to challenge traditional religious assumptions, the belief in an afterlife declined, and people thus sought new ways to manage death. One way to do this was to make the act of dying into an elaborate aesthetic spectacle. Through various means — memorial art and jewelry, glass-sided hearses and coffins, and mortuary photography, for example — bereavement was replaced by a physical attachment to the deceased. These rituals and customs were a response to the erosion of belief in a sacred, divinely intended death. In Dreiser's novel, the deaths of virtually everyone to whom Jennie is close leave her alone in a world that she does not understand. Thus, as her contemporaries did, she domesticates or secularizes death so that its force is blunted. In *Jennie Gerhardt,* the reality of death becomes muted, and the act of dying becomes beautified.

Illness and the threat of death are present in each phase of Jennie's life. There is a pattern in the novel of Jennie's becoming dependent on someone (both emotionally and financially), losing that person, and having to start a new life elsewhere. This pattern of loss and displacement reinforces the tenuous, day-to-day existence of Jennie and her family. The cycle begins on virtually the first page of the novel, when we learn that old Gerhardt's poor health makes it difficult for him to work steadily; the Gerhardts' precarious existence is jeopardized further by the illness of little Veronica, who contracts measles and nearly dies. These events set in motion Jennie's plight: to support the household, Jennie and her mother go to work at the Columbus House, where Jennie meets Senator Brander and is eventually impregnated by him. Brander becomes a financial provider for Jennie and her family as well as a surrogate father. He usurps the role of the ineffectual Gerhardt as head of the household when he provides food and money for the family. Brander's death, however, leaves the family impoverished again — although it also makes possible Jennie's meeting Lester Kane when she goes to work as a maid at Mrs. Bracebridge's home. Once involved with Lester, Jennie, and soon her family, become financially dependent on him, and he provides for them in the same way that Senator Brander did. This time, the male provider figure makes it possible for the family to move to Cleveland, where the Gerhardts feel as though they "could start life all over, as it were. They could be decent, honorable, prosperous" (98). Lester also causes Jennie to live with him on the North Side of Chicago. Here Dreiser again points out that Jennie's "old life had ended and [her] new one had begun" (175).

This cycle continues throughout Jennie's life: the death of Mrs. Gerhardt breaks the family apart geographically as well as emotionally, and soon thereafter Jennie moves with Lester to Hyde Park, where old Gerhardt joins them. The death of Archibald Kane likewise causes displacement in Jennie's life: she and Lester travel through Europe, while Lester considers the ultimatum delivered by his father from the grave, via his will. Jennie is thus again affected by someone's death. After the death of old Gerhardt and the visit to Jennie by Mr. O'Brien, the Kane family lawyer, Jennie leaves Lester and moves with Vesta to Sandwood. After Vesta dies, Jennie not only moves again, this time to the South Side of Chicago, but she also reinvents herself. She becomes Mrs. J. G. Stover and adopts a child, Rose Perpetua. (Her adopted daughter's name suggests permanence — or an eternal life, unlike the life of Vesta, which was cut short.) With the death of Lester at the end of the novel, Jennie sees stretching before her "a vista of lonely years" (418).

Because these various people die, Jennie for a time has no financial stability, no one to love (except her adopted child), no respectable status in society, and sometimes no home to go to. Ultimately, she has no direction or sense of purpose in life. She is at the mercy of those who die, a victim of the forces of death. "She was never a master of her fate," Dreiser tells us near the end of the novel. "Others invariably controlled" (413). It can therefore be said that the deaths that Jennie witnesses or that she is affected by leave her without the emotional nourishment she craves. They perpetuate the tenuous existence that she has known since her youth.

One is also struck by the suddenness and mystery of the deaths that occur in the novel. Especially as the novel draws to a close, it seems almost as if Dreiser is expeditiously killing off his characters to tie up the loose threads of the plot. This abruptness, however, does serve an important thematic purpose: it affirms Dreiser's strong philosophy of determinism and his innate belief in an all-powerful, uncontrollable fate. It is natural, for example, that in Dreiser's universe of chance, all of the fatal illnesses that his characters contract are either untreatable or cannot be diagnosed with much accuracy. Senator Brander, for example, is first "seized with a slight attack of fever" that his doctors do not think is dangerous. It is then discovered that he is actually "suffering from a virulent form of typhoid"; during his convalescence, he is "seized with a sudden attack of heart failure" and never regains consciousness (78). Vesta also suddenly contracts a fever, and it too develops into typhoid. Although Vesta is thought to be "strong enough constitutionally to shake it off," her heart and kidneys eventually are invaded by the illness, and the physicians who attend her cannot save her (384, 385). Lester's illness, like Senator Brander's, is misdiagnosed: after his death, it is discovered that "it was not the intestinal trouble which killed him, but a lesion of a major blood vessel in the brain" (412). The fatal illnesses of Mrs. Gerhardt and old Gerhardt are of vague origins, and in all these cases what Dreiser refers to as the "usual remedies" or "favorite remedies" are ineffective.

The pertinent point is that in the novel death is linked with a universe of force that controls one's fate and that affects Jennie directly. When Senator Brander dies, for example, Jennie is unable to "get a full conception" of the "vigor of the blow" that fate has dealt her (79). Vesta's death is likewise an "additional blow" that fortune "inconsiderately" administers to Jennie (387). The fragile and transitory state of life in the novel explains the attention that various characters pay to omens or imminent warnings of death. Nearly all of the characters have such premonitions: when Lester falls ill, for instance, he has the feeling "that he would not see [Letty] again"

(407). Similarly, Vesta's illness begins on "one of the first premonitory chilly days" in October (384). Mrs. Gerhardt is convinced that she will die when on a carriage ride with Jennie she notices "the fading autumn scenery," which depresses her: "'I don't like to get sick in the fall,' she said. 'The leaves coming down make me think I am never going to get well.'" For her mother's sake, Jennie tries to play down the significance of such an omen, but Dreiser tells us that Jennie "felt frightened nevertheless" (179–80). Dreiser believed strongly in the validity of such signs. He was reared by a mother who instilled such beliefs in him, and later in life he dabbled in spiritualism. According to his autobiography, *Dawn,* Dreiser's last days with his mother were much like those of the fictional Jennie with her mother. Mrs. Gerhardt's remark about the leaves of autumn, in fact, is almost precisely the same as Dreiser's recollection in *Dawn* of his mother's statement about dying in the fall (see Lingeman 81).

The most important scene of this type takes place in chapter LIX, when Jennie receives word of Lester's illness. Dreiser tells us that "several nights" earlier Jennie had had a dream, which she recalls vividly:

> She was out on a dark, mystic body of water, how or in what vessel was not clear, but there was water—still and smooth and lovely everywhere—a vast body of silent water over which was hanging something like a fog, only it appeared to be more of a pall of smoke or haze. . . . Then out of the surrounding darkness a boat appeared. It was a little boat, oarless, or not visibly propelled, and in it were her mother and Vesta and someone whom she could not make out. . . . Then suddenly Jennie realized that the third occupant of the boat was Lester. He looked at her gloomily . . . and then her mother remarked, "Well, we must go now." The boat began to move, and a great sense of loss came over her, and she cried, "Oh, don't leave me, Mama." (408)

Dreiser was probably drawing here on the folkloric significance of such a dream. A boat was thought to symbolize a coffin (owing to their similarities in shape), and the miasma of water and fog that Jennie sees would have represented a transitionary otherworld (Coffin 201). The boat and the body of water are the means by which the soul is transported from death to the afterlife. The presence of Mrs. Gerhardt, Vesta, and Lester in such a place in Jennie's dream at once suggests a tendency to believe in an afterlife yet, paradoxically, projects a frightening image rather than a consolatory one.

Beliefs in such intimations of death are in large part attempts by the characters to give themselves the illusion of controlling death and to prepare for loss. Since the characters think themselves to be at the mercy of an all-powerful fate, it is natural that there is much philosophical musing in the novel about whether one can control what happens to one after death. Dreiser uses these passages to explore the dichotomy between orthodox religion and scientific naturalism. Between 1880 and 1910, the period during which the novel is set, this issue was much on the minds of Americans. The theories of evolution and natural selection espoused by Darwin, Thomas Huxley, and Herbert Spencer (whose *First Principles* had a formative influence on Dreiser's thinking) helped erode the once strong faith in religion. The notion of an afterlife, once thought to be a virtual certainty, now seemed implausible.

Dreiser gives the voice of orthodox religion in the novel to old Gerhardt—a stern, devout Lutheran who believes that "everything spoken from the pulpit of his church was literally true" (52). Old Gerhardt is obsessed with death. When Mrs. Gerhardt is dying, Dreiser says that old Gerhardt "hung about like one expectant of and greatly awed by the possibility of disaster" (180). His macabre interest in the topic grows out of his religious faith:

> He believed . . . that the problem of the future life was the all-important question for man. Death was an awesome thing to him. He had lived in dread of the icy marvel of it ever since his youth, and now that the years were slipping away and the problem of the world was becoming more and more inexplicable, he clung with pathetic anxiety to the doctrines which contained a solution. (52)

Gerhardt represents that generation of people in Dreiser's time who were raised to believe in the traditional Christian notion of a Judgment Day and an afterlife. Such characters as Lester and Senator Brander, by contrast, evince a more skeptical turn of mind, and both men embrace a carpe diem philosophy. In desiring Jennie, Senator Brander considers that he has "not so very many more years to live. Why die unsatisfied?" (40). Lester also wants to "keep young or die young" and not "dry up into an aimless old age" (270)—precisely what happens to old Gerhardt by stubbornly clinging to the doctrines of his faith in the face of contradictory empirical evidence. On his deathbed, Gerhardt resolutely maintains his "very dogmatic religious convictions," which, although not "upset by the direct testimony of life," nevertheless have been "shaken, confused, made anomalous." He asks, "What was this thing—life? What did it all come to, after struggle and worry and grieving? Where does it all go to? People die. You hear nothing more from them. His wife, now, she was gone. Where had her spirit taken its flight?" (242).

Dreiser is hard on organized religion in the novel, particularly old Gerhardt's grim, fanatical Lutheranism. Religion offers no consolation, for example, to Mrs. Gerhardt when Veronica falls ill with the measles. In fact it does the opposite: when the prognosis for Veronica looks bleak, the Lutheran minister, Pastor Wundt, visits the Gerhardts and brings "an atmosphere of grim ecclesiasticism into the house." Rather than hold out the hope of life, he and the physician attending Veronica affirm the reality of death. "They were the black-garbed, sanctimonious emissaries of superior forces. Mrs. Gerhardt felt as if she were going to lose her child, and watched sorrowfully by the cot-side" (6).

In the late nineteenth century, scientific naturalism not only diminished religious faith; it became the crucial catalyst in the culture of death in America. As religion began to lose its consolatory force and belief in an afterlife began to decline, death assumed a disquieting power over the imagination of nineteenth-century Americans. To compensate for the loss of a loved one, people secularized and domesticated death. They made the act of dying and the subsequent rituals of funeral services, burial, and mourning into an extended aesthetic spectacle. These customs explain many of the elaborate descriptions of mourning that Dreiser renders in the novel. The purpose of such pageantry was to control and soften the bleak reality of death and, in many cases, to replace bereavement with a physical — almost fetishistic — attachment to the dead body.

The traditional emphasis on death and the afterlife shifted to a new concern with the life of the person before he or she died, as well as to the ties between the deceased and the bereaved. Beginning in the 1870s, obituaries (such as the one about Senator Brander in chapter VIII) began to focus on the period of dying rather than on the moment of death, and they also emphasized the person's secular achievements instead of rhapsodizing about a new life in heaven (Farrell 190). Cemeteries at the time were transformed from crowded, poorly maintained lots in urban areas to beautifully landscaped tracts of land resembling parks or country estates (French 73ff). The impetus behind the so-called rural cemetery movement of the 1850s and 1860s was a concern for the physical comfort of the deceased and for the consolation of the bereaved. The new cemeteries drew attention away from the mystery of what happens after death by placing the physical remains of the departed in an environment that was meant to symbolize and reinforce living.

The most striking manifestations of this interest in death were various means by which mourners attempted to remain attached to the deceased.

Jennie exhibits this tendency after Lester's death, for example, when she is disconsolate about not being able to view his corpse: "She would have liked so much to have gone and seen him again, to have had him buried in Chicago, where she could go to the grave occasionally, but this was not to be" (413). We also see this tendency when Jennie reacts to the death of Vesta by considering a move to "a cottage somewhere near the Cemetery of the Redeemer," where "she could be near Vesta and Gerhardt. . . . She could not live alone here" (389). Most striking of all is Jennie's desire to look at Vesta's corpse, which lies on the deathbed "for a day or two after the end":

> [Jennie] would come into the pink and white bedroom where the bright waters of the lake were visible in the distance, shining in the sun, and look at this sylph-like figure, terribly thinned by sickness, and wonder where she was. What had become of all that she was? Vesta's hand would rest under hers, stiff and cold. (388)

Such an act seems almost ghoulish to us today, but it was common at the time.

Several developments in the management of death in the late nineteenth century combined to create this interest in the physical remains of the deceased. It was commonplace for people to die at home — fewer than one in fifty died in hospitals. Funeral homes, which did not become widespread until the 1920s, were created to give domestic comfort to the mourner who normally would have stood watch over a loved one as he or she died at home, usually on his or her own bed — as Jennie stands watch over her mother, her father, Vesta, and Lester. More evidence of the strong ties between the deceased and the living can be seen in the average length of time that passed between death and burial — usually at least three days, sometimes four. The Kane family, for instance, decides to hold the body of Lester for four days so that they may then have private funeral services at the residence of his sister Imogene. As nominal upper-class Catholics, the Kanes encounter no resistance from the Church; public ceremonies are held in "one of the wealthy Roman Catholic churches of the North Side"; the body is then transported by train to Cincinnati, where it is to be interred in the Pace family vault (412–14). There was an aspect of social class to this preference for the deferred funeral: whereas nearly 90 percent of the funerals for white-collar workers took place two or more days after death, for farmers and for blue-collar workers this figure was only 27 percent and 46 percent respectively (Farrell 208). These statistics suggest that the less well-educated classes still clung to a belief in the afterlife and saw death merely as a passing, a movement toward a more important fate. Thus there were no attempts by such people to preserve the deceased a little longer. The upper class and the emergent middle class, by contrast, wanted to think of the deceased as still being alive, at least in their own minds, in the days immediately following death.

Even more elaborate measures were taken to remember the departed in life rather than in death—and more specifically to have some material remembrance of the deceased. One of the most common practices was that of premortem and postmortem photography, particularly of children. Often the parents would pose for photographs of themselves with their dying child, and just as often would be photographed in the moments immediately following death. In *Sleeping Beauty,* a fascinating collection of such photographs published in 1990, Stanley Burns notes that if circumstances prevented a parent from being available to be photographed with the dying child, then the body would be preserved at home for as long as nine days to have the photograph taken. Other memorials proliferated in the nineteenth century: samplers, vases, jewelry, cartes de visite etched in black with a miniature of the face of the deceased printed on them, even floral arrangements woven with locks of hair from the deceased. An entire iconography of loss was generated by these attempts to remain in touch with the departed. Mourning art, in fact, became so commonplace that Mark Twain was moved to satirize its lugubriousness in *Adventures of Huckleberry Finn* when Huck sees such memorials in the parlor of the Grangerford house. The daughter of the family, Emmeline, writes lachrymose consolation poems in tribute to the Confederate dead, and the house is decorated with such memorials as dark-hued paintings of women leaning over gravestones and weeping into handkerchiefs. Below the pictures are inscribed such mottos as "I Shall Never See Thee More Alas."

The funeral, burial, and process of mourning also assumed major significance at this time. When a death in the family occurred, typically the house would be done over in black, with a scarf or an arrangement of crepe on the door; deeply colored veils were often hung in the entranceway as well. For the bereaved, black funeral crepe, black silks, and blue-black alpacas were used to make mourning garments. These clothes were worn during several clearly defined periods of mourning. The first six months were commonly known as the period of deep mourning and carried a proscription against participating in any social or recreational activities. Even correspondence fell under the regulation of mourning custom: stationery was white or grey with a black border, and elaborate lettering or coloring of any kind was prohibited. During the second six months of mourning, these restrictions were lifted, but the mourner was still expected to wear only clothes with a dull black finish. In the first six months of the second year, less funereal habiliments were permitted, and after two years the mourner could wear ordinary garments (Habenstein and Lamers 92). A funeral procession, like Lester's in the novel, was carried out with much pomp and fanfare (414–15). Often the deceased reposed in a glass-sided hearse, enabling mourners to gaze upon the remains; open-casket viewings were, of course, customary. All these rituals bonded the mourner to the deceased and distracted the mourner from the question of what happened to a person after death. The funeral and the burial thus became more than utilitarian events. Robert Habenstein and William Lamers point out that the very word "casket"—which at this time replaced the more pedestrian "coffin"—signified a box or container for something precious; "the preciousness of the human body was felt to be best expressed to the world *symbolically* by the aesthetic luxury of the casket, and *dramatically* to the world by the funeral ceremony" (95). Appropriately, Lester's body lies in a large black casket "with silver handles"; it is covered by a white shroud "bearing the insignia of suffering, a black cross" (414, 415).

These various customs and rituals not only offer Jennie and the other characters consolation during a time of loss, but also soften the harsh reality of death and give an illusion of control over something uncontrollable—an all-powerful fate. In a time when religion had lost much of its consolatory power, the domestication and secularization of death helped Americans manage the emotional and intellectual confusion brought on by scientific naturalism. The pain of being left alone in the world, which is a constant recurrence in Jennie's life, is to a large degree mitigated by these physical and emotional attachments to the lost loved ones.

Bibliography

Burns, Stanley B. *Sleeping Beauty: Memorial Photography in America.* Altadena, CA: Twelvetrees Press, 1990.

Coffin, Margaret M. *Death in Early America: The History and Folklore of Early Medicine, Funerals, and Mourning.* Nashville, TN: Thomas Nelson, 1976.

Farrell, James J. *Inventing the American Way of Death, 1830–1920.* Philadelphia: Temple University Press, 1980.

French, Stanley. "The Cemetery as Cultural Institution: The Establishment of Mount Auburn and the 'Rural Cemetery' Movement." In *Death in America,* edited by David E. Stannard. Philadelphia: University of Pennsylvania Press, 1975.

Habenstein, Robert and William Lamers. "The Pattern of Late Nineteenth-Century Funerals." In *Passing: The Vision of Death in America,* edited by Charles O. Jackson. Westport, CT: Greenwood, 1977.

Lingeman, Richard. *Theodore Dreiser: At the Gates of the City, 1871–1901.* Vol. 1. New York: G. P. Putnam's Sons, 1986.

Checklist: Criticism of the 1911 Text

Calvert, Beverlee. "A Structural Analysis of *Jennie Gerhardt*." *Dreiser Newsletter* 5(Fall 1974):9–11.

Casagrande, Peter J. "'The Pathetic Side of the World': Hardy and Theodore Dreiser." In Casagrande, *Hardy's Influence on the Modern Novel*, 173–203. Totowa, NJ: Barnes and Noble, 1987.

Dance, Daryl C. "Sentimentalism in Dreiser's Heroines, Carrie and Jennie." *CLA Journal* 14(December 1970):127–42.

Deegan, Dorothy Yost. "Jennie Gerhardt." In Deegan, *The Stereotype of the Single Woman in American Novels*, 49–56. New York: King's Crown Press, 1951.

Elias, Robert H. *Theodore Dreiser: Apostle of Nature*. Emended ed., 18–19, 122–25, et passim. Ithaca: Cornell University Press, 1970.

Gerber, Philip. "The Washerwoman's Daughter: *Jennie Gerhardt*." In *Theodore Dreiser Revisited*, 35–45. New York: Twayne, 1992.

Graham, Don B. "Dreiser's Use of the 'English Jefferies' in *Jennie Gerhardt*." *Dreiser Newsletter* 8(Spring 1977):6–8.

Hapke, Laura. "Dreiser and the Tradition of the American Working Girl." *Dreiser Studies* 22, 2(Fall 1991):2–19.

Hussman, Lawrence E., Jr. "*Jennie Gerhardt*." In *Dreiser and His Fiction: A Twentieth-Century Quest*, 50–69. Philadelphia: University of Pennsylvania Press, 1983.

Kazin, Alfred. Introduction to *Jennie Gerhardt*. New York: Dell, 1963.

Lehan, Richard. "*Jennie Gerhardt*." In *Theodore Dreiser: His World and His Novels*, 80–96. Carbondale: Southern Illinois University Press, 1969.

Lingeman, Richard. "Jennie Redivivus." In *Theodore Dreiser: An American Journey, 1908–1945*. Vol. 2, 33–43. New York: G. P. Putnam's Sons, 1990.

Marcus, Mordecai. "Loneliness, Death, and Fulfillment in *Jennie Gerhardt*." *Studies in American Fiction* 7, 1(Spring 1979):61–73.

Mitchell, Lee Clark. Introduction to *Jennie Gerhardt*. Oxford: Oxford University Press, 1991.

Pizer, Donald. "Dreiser and the Naturalistic Drama of Consciousness." *Journal of Narrative Technique* 21, 2(Spring 1991):202–11.

———. "*Jennie Gerhardt*." In *The Novels of Theodore Dreiser: A Critical Study*. Minneapolis: University of Minnesota Press, 1976.

Schwartz, Carol A. "*Jennie Gerhardt*: Fairy Tale as Social Criticism." *American Literary Realism* 19, 2(Winter 1987): 16–29.

Wadlington, Warwick. "Pathos and Dreiser." *Southern Review* 7(Spring 1971):411–29.

Ward, Joseph A. "'The Amazing Hotel World' of James, Dreiser, and Wharton." In

Leon Edel and Literary Art, edited by Lyall H. Powers and assisted by Clare Virginia Eby, 151–60. Ann Arbor: University of Michigan Research Press, 1988.

West, James L. W., III. "C. B. De Camp and *Jennie Gerhardt.*" *Dreiser Studies* 23, 1 (Spring 1992):2–7.

———. "Double Quotes and Double Meanings in *Jennie Gerhardt.*" *Dreiser Studies* 18, 1 (Spring 1987):1–11.

Yglesias, Helen. Introduction to *Jennie Gerhardt.* New York: Schocken Books, 1982.

Contributors

SUSAN ALBERTINE is Associate Professor of English at Susquehanna University. Her essays on American literature and life writings have appeared in *American Literary History* and *Review*; her edited collection *A Living of Words: American Women in Print Culture* was published in 1995.

NANCY WARNER BARRINEAU is Associate Professor of English at Pembroke State University. She is past Editor of the *Dreiser Society Newsletter* and has a book in progress on women in Dreiser's fiction. Her edition of Dreiser's writings for *Ev'ry Month* is in press.

DANIEL H. BORUS is Assistant Professor of History at the University of Rochester. He is the author of *Writing Realism: Howells, James, and Norris in the Mass Market* and is at work on a book about the politics of the arts between 1860 and 1930.

ARTHUR D. CASCIATO is Associate Professor of English at Miami University of Ohio. He has written on American literature of the 1930s and 1940s and has in progress a study of the League of American Authors.

LEONARD CASSUTO is Assistant Professor of English at Fordham University. He has published articles on Dreiser and other American naturalist authors, and is currently finishing a book on the antebellum racial grotesque.

EMILY CLARK is Associate Librarian at the Chicago Historical Society. She was co-curator of an exhibition on Samuel E. Gross there in 1992 and co-author of an article on him which appeared in *Chicago History*.

CLARE VIRGINIA EBY is Associate Professor of English at the University of Connecticut, Hartford. She is completing a book that uses Veblen's theories to construct a matrix within which to read Dreiser's work.

ROBERT H. ELIAS is Goldwin Smith Professor Emeritus of English and American Studies, Cornell University. He wrote the first full-length biography of Dreiser, *Theodore Dreiser: Apostle of Nature,* and edited the standard three-volume collection of Dreiser's letters.

PHILIP GERBER, Professor of English at the State University of New York at Brockport, is the author of books on Cather, Frost, and Dreiser. He is coediting *The Financier* for the Pennsylvania Dreiser Edition and is at work on a history of Dreiser's Trilogy of Desire.

MIRIAM GOGOL is Associate Professor of English at SUNY Fashion Institute of Technology. She has edited a forthcoming collection of essays entitled *Theodore Dreiser: Beyond Naturalism* and is cofounder and past president of the International Dreiser Society.

YOSHINOBU HAKUTANI, Professor of English at Kent State University, is the author of *Young Dreiser* and editor of a two-volume collection of Dreiser's magazine writings. His book *Richard Wright and Racial Discourse: A Multicultural Criticism* and his edition of Wright's haiku are forthcoming.

JOHN B. HUMMA is Professor of English at Georgia Southern University. He is the author of *Metaphor and Meaning in D. H. Lawrence's Later Novels*; his articles have appeared in *PMLA,* the *South Atlantic Review,* and *Studies in the Novel.*

LAWRENCE E. HUSSMAN is Professor of English at Wright State University. His book *Dreiser and His Fiction: A Twentieth-Century Quest* was published in 1983 by the University of Pennsylvania Press.

JAMES M. HUTCHISSON, Associate Professor of English at The Citadel, is coeditor of the Pennsylvania Edition of Dreiser's *The Financier.* Hutchisson's articles on Dreiser have appeared in *PBSA* and *Papers on Language and Literature*; his book *The Rise of Sinclair Lewis* is forthcoming.

JUDITH KUCHARSKI is a Ph.D. candidate in English at the University of Virginia in modern American literature and culture.

RICHARD LINGEMAN, Executive Editor of the *Nation,* is the author of the two-volume biography *Theodore Dreiser: At the Gates of the City, 1871–1907* and *Theodore Dreiser: An American Journey, 1908–1945.* An abridged one-volume paperbound edition was published in 1993, *Theodore Dreiser: An American Journey.*

VALERIE ROSS is Assistant Professor of English, Miami University of Ohio. Her essays have appeared in *American Literary History* and in a recent collection on biographical writing entitled *Contesting the Subject.* She has a book in progress about sentiment, biography, and the discipline of literature.

JAMES L. W. WEST III is Distinguished Professor of English at Pennsylvania State University, where he directs the Penn State Center for the History of the Book. He has recently published an edition of Dreiser's *Jennie Gerhardt* and is general editor of the Cambridge Edition of the Works of F. Scott Fitzgerald. His biography of William Styron is in progress.

CHRISTOPHER P. WILSON, Professor of English at Boston College, has published *The Labor of Words: Literary Professionalism in the Progressive Era* and *White Collar Fictions.*

Index

This book has been set in Linotron Galliard. Galliard was designed for Mergenthaler in 1978 by Matthew Carter. Galliard retains many of the features of a sixteenth-century typeface cut by Robert Granjon but has some modifications that give it a more contemporary look.

Printed on acid-free paper.